A HISTORY OF
ORGANIZED LABOR IN CUBA

A HISTORY OF ORGANIZED LABOR IN CUBA

Robert J. Alexander

Westport, Connecticut
London

Library of Congress Cataloging-in-Publication Data

Alexander, Robert Jackson, 1918–
    A history of organized labor in Cuba / Robert J. Alexander.
      p.   cm.
    Includes bibliographical references and index.
    ISBN 0–275–97703–X (alk. paper)
    1. Labor unions—Cuba—History. 2. Labor movement—Cuba—History.
    3. Working class—Cuba—History. I. Title.
    HD6577.A44   2002
    331.8′097291—dc21   2002067943

British Library Cataloguing in Publication Data is available.

Library of Congress Catalog Card Number: 2002067943
ISBN: 0–275–97703–X

First published in 2002

Praeger Publishers, 88 Post Road West, Westport, CT 06881
An imprint of Greenwood Publishing Group, Inc.
www.praeger.com

Printed in the United States of America

The paper used in this book complies with the
Permanent Paper Standard issued by the National
Information Standards Organization (Z39.48–1984).

10 9 8 7 6 5 4 3 2 1

To Lyndsey Erin Alexander

Contents

Preface

This is the first of a planned series of volumes on the history of organized labor in Latin America and the Caribbean. These deal with a subject that more than half a century ago first caused me to become interested in the societies, economics, and politics of the nations that make up the Western Hemisphere south of the United States.

My attention first focused on Latin American organized labor when I took a course in Latin American History from Professor Frank Tannenbaum at Columbia University in the late 1930s. I wrote a term paper for Professor Tannenbaum on the history of Argentine labor movement. When I completed this study, which totaled something more than 100 pages, I made the surprising (and not unpleasant) discovery that I was an "expert" on the subject—for the simple reason that it appeared that no one else in this country—except a real expert in the U.S. Department of Labor—knew anything about it.

I continued to look into the labor movements of Latin America by writing my M.A. thesis on the history of Chilean organized labor. Then, after an "extended vacation" from concentration on intellectual matters while spending three and a half years in the United States Army Air Force during World War II, I returned to the subject by writing my Ph.D. dissertation on labor relations in Chile. To collect material for that work, I made my first extended trip to Latin America in 1946–1947, spending half of that year in Chile, and first visiting Cuba on the way home.

Subsequently, during my early years as a member of the Economics faculty of Rutgers University, I had the good fortune of having an association with two people who greatly facilitated my continuing and developing study of Latin America, and particularly of the Latin American labor movements. These were Serafino Romualdi, the Latin American representative of the American Federation of Labor (and subsequently of the American Federation of Labor-Congress of Industrial Organizations [AFL-CIO]), and Jay Lovestone, who was for many years the virtual "foreign minister" of the AFL and then of the AFL-CIO.

Mr. Romualdi engaged my part-time services to help him edit the English-language periodical of the Interamerican Confederation of Workers (CIT), and then that of the Interamerican Regional Organization of Workers (ORIT). Mr. Lovestone employed me on a number of occasions during the Rutgers vacation periods to travel to various parts of Latin America to report to him what I observed there about the trade union situation (as well as general economic and political conditions) in the countries that I visited. With the help of these two gentlemen I was able to expand and intensify my firsthand acquaintanceship with the labor movements of Latin America and the Caribbean. Subsequently, for several additional decades, I continued to visit Latin America and the Caribbean and to maintain and broaden my study of the subject.

In traveling more or less frequently to Latin America and the Caribbean, renewing and expanding my contacts with organized labor in the nations, I kept extensive notes on conversations I had with union leaders, politicians, and others who could shed light on the labor movement, as well as comments on particular situations that I was able to observe. These notes and comments have provided an important part of the material that appears in this book. So do trade union related documents that I collected on my visits.

Of course, I am obliged to many people who had made it possible for this book to be written and published. To start with, I owe much to the many people who, over the years, talked with me and told me about details of the history of Cuban organized labor with which they were acquainted or in which they had participated. The names of many of these can be found in the chapter notes and Bibliography.

I am much obliged to Dr. Efrén Córdova, who himself has chronicled the story of Cuban organized labor and who was kind enough to read parts of the manuscript of this book, and to give me a worthwhile critique of them. Of course, he bears no responsibility for any errors of fact or judgment that appear in these pages. That responsibility is only mine.

I also owe much to my friend and former student, Eldon Parker, who has put the manuscript into camera-ready condition, and has done invaluable work in proofreading it, and helping in various other ways to get the book through the production process.

I likewise owe much to people in Greenwood Publishing who were instrumental in bringing this book to print. As has frequently been the case in the past, I must thank Dr. James Sabin, who decided that this work was worthy of publication. I must also thank Susan Thornton for copyediting and Lynn Zelem who otherwise pushed forward the process of converting a manuscript into a published book.

Finally, I am as always indebted to my wife, Joan, who bore with me while I worked on this book instead of doing other things that she might have thought more worthwhile.

Rutgers University
New Brunswick, NJ

1

Organized Labor in the Colonial Period and Early Republic

Cuba, together with Puerto Rico, were the last parts of the American empire to be lost by Spain. Cuba did not fall until what the Cubans call the Cuban-Spanish-American War of 1898.

During almost all of the nineteenth century, the Spaniards continued to rule in the island. During that period, the Cuban economy began to center particularly on the production and export of sugar and tobacco. In the last decades of the century, investments, particularly in sugar, by United States citizens and companies increasingly challenged Spanish control of the Cuban economy.

The labor force, particularly in the sugar industry, continued until very late in the nineteenth century to be made up to a large degree of black slaves from Africa. Although the Cuban First Republic declared the emancipation of the slaves in 1868, not until 1886 did slavery effectively end. Cuba was the next to last American country to abolish slavery. So long as slavery existed, it greatly hampered the development of an organized labor movement.

By the middle of the nineteenth century, Cuban politics began to become a reality. Political opinion was divided among three groups. There were those who supported the continuation of Cuba as a Spanish colony; those who, without breaking the ties with the "mother country," sought the establishment of an autonomous regime on the island; and those who advocated establishment of a Cuban republic, independent of Spain. The Spanish government did little to placate those who held the latter two points of view.

The upshot of the situation was the outbreak in 1868 of the Ten Years War, the island's first struggle for independence. Under the leadership of a landowner on the eastern part of the island, Carlos Manuel de Céspedes, the First Cuban Republic was proclaimed, and for some time the rebels controlled much of the eastern half of the island. It took a decade for the Spanish authorities to defeat the rebels.

However, the military defeat of the republic did not end the struggle against the colonial rule that Spain had exercised over the island for almost four centuries. Finally, the Liberal Party government, which came to power in Spain in 1897, recognized this fact. That administration negotiated with the Autonomist parties in both Cuba and Puerto Rico and early in 1898 established more or less elected autonomous regimes in both islands.

However, in Cuba it was too late. The military struggle for reestablishment of the Cuban Republic had been resumed. This time, the spark plug of the independence forces was José Martí. After more than a decade of organizing the independentist forces from exile, and of traveling throughout the Western Hemisphere arguing the cause of the Cuban Republic, he had succeeded in launching a second war of independence in 1895. Although Martí was killed early in the struggle, the war went on.

The Second Cuban War of Independence aroused much attention and sympathy in the United States. There had always been those North Americans who felt that "manifest destiny" dictated that Cuba become part of the United States, and there were by 1898 those who felt that the Cuban revolutionary war presented the chance of that destiny's being fulfilled. There were by that time, too, important United States economic interests in the sugar industry and elsewhere that welcomed the chance to "free" Cuba from Spanish rule. Finally, there were some idealistic sympathizers with the Cuban struggle for independence, whose number was greatly augmented by the vivid descriptions by an important part of the United States press of the bravery of the rebels and the cruelty of the Spanish "oppressors."

The United States became involved in the struggle in Cuba as the result of the explosion in the Havana harbor of the U.S. battleship *Maine*, the exact cause of which remained a mystery a century after it occurred. However, whatever the cause, the government of President William McKinley took the incident as a casus belli, and war was soon declared on Spain by the United States Congress. After a conflict lasting about three months, the United States forces controlled not only Cuba, but also Puerto Rico, as well as the Philippine Islands and Guam, Spanish possessions in the Pacific Ocean.

For four years after the United States occupation, Cuba was under U.S. military government. The United States Congress refused to end that regime until the Cuban assembly, which was writing a constitution for the Republic of Cuba, would adopt the Platt Amendment, which provided for the right of the United States government

to intervene for the conservation of the independence of Cuba, the maintenance of a government adequate for the protection of lives, property and individual liberty and to fulfill the obligations which with respect to Cuba have been imposed upon the United States by the Treaty of Peace and which now must be assumed and fulfilled by the Government of Cuba.[1]

Of course, the treaty of peace had been signed by the United States and Spain, with no participation by the Cubans.

In 1902 the Republic of Cuba was formally launched, with Tomás Estrada Palma, a man who had lived for many years in the United States, as its first president. During the first U.S. military occupation of Cuba and the Estrada Palma administration the trade union movement began to take shape.

As the end of his administration approached, it became evident that Estrada Palma wanted to have a second four-year term. However, this aroused great opposition, and even armed revolt. That situation was used as justification of a second military occupation of Cuba by the United States under the terms of the Platt Amendment, which lasted from 1906 to 1909.

This second occupation ended in 1909, when General José Miguel Gómez, a Liberal, was elected president. He was succeeded by General Mario García Menocal, a Conservative, who remained in office until 1921. Neither Gómez nor García Menocal was favorably disposed toward the existing labor movement.

During the nearly two decades of the Cuban Republic, the Cuban economy became overwhelmingly concentrated on the production and export of sugar. United States companies invested heavily in that industry, as did Cuban landowners. During World War I the sugar industry grew particularly rapidly, to provide the sugar needed by both the United States and Allied Europe, which had been to a large degree cut off from other sources of supply by the war. This boom came to a sudden end in 1920, and Cuban sugar suffered from an economic crisis that lasted for more than a decade and a half.

One effect of this crisis was that a large proportion of Cuban sugar producers lost control of their estates. Having borrowed very heavily from the foreign banks—American, Canadian, and Spanish, among others—that made up most of the financial sector to expand their operations during the war, producers were unable to repay these loans after 1920 and lost their properties to the banks. The banks held them until World War II, which generated another sugar boom and allowed Cuban companies and individuals to purchase the sugar properties from the foreign financial institutions.

Meanwhile, the United States government had intervened once again in Cuban political life, sending General Enoch Crowder to Havana virtually to establish a protectorate regime, in which he in effect gave orders to President Menocal, and his successor, President Alfredo Zayas. This was precipitated by growing opposition to Menocal and the spread of massive corruption and what was seen from Washington as a growing financial crisis.

At the end of Zayas's administration, General Gerardo Machado was elected. Although at first he enjoyed substantial popular support, he was no friend of organized labor. As minister of interior under President Gómez he had treated the labor movement very arbitrarily. On becoming president, he made it known that no strike would be allowed to last more than twenty-four hours.[2]

During his more than eight years in the presidency, Gerardo Machado established one of the worst dictatorships under which Cuba suffered in the twentieth century. He altered the constitution to permit his staying in office after his term ended. He established a fearsome secret police force that jailed, tortured, and murdered people, extending its range of killings not only throughout Cuba but also into several neighboring countries. Among its victims were many leaders of organized labor.

Finally, in August 1933, President Machado was overthrown by the country's first successful military coup. This occurred while the dictator was faced with an almost universal general strike, which he unsuccessfully tried to halt by making a deal with the Communist leadership of the Confederación Obrera Nacional de Cuba (CNOC); and the coup was encouraged, if not engineered, by the United States ambassador, Sumner Welles.

Welles installed a new "safe" conservative administration headed by Carlos Manuel de Céspedes, grandson of the president of the First Cuban Republic of 1868–1878. However, that short-lived regime was itself overthrown by an insurrection of army enlisted men led by Sergeant Fulgencio Batista and university students. They installed a provisional government headed by Professor Ramón Grau San Martín of the University of Havana Medical School, which consisted in large part of university students and recently graduated alumni. This first Grau San Martín government was nationalist and socially oriented, with wide popular support, including that of much of the labor movement.

However, the Grau San Martín regime had two powerful enemies—the Communist Party and the United States government. The first sought to launch its own rural revolution, and the latter—at the urging of Ambassador Welles and his successor, Jefferson Caffery—convinced the State Department not to grant diplomatic recognition to the Grau administration. Finally, Caffery convinced the former Sergeant—by then Colonel—Batista to oust Grau and put in his place an old-style Cuban politician, Colonel Carlos Mendieta.

There was widespread popular opposition—particularly from the labor movement—to the Mendieta regime. This culminated in a revolutionary general strike in March 1935, which was put down with extreme brutality. For a couple of years, the regime— run from behind the scenes by Colonel Batista—was very oppressive and sought all but to destroy the labor movement.

However, in 1937 Colonel Batista began to modify his regime. He reached an agreement with the Communists and the remains of the CNOC leadership whereby he allowed the reorganization of the labor movement under predominantly Communist direction and the legal recognition of the Communist Party and began to make arrangements for the election of a new constitutional assembly.

As a result of this agreement, in January 1939, a congress was held that established a new central labor organization, the Confederación de Trabajadores de Cuba (CTC), which soon included virtually all of a greatly expanded labor movement within its ranks. Later that year, elections were held for a constituent assembly, which fashioned what came to be seen as one of the most progressive constitutions in Latin America, that of 1940.

Later that year Colonel Batista was elected president. He presided over a democratic regime, which in 1944 held honest elections that were won by the opposition presidential candidate, Ramón Grau San Martín. Although Grau's election was at first greeted with much euphoria by a large part of the population, disillusionment quickly followed. Not only did it fail to carry out most of the program of social and economic change on which it had been elected, but it evidenced a degree of corruption hitherto unmatched in Cuban history. From the point of view of the labor movement, it was most important because it saw the substitution of control over organized labor by President Grau's own party, the Partido Revolucionario Cubano (Auténtico), popularly called the Auténticos, for that of the Communists.

President Grau was succeeded in 1948 by President Carlos Prío Socarrás, also an Auténtico. Although Prío's government was also characterized by substantial corruption, it did carry out

much of the Auténtico program, establishing a Cuban central
bank and a Bank of Agricultural and Industrial Development, as
well as setting up the Tribunal de Cuentas, provided for in the
Constitution of 1940 and designed to keep track of government
expenditures to prevent corruption.

The Auténticos might well have won a third term in elections
scheduled for June 1952. But those elections were never held. On
March 10, General Batista engineered a military coup that ousted
President Prío—who offered little resistance—and installed the
general as Cuban chief executive once again. He engineered and
managed presidential and parliamentary elections in 1954 that he
won when Ramón Grau San Martín, his only opponent, withdrew
a few days before the election, charging that its results had been
rigged.

During the second Batista dictatorship, organized labor suffered a catastrophic crisis. At first trying to launch a general
strike against Batista's coup of March 10, 1952, the Auténtico
leaders of the CTC quickly made a deal with General Batista, feeling that that was the only way of preserving the labor movement.
However, as time went on, the top CTC leadership, headed by Eusebio Mujal, became, objectively at least, one of Batista's most
important supporters, leading subsequently to their complete dis-
crediting.

The opponents of the Batista dictatorship were divided into
four groups, insofar as strategy to overthrow the dictatorship was
concerned. One, headed by the former President Grau San
Martín, sought to repeat the 1944 experience and defeat him at
the polls. A second, led by former President Prío, attempted to
engineer a military coup against him. A third element, based on
the university students' organization, the Directorio Revolucionario, relied on terror, including a major attempt to kill the tyrant.

The fourth group of opponents of Batista sought to organize a
guerrilla war against the dictatorship. The most prominent—and
successful—of those supporting this strategy was Fidel Castro,
whose 26th of July Movement in November 1956 launched such a
guerrilla effort—to be followed soon by smaller contingents of people of the Directorio Revolucionario and some ex-followers of
President Prío, in separate guerrilla forces. This strategy finally
proved successful on January 1, 1959, when, after a major military defeat, Batista fled into exile.

The first months of the regime dominated by Fidel Castro and
the 26th of July were in a real sense transitional. It was not
clear—perhaps not even to Castro himself—in what direction the
new leaders wished to take Cuba. In that period, the 26th of July

more or less completely dominated organized labor, and demonstrated to a large degree the uncertainty of direction of the regime.

However, by the last months of 1959, Fidel Castro and the principal figures in the regime had determined that they were going to lead the Cuban Revolution in a Marxist-Leninist direction. Obviously, this had grave repercussions in the labor movement, which eventually resembled those of other Communist-led regimes.

ANTECEDENTS OF CUBAN ORGANIZED LABOR

Mario Riera Hernández professed to see as a forerunner of the modern labor movement in Cuba a strike in 1574 of stonecutters employed in building a military fortification that was resolved by granting the workers involved an increase in pay and a reduction of working hours.[3] However, there was in fact no permanent organization that resulted from this incident; nor did it in any other way leave any traces in subsequent Cuban history. Three centuries would pass before the beginnings of a modern labor movement.

Until very late in Cuban colonial history, slavery remained a major impediment to the establishment of any kind of labor organization. Although there were undoubtedly from time to time isolated slave rebellions, the slave system did not have room for any organization of the enslaved workers for the purpose of ameliorating their lot.[4]

Among the island's free workers, the Spaniards attempted to establish *corporaciones* or *gremios*, organizations similar to the guilds that had existed in medieval Spain and continued in that country for several centuries thereafter. These groups, of course, were made up of masters, journeymen, and apprentices, dominated by the first of these groups. According to Efrén Córdova, there did not develop in Cuba any kind of specific journeymen's groups that could be precursors of a modern labor movement such as those that emerged in France. Indeed, the only possible connection of the *corporaciones* with the emergence of the labor movement was the support that a few of them gave to the establishment of mutual benefit societies in the early decades of the nineteenth century.[5]

As in most of the rest of Latin America, it was the mutual benefit societies, and what Córdova called the "artisans' societies," that were, at least in some cases, the direct antecedents of trade unions. Córdova distinguishes between the mutual benefit societies, which were made up of workers in various trades, and the artisans' societies, consisting of workers who had a particular specialty. These began to appear in some numbers between 1848 and 1850. Both kinds of organizations were principally concerned with providing financial help to their members in case of sickness and aid to families on the death of breadwinners. Some also took an interest in establishing cooperatives.

Córdova notes:

Even more interesting was the fact that along with the classic purposes of protecting the members, there began to appear in some artisans' societies and those of mutual benefit, the purpose of defending the group. This was not yet expressed in a militant form or too explicitly, but the fact that some of these societies were in fact transforming themselves in practice into *resistance societies* pointed to another form of evolution in the direction of trade unionism.[6]

THE BEGINNING OF THE LABOR MOVEMENT

At the end of 1865 the first labor newspaper in Cuba, *La Aurora*, was established by Saturnino Martínez. He was a Spanish worker from Asturias, who had had some contact with the labor movement already in existence in his homeland and had worked for a number of years in the tobacco industry in Havana.

La Aurora circulated particularly among the tobacco workers. It published information about the bad working conditions of those employed in that industry, as well as in some others. It also emphasized Saturnino Martínez's belief that one of the things that the workers needed to improve their situation was education. The paper argued strongly for the establishment by the workers of schools in which they and their children could become literate and acquire other kinds of knowledge.

Martínez also advocated strongly something that was to become common in the Cuban tobacco industry where newspapers, books, and magazines were read to the workers. Although the Spanish government in Cuba at first allowed the practice of reading in the tobacco shops, in 1867 it outlawed it on the grounds that the workers were being imbued with "subversive" ideas. Subsequently, however, the regime allowed the renewal of the practice.

A close associate of Saturnino Martínez was José de Jesús Márquez, a Cuban who had lived for a number of years in the United States and had returned home with new ideas. He was particularly strong in his adherence to the notion that the workers should establish cooperatives, particularly consumers' cooperatives. These ideas were circulated through *La Aurora*.

Labor journalism was not the only interest of Saturnino Martínez. In August 1865 there had occurred spontaneous strikes in the important tobacco enterprises in Havana. After these, Martínez undertook the leadership in the formation of what Efrén

Córdova calls "the first Cuban trade union," the Asociación [or Gremio] de Tabaqueros de La Habana, established in June 1866. The association presented demands to a number of the employing firms in the tobacco industry, and although it lasted only six months as a result of disputes within its membership, it set what became a pattern for Cuban labor organizations. It conducted a number of strikes, during which employers used the ranks of a dissident group, the Unión Obrera, to provide strikebreakers.[7]

Carlos del Toro has written that

at the beginning of the Ten Years War . . . the organization of the Cuban proletariat was fragmented in diverse mutualist, cooperative and craft organizations of ephemeral existence or which fought to survive under difficult conditions, especially in the tobacco industry. Where they appeared, they were oriented to improvements of a moral, economic and hygienic nature. The regime of slavery weighed heavily on the process of development and increase of the Cuban working class.[8]

The first Cuban war of independence, the Ten Years War (1868–1878), served to curb the first growth of trade unionism. The Spanish colonial government adopted draconian measures against "treason," evidence of which included "coalition of laborers or workers and leagues."[9] Although there were walkouts during those years, particularly in 1872 and 1876, among tobacco workers, shoemakers, coach drivers, and other groups of workers, these were severely repressed, and numerous strikers were jailed by the authorities.[10] Saturnino Martínez, who was by then publishing the periodical *La Unión*, was deported to Spain for publishing articles in sympathy with the First International in that newspaper.[11]

After the Ten Years War the labor movement began to expand considerably. Not only the tobacco workers and the printing trades workers, who in the 1860s had been the first groups to organize, established new unions; so did construction workers, railroad workers, port workers, and as well as a number of artisan groups such as tailors, bakers, shoemakers, and coach drivers.[12] One example of these organizations was the hotel and restaurant workers union of Havana, which was founded in 1889 as a *Gremio*, rather than a "resistance society." In one form or another it continued to exist for at least the next sixty years.[13]

The labor movement began to expand outside the capital city of Havana, where it had formerly been concentrated, into nearby municipalities and the provinces of the interior. Efrén Córdova comments, "By the middle of the decade of the '80s, it was difficult to find a city of importance in Cuba where there were not groups of workers."[14]

This spread of trade unionism was confined almost totally to the cities and large towns. Most particularly, it had little impact on the sugar industry, the largest segment of the Cuban economy. Certainly one reason was that slavery was not finally abolished until 1886, and a substantial portion of the sugar workers were slaves. Others were people imported from China and even from the Yucatan Peninsula of Mexico, whose status in the sugar plantations was not far removed from slavery.

Even after emancipation, trade unionism had little immediate impact among the sugar workers. Another generation had to pass before unionization among them began to be widespread.

The United States anthropologist John Dumoulin described the situation among the sugar workers in the area of Cruces, near the city of Cienfuegos in Central Cuba in the period between the two Wars of Independence. He noted that the workers tended to organize principally on the basis of ethnicity. Thus, there existed a Club Español, a Club Asiático, and a Circulo Africano. There also existed a Club de Obreros, consisting largely of black workers and mulattoes who were oriented toward assimilation to the predominant Cuban values of the time. All of these organizations were social groups, with an orientation toward self-education and uplift. Only among the Spaniards was there some evidence of the beginning of anarchist influence.[15]

As the labor movement spread, it exhibited two ideological tendencies. One, usually referred to as "reformist," included Saturnino Martínez, who had returned to Cuba in 1878 and revived the tobacco workers' organization in Havana, now called the Gremio de Obreros del Ramo de Tabaquerías, of which he became the leader, as he had been a decade earlier.[16]

The other tendency in the labor movement after 1878 was anarchism. Stimulated in part by workers who had been active in the anarchist labor movement in Spain and had migrated to Cuba, anarchism also gained many recruits among native Cubans. One of the most outstanding Cuban anarchists was Enrique Roig San Martín, who had worked in both the sugar and tobacco industries. He became an early labor journalist, writing in *El Obrero* and the *Boletín del Gremio de Obreros*, the periodical of the Gremio de Obreros del Ramo de Tabaquierías, which, although it had been founded by Saturnino Martínez, quickly passed into the control of the anarchists. In 1887, Roig founded *El Productor*, which for some years was the leading labor publication in Havana.[17]

In 1879, the anarchist labor leaders established in Havana the Junta Central de Artesanos, which later changed its name to Junta Central de Trabajadores. It drew together not only the nascent trade unions but also mutual benefit organizations. It had as its objectives the spread of labor organization and the provision of a united voice for the city's workers. After a decline, the Junta was reorganized in 1885; it was given some government recognition in October of that year.

A somewhat different kind of central group was established in Havana in February 1885. This was the Círculo de Trabajadores de La Havana, which was dedicated particularly to labor education, urging the unions to establish cultural activities and libraries for their members. Like the Junta, the Círculo had an anarchist orientation, including among its leaders some of the leading anarchists of the period, including Enrique Messonier, Enrique Crecci, and Máximo Fernández.

Soon after the establishment of the Círculo de Trabajadores, Messonier and Crecci toured the interior of the country, trying to encourage labor organization, as well as the establishment of specifically anarchist groups. They were successful principally in the provinces of Havana and Santa Clara.[18]

THE LABOR CONGRESSES OF 1887 AND 1892

The Congress of 1887, which is generally seen by historians of the Cuban labor movement as the first such conclave, was in fact a series of meetings held in Havana and neighboring towns. These were held under the aegis of the Spanish anarchist group, the Federación de Trabajadores de la Región Española. Representatives chosen by each of these meetings gathered in Havana in November 1887 to adopt a statement of principles, which reflected the anarchosyndicalist origins of the sponsors of the gathering.[19] According to the more or less official history of the Cuban organized labor published by the Castro Communist Party (as opposed to the earlier Communist Party), it was this "1887 Congress" that marked the end of control of "reformist" leaders over the Cuban labor movement.[20]

The congress that met in Havana in January 1892 can be better regarded as the first national meeting of the Cuban labor movement, since there were present delegates from the unions from all over the country, except the city of Santiago de Cuba. The agenda for the meeting included three points: discussion of the eight-hour workday and means of obtaining it, the type of national organization the workers should establish, and any other matters that the delegates wished to suggest.

Much of the discussion of the meeting centered on the eight-hour-day question. Opinion was unanimous that workday should be limited to eight hours, not only to improve workers' health, but to allow them to educate themselves and otherwise improve their lives. The meeting expressed the opinion that the only way to achieve this goal was a national general strike, although no steps were apparently approved to bring about such an event.

The resolution concerning future organization of the workers of the island that was adopted clearly reflected the anarchosyndicalist point of view. It urged that in each locality there to be established a workers' organization that would be divided into branches of workers in a particular trade or industry; all of these regional groups would be joined to form the Federación de Trabajadores de Cuba. However, each local unit of the organization should have full autonomy, and no central group should be able to impose its ideas or control on any subordinate element in the federation.

A variety of resolutions concerning other issues and problems were discussed and adopted. One of these committed Cuban organized labor to "revolutionary socialism," a phrase frequently used by the anarchosyndicalists to describe their own ideology. Another expounded extensively on the need for equality among the white and black workers of the island. Finally, a resolution that was presented argued that seeking the emancipation of the individual, as congress aspired to do "could never become an obstacle to the aspirations of the emancipation of the people."

It was perhaps this last resolve of the congress that caused the Spanish colonial government to order the dissolution of the meeting before it had concluded its business. Orders were also issued for the arrest of the delegates to the congress.[21]

LABOR ACTIVITIES BEFORE THE SECOND INDEPENDENCE WAR

The new Cuban labor movement engaged in a variety of different activities in the years before the outbreak of the Second War for Independence in 1895. In 1887, the Círculo de Trabajadores raised funds to send to the families of the "martyrs of Chicago," the union leaders who were put on trial after the Haymarket Massacre in Chicago. Then in 1890, the Círculo sponsored Cuba's first May Day demonstration in Havana, both to protest the execution of the Chicago martyrs and to advocate the institution of the eight-hour workday. Some three thousand workers gathered in a park, then marched to a theater, where twelve orators delivered speeches. There were also May Day demonstrations in the three succeeding years.[22]

Strikes were relatively frequent in the 1880s and early 1890s. Between 1879 and 1900 there were eighty-three recorded strikes, of which sixty-six took place in Havana, and twenty-seven were walkouts of tobacco workers.[23] During this period, the other workers involved in walkouts included railroaders, millers, milk workers, hotel and restaurant employees, painters, port workers, metal workers, and coach drivers.[24] There were even two strikes recorded in the sugar industry: one of white workers in two sugar mills in the province of Matanzas in 1880, and another by black workers in another Matanzas mill three years later.[25]

Wages and hours were the most frequent causes of strikes. Wages generally were very low in Cuba in this period, and working hours were frequently twelve to fourteen a day. However, general working conditions, complaints about housing and meal conditions, as well as abusive treatment of workers by management also caused the workers to walk out.[26]

Several strikes of the period are of particular interest. In 1882 there was a walkout of tailors in Havana and employers sought to recruit strikebreakers in New York City, but when the Cuban strikers appealed to their fellow workers in New York, the employers were only able to recruit seventeen scabs.[27]

One of the most important strikes of the period was that of the coach drivers of Havana in October 1890. Some four thousand workers were involved, and they gained support from tobacco workers, bakers, bricklayers, and other groups who called sympathy strikes. However, the Spanish civil governor supported the employers' efforts to break this strike, prohibiting all meetings or demonstrations and threatening to draft the strikers into military service. As a consequence, the walkout was lost.[28]

Two tobacco worker walkouts in Havana were particularly notable. One, in 1886, first involved workers employed in shops that used relatively inferior tobacco grown in the vicinity of Havana (second category), whose products sold at lower prices than those made with finer tobacco from the province of Pinar del Río (first category), where workers had lower wages than their fellows in first category plants. The strikers demanded to be paid the same wages as first category workers, a demand that was first supported by employers of first category shops, on the assumption that if their competitors were forced to pay higher wages, they would have to raise the prices of their products. But when workers in first category shops began to join the strike, the tobacco employers generally declared a lockout, defeating the walkout. This defeat greatly weakened the position of the reformist union leader Saturnino Martínez, who until then had been the principal tobacco workers' leader in Havana.

The use of the lockout also played a major role in another tobacco strike, in July 1888. When employees of the employers' association, the Unión de Fabricantes de Tabaco de La Habana, demanded wage increases, the head of the association dismissed the workers who presented the demands. This act provoked a strike, which was soon joined by workers of many other tobacco firms, whereupon the employers' association declared a general lockout and refused to negotiate at all with the unions. However, the strikers sought direct negotiations with individual factory owners and soon reached agreements with more than one hundred of them, representing a serious defeat for the employers' organization.[29]

During this 1888 strike, the tobacco workers became divided into two rival groups. One was the Alianza Obrera, of anarchist orientation and headed by Enrique Roig San Martín, Enrique Messonier and Enrique Crecci. It urged formation of a federation that included all the tobacco worker unions, as well as insisting on the equality of all workers in the industry, whether white or black, native born or immigrants. The other group was the Unión Obrera, of which the principal leader was Saturnino Martínez, the veteran reformist leader. For some time, there were serious clashes, sometimes involving the use of force, between these two workers' groups.[30]

Carlos del Toro noted that by 1889

there were workers organizations in the principal centers of the Island of Cuba, even in the Oriente region which was hard to get to because of primitive transport conditions and communication facilities. The Círculo de Trabajadores maintained fraternal relations with the different proletarian societies in Cuban territory and even with the tobacco workers of Tampa and Key West, who were accused of being separatist and revolutionary elements.[31]

ORGANIZED LABOR DURING THE FIRST U.S. OCCUPATION

The organized labor movement suffered greatly during the Second War of Independence. According to the official history of the labor movement of the Castro Communist Party: "The organizational state of the workers of Cuba at the beginning of the North American occupation was chaotic. Very few organizations were able to survive the systematic persecution of the Spanish authorities during the period of the war; only a few remained . . . which were fundamentally made up of and led by Spaniards."[32]

However, with the end of Spanish rule, the labor movement began to revive. The Círculo de Trabajadores of Havana, which had been outlawed during the war, was revived, as were a number of unions that had also been suspended during the conflict,

particularly those of tobacco workers, but also including organizations of railroaders, bakers, typographers, construction workers,
tailors, and others. By the end of the occupation, there were more
than thirty unions functioning in the province of Havana. However, the resurgence of unionism was not confined to the capital
and its environs, but also took place in provincial cities such as
Cardenas, Cienfuegos and Santiago de Cuba.[33]

An organization that sought to unite the labor movement
throughout the island, the Liga General de Trabajadores, was
established in September 1899. It was organized on a regional
basis, with local groups in various cities joining not only unions
but other working-class organizations. Its leaders traveled in the
interior, stimulating the revival of the labor movement.

The Liga General de Trabajadores did not have any very clear
ideological orientation. However, it did oppose those who were
then advocating that Cuba be annexed to the United States and
fought for equal treatment of Cuban and Spanish workers in the
island. For some years, its periodical, *Alerta!*, carried articles reflecting the various ideological tendencies then extant in the labor
movement: anarchosyndicalism, Marxism, and reformism. At its
high point, the Liga had between 10,000 and 15,000 members.
However, it did not long survive the end of the first U.S. occupation of the island.[34]

There were dozens of strikes in Cuba during this period.
Among the most frequent demands of the strikers were increases
in wages, reduction of working hours, ending of discrimination
against native Cuban workers, general improvement of working
conditions, and protection of jobs against import competition.

The first strike after formal occupation of the island, took
place in January 1899 among the port workers of Cárdenas, in
the province of Matanzas, which was then the major city for export of sugar. The workers demanded payment in U.S. dollars
instead of Spanish pesos, which circulated at a considerable discount, and an increase in their wages. After seventy-two hours,
the walkout was settled on the basis of payment in dollars, but
without a formal wage increase.

One of the most important strikes of the period was that of
the construction workers of Havana, some 1,500 of whom walked
out, demanding wage increases, payment in U.S. dollars, and establishment of the eight-hour day. The walkout had the backing
of a number of other Havana unions, and a variety of meetings
were held in its support. However, the U.S. military authorities
reacted strongly against the walkout and arrested a number of
the strike leaders, who were forced to appear on a balcony and
urge their followers to call off the walkout. The Liga General de

Trabajadores Cubanos did not support the strike, and it was finally lost.[35]

There even occurred a few isolated strikes among sugar workers. In the Cruces area there was such a walkout in 1902. It was
held by members of the Club Africano, evidencing the melding of
ethnic and trade union consciousness, and was centered among
the field hands rather than the mill workers.[36]

THE APPRENTICE STRIKE

The Cuban Republic, under President Estrada Palma, was officially launched on May Day 1902. Almost exactly six months
later there occurred the first major strike of the republic's history,
which, starting with the tobacco workers, became virtually a general strike in Havana and some provincial cities.

The walkout was known as the Apprentice Strike, since the
principal demand put forward by the tobacco workers was an end
to the system whereby only young Spanish immigrants were allowed to become apprentices, thus giving them ultimate access to
the better paying jobs in the industry, while Cubans were limited
to the poorer paying positions. The strikers also demanded that
the number of apprentices in any tobacco shop be limited to 5
percent, and that the employers recognize the unions and meet
regularly with union representatives to handle problems that
might arise.

By this time, two-thirds of the tobacco industry was in the
hands of two large companies, one British and one North American; while the rest of the shops, in the hands of Cubans, were
generally referred to as independents. All of the employers absolutely refused to negotiate the issues that the workers' unions
had raised. When the unions presented their demands to President Estrada Palma, he refused to intervene, claiming that the
issue should be dealt with by the mayor of Havana.

In the face of this situation, when a strike broke out early in
November in one of the North American tobacco plants over an
issue unrelated to these general demands, the union leaders, who
for some time had been planning for a general strike of tobacco
workers, decided to call such a walkout. Quickly, all of the United
States–owned plants were closed down, followed quickly by those
of British ownership, and then the independents. Cuban tobacco
workers in Key West and Tampa, Florida, quickly sent funds to
help their striking colleagues.

The Liga General de Trabajadores Cubanos immediately declared its support for the tobacco workers' strike, and various
other workers' groups also went out on strike. The movement

spread to the province of Santa Clara, where workers of Cienfuegos and Cruces joined the walkout, even including some sugar workers near the latter city, who went on strike.

On November 22, 23, and 24, 1902, the economic life of Havana was virtually closed down. The government responded to this general strike with violence. It sent out not only the urban police and army units, but also elements of the Guardia Rural to combat the walkout. Police and soldiers fired on demonstrating strikers, killing many and wounding hundreds.

Finally, a group of veterans of the Second War of Independence, headed by Máximo Gómez, decided to intervene in the situation. They negotiated with the strike leaders and President Estrada Palma, getting from the latter a promise that he would push through Congress a law opening up the ranks of apprentices to Cubans regardless of race and fixing their number at 5 percent of the work force. In the light of that promise, the strike leaders called off the walkout on November 28.

However, President Estrada Palma did not honor his promise. Instead, the government persecuted the strike leaders, arresting many of them and forcing others to flee abroad to avoid being jailed. It was not until 1933 that the apprenticeship issue was resolved when the first government of President Ramón Grau San Martín enacted a decree providing that the great majority of employees in any firm had to be native Cubans.

This "solution" of the Apprentice Strike was in fact a major defeat for organized labor. The most obvious early result of this defeat was that the Liga General de Trabajadores went out of existence a few months later.[37]

However, the defeat of the Apprentice Strike by no means put an end to all trade union activity and militancy. There were several significant strikes in the years immediately after the 1902 general walkout. These included work stoppages in some sugar plantations in the province of Las Villas in the areas of Cruces and Lajas, one by railroaders in the Pinar del Río and another by shoemakers in the same province. During this period, the anarchist labor leaders sometimes used the boycott instead of the strike as a weapon against employers who were not willing to negotiate or to bargain effectively with the unions.[38]

THE LABOR MOVEMENT DURING THE SECOND AMERICAN OCCUPATION

As a consequence of the political disturbances surrounding President Estrada Palma's unsuccessful attempt to extend his term in power, the second U.S. military occupation of Cuba began on September 28, 1906. Far from resulting in a suppression of trade union activity, this second Yankee intervention seems to have served to reanimate the Cuban labor movement. In December 1908, the U.S. governor, Charles Magoon, wrote, "The industrial situation has been complicated by numerous strikes." According to him, these had occurred among tobacco workers, railroaders, masons, and several other groups.[39]

The most famous strike during this period was that of the Havana tobacco workers in February 1907, which was popularly known as the Money Strike, since the principal matter of dispute was the kind of money in which the workers should be paid. They demanded to get their wages in U.S. dollars, instead of in the depreciated Spanish pesetas that still circulated in the island. This walkout lasted from February until July 1907. It received wide support from other labor groups, who raised funds to help the workers who were out on strike, including a contribution from Cuban tobacco workers in Key West, as well as from the Partido Socialista de Cuba. As the strike lingered on, Samuel Gompers, the president of the American Federation of Labor (himself an old cigar maker) went to Havana to express the U.S. labor movement's strong support for the walkout.

The British and American employers whose workers were out on strike remained adamant for a considerable period. They finally convinced the independent cigar makers to close down their operations, thus increasing the number of unemployed tobacco workers, but that move did not break the strike because of the financial and other aid the strikers received.

U.S. Military Governor Magoon did nothing to try to break the tobacco workers strike. Finally, he made it clear that he thought that the demand of the workers to be paid in the currency that would give them a higher income was a reasonable one. The employers finally gave in and settled the walkout on the basis of agreeing to pay the workers in dollars.[40]

This success of the tobacco workers stimulated other workers to go out on strike. These included railroaders, masons, and commercial employees. The results of these walkouts varied from case to case. One notably successful strike was that of the masons of Havana in January 1908, which won wage increases and the eight-hour working day.[41]

The success of the Money Strike also led to the formation of the Comité Federativo. This was a loosely organized body that had the objective of forming a nationwide labor federation. Although it succeeded in rallying support for a number of the strikes of this period, it did not succeed in establishing a national labor organization.[42]

Considerably less influential, but with a following in some localities and among some kinds of workers were the more or less Marxian Socialists. The first attempt to establish a Socialist Party had been made in March 1899, with the organization of the Partido Socialista Cubano by Diego Vicente Tejera, who had been working with José Martí in exile and returned to Cuba soon after the end of the Spanish-Cuban-American War. Tejera was by no means an orthodox Marxist, but he did seek to have his party represent the working classes. It was of only a few months duration, however, and in 1900 Tejera established a second party, the Partido Popular, which took a strong position against continuing United States occupation of the island. It, too, was of very short duration, and Tejera died in 1903.[48]

In the year of Tejera's death, Carlos Baliño, who already had a substantial career as a labor organizer, established the Club de Propaganda Socialista. It became active in the Partido Obrero, which was established by a group of workers in Havana in 1904. In 1905, the Partido Obrero proclaimed its objective to be "the possession by the proletarian class of political power . . . so that society is organized on the basis of an economic federation . . . abolishing social classes so that there only exists one of workers, owners of the fruit of their labors, free, honorable, intelligent and equal." The party also changed its name to Partido Obrero Socialista, and Baliño became one of its principal figures.

Also in 1905, a group of Spanish immigrants who had belonged to Pablo Iglesias's Socialist Party in Spain established the Agrupación Socialista Internacional, which merged with the Partido Obrero Socialista to establish in November 1906 the Partido Socialista de la Isla de Cuba. Its periodical, *La Voz Obrera*, which had previously been published by the Partido Obrero, became one of the major advocates of the labor movement, and the Socialists' role in it.

Although the Partido Socialista de la Isla de Cuba described itself as Marxist, it was criticized by Carlos Baliño (and subsequently by the official history of Cuban labor of the Castro Communist Party) for mixing its Marxism with some ideas of Ferdinand Lasalle, for being insufficiently aware of the race problem in Cuba or of the discrimination against native-born Cubans that then existed, and for being insufficiently active in the organized labor movement.

Of more purely Marxist orientation was the Partido Socialista de Manzanillo, headed by a former anarchist, Agustín Martín Véloz, a tobacco worker. Established in 1906, it was thereafter very active in the local labor movement, taking the lead in organizing the Federación Obrera de Manzanillo and directing a number of strikes in the area. Some of its leaders would subsequently be among the founders of the Cuban Communist Party.[49]

The reformists were the second largest element in the labor movement in the two decades of the twentieth century. Unlike the anarchists and the Socialists, they were willing to work with the government. In fact, they received government aid, financial and otherwise, in organizing the largest national gathering to be held up until that time, the Congreso Obrero of August 1914. President Mario García Menocal provided 10,000 pesos for the organization of the congress, and the City Council of Havana declared the delegates "honored guests of the city" and appropriated 7,000 pesos to pay for their travel costs and their housing during the sessions of the congress. Subsequently, the organizers of the meeting published an extensive record accounting for how these funds had been spent. In the official report of the Congreso its Organizing Committee expressed their "profound thanks" to President Menocal; his secretary of justice, Dr. Cristóbal de la Guardia, who addressed the first session of the congress; and various other officials.[50]

A leading role in summoning this congress was that of the Asociación Cubana para la Protección Legal del Trabajo, established in February 1914. It was set up by some reformist labor leaders, as well as some professional people interested in labor problems, and even some people associated with the Menocal administration who also supported the passage of some labor legislation. The Asociación had relations with the International Association for the Legal Protection of Labor, which had headquarters in Switzerland.[51]

About 1,400 delegates attended this Congreso. Almost all of them represented organizations with reformist leadership. Anarchist-controlled unions refused to have anything to do with it, and there was only a sprinkling of people from Socialist-led organizations.[52]

Preceding the congress, an invitation had been issued not only to labor groups from all the country to send delegates, but also to individuals to submit short essays on problems that they thought faced the nation's working class. Prizes were awarded at the Congreso to those who had sent in the best essays, which included a wide range of subjects, including labor accidents, immigration, protection of jobs for native Cubans, problems of women and children workers, discussions of problems of particular workers' groups, and even one on the question of tariff protection for national industries. These essays were subsequently published, together with the minutes of various sessions of the congreso.[53]

One of the last resolutions passed by the congreso was a call for establishment of a Partido Democrático Socialista, to be the political representative of the workers. Right after the adjournment of the congress, a number of the delegates met again to launch the new party. This action drew strong condemnation in the press from government elements who had originally patronized the congreso. The party did not survive long.[54]

The leadership of the reformist element in the labor movement in this period was not homogeneous and had no cohesive ideology. For some time, Carlos Loveira, a railroader, was one of their outstanding figures, but he left the country after the outbreak of the Mexican Revolution, going to Yucatan, and subsequently to the United States, where he helped to organize the Pan American Federation of Labor, of which he became an official. The port workers' leader, Juan Arévalo, was another figure of significance among the reformists, although he sometimes proclaimed himself a Socialist. Efrén Córdova names Ramón Rivera, Feliciano Prieto and Manuel Candoya as other important reformist figures.[55]

Efrén Córdova noted that the reformers were the most influential among the tobacco workers, in a few sugar mills, among railroad and port workers, as well as among such craft groups as the meat workers, bakers, shoemakers, and tailors. He added that "some of these groups, principally the railroaders, port workers and skilled workers in the sugar mills were among the best paid in the country, which may in part explain their support of the reformist thesis."[56]

ORGANIZED LABOR IN WORLD WAR I AND IMMEDIATELY THEREAFTER

The First World War had a great impact on the Cuban economy. On the one hand, it resulted in a very great stimulus to sugar production, as access to sugar for the United States and the Allied countries of Europe from other areas was curtailed, thus generating a rapidly increased demand for Cuban sugar, the price of which rose considerably. On the other hand, the demand for Cuban tobacco declined sharply, as Britain in particular sharply limited the amount of tobacco that could be imported into the country, because of limitations on shipping space resulting from the war. Also, particularly during the last two years of the war, and for a year or so thereafter, there was substantial inflation, resulting, other things being equal, in a considerable fall in real wages.

Another factor was important for the labor movement, particularly in the sugar industry, during the war and immediately

afterward. The sugar employers persuaded the government to au-
thorize importation of very substantial numbers of workers,
particularly for labor in cutting and transporting cane, from Jamaica
and Haiti. It was estimated that between 1917 and 1921, some
230,000 such workers entered the country.

Organized labor expanded and was increasingly militant during this period. It was estimated that by the end of the war there
were between four hundred and four hundred fifty unions in
Cuba.

There were a number of important strikes during and immediately after the war. There were more than two hundred twenty
walkouts between 1917 and 1920. Many were strikes in individual enterprises; some were much more extensive.

Several strikes were particularly important. One of the first of
these was the walkout of 2,500 construction workers in Havana
in October–November 1916. Their demands were for a reduction
of working hours from nine to eight, and a 5 percent increase in
wages, and the strike was generally successful. However, in 1919
there was a further construction workers walkout in the capital,
particularly to force recalcitrant employers to conform to the earlier agreement, and to gain a further wage increase.

One of the most extensive strikes of the period was that of the
sugar workers, particularly those of the province of Las Villas, but
including some in the neighboring provinces of Matanzas and
Camaguey, in 1917. This walkout was concentrated among the
employees of the sugar mills, where imported foreign workers
were concentrated. This walkout was led by reformist leaders and
was in many cases more or less spontaneous, rather than organized by the unions. The government reacted with particular
violence against this strike, sending in troops and in some cases
using them as strikebreakers. Most of the people leading the
walkout were arrested. Finally, U.S. marines were landed in some
areas, allegedly to "protect" United States–owned plantations.
However, the American firms involved were not successful in efforts to recruit strikebreakers from the United States. The strike
was lost.[57]

A curious aspect of this sugar strike was the use apparently
made of it by President Menocal in negotiations with the U.S. government. At that time, the United States was buying all of the
Cuban sugar crop at a fixed price, a price that made both the
sugar producers and Menocal unhappy. He apparently used the
strike as an argument for pushing up the price.[58]

Late in 1917 there was a strike of railroad men in the province
of Camaguey. The railroad companies involved recruited four to
five hundred skilled workers from the United States to act as

strikebreakers. When the strike leaders contacted Samuel Gompers, president of the American Federation of Labor, to protest this, he went to Cuba, lodged a protest with the Cuban government, and personally addressed the American workers, urging them not to allow themselves to be used to break the strike, as a result of which they returned home.[59] The strikers gained a victory on only "some points" in their demands.[60]

Late in 1918 there was a walkout of the port workers of Havana, who were demanding wage increases. Although the government of President Menocal first used force against the walkout, arresting the strike leaders and deporting those who were not native-born Cubans, it soon relented, fearing that Cuba's foreign trade would be seriously damaged. It appointed an arbitration commission, which rendered a decision not only granting the union demands, but also establishing a system of rotating employment among longshoremen, replacing daily competition for jobs.

In 1919 there were three strikes of printing trades workers of Havana. The first of these arose when a number of employers refused to pay double wages to workers who went to their jobs on a "day of mourning" officially decreed by the Menocal government at the time of the death of Theodore Roosevelt. The second was in protest against the very low wages and ill treatment of apprentices by some employers. The third occurred when the employers rejected a series of demands by the Asociación de Tipógrafos. All three walkouts were won by the unionists, the first two by mutual agreement with the employer, the third as a result of an arbitrator's decision.

The strike was not the only weapon used by the unions during and right after the First World War. Some organizations, particularly those under anarchist leadership, used the boycott; in still other cases there was some resort to sabotage. The sympathy strike was also frequently used, provoking a strong attack on the idea by President Menocal.

The Menocal government more frequently than not resorted to various degrees of force to try to curb the strikes. Troops were sometimes used, as we have noted, and there was frequent resort to arrest of strike leaders and deportation of those who were foreigners. However, in a number of cases, the government appointed conciliators and/or arbitrators to try to seek a solution or to impose one if conciliation was not effective.[61]

THE FEDERACIÓN OBRERA DE LA HABANA AND
OTHER NEW ORGANIZATIONS

During World War I and the immediate postwar years, a number of important new labor groups were organized both in Havana and in the provinces. Among the latter were the Sindicato de Trabajadores de la Provincia de Camaguey, the Federación Obrera de Cienfuegos, the Unión General de Trabajadores Agricolas e Industriales de la Provincia de Matanzas, and the Gremio de Mineros de Pinar del Río.

One of the most important new organizations in Havana was the Federación Obrera de la Bahía de La Habana, of the port workers of the capital city. They were a particularly militant group in this period, although they were under so-called reformist leadership, headed by Juan Arévalo. According to the captain of the Port of Havana, there were in September 1918 some 5,430 organized port workers. Even the official history of organized labor published by the Castro Communist Party recognized, "In spite of being partisans of conciliation and arbitration, these leaders directed numerous successful actions of the port workers in favor of their demands."

Another key group established in Havana during this period was the Sindicato General de Obreros de la Industria Fabril, established in August 1917, which was "one of the most combative organizations of the period" and was under anarchist leadership. It had in its ranks groups of factory workers in the candy, soap, paper, cigar, and beer industries, among others. Among its principal leaders were Angel Arias and Margarito Iglesias.

An important organization was also established among the tobacco workers. This was the Federación de Torcedores de las Provincias de la Habana y Pinar del Río, covering one of the important craft groups among the tobacco workers in both Havana and the province of Pinar del Río.

Finally, the railroad workers succeeded in forming a single national organization in 1924, the Hermandad Ferroviaria (Railroaders Brotherhood). Obviously, its name indicated that it was much influenced by the railroad brotherhoods of the United States, although unlike them it organized the workers in a single group instead of individual crafts.[62]

The most important labor organization established in this period was the Federación Obrera de La Habana, which drew together a varied group of unions in and around the capital city. The precursor to the foundation of this federation was the Labor Congress of 1920, which was attended by delegations from 102 organizations in various parts of the country.

The meeting originally had on its agenda two questions: how to combat the rising cost of living, and whether or not to send delegates to the Second Congress of the Pan American Federation of Labor, which had been founded in December 1918. The delegates to the 1920 congress were unanimous in their belief that drastic steps needed to be taken to deal with the inflation that was then rampant. They adopted a number of resolutions suggesting government action to that end. However, there was no such unanimity concerning the Pan American Federation. Although some delegates led by Juan Arévalo strongly urged that delegates be sent to its meeting, a larger group of more radical congress members, led by the anarchosyndicalist Alfredo López, opposed the idea, and it was defeated.

The 1920 congress went on to discuss many other issues that were not on its original agenda. The most important was the need for establishing a national labor confederation. It was agreed to call a congress of labor organizations of all ideological orientations to establish such a confederation; a provisional committee was elected to organize a congress for that purpose. However, the Menocal government was strongly opposed to the idea and arrested most of the members of the provisional committee, putting an end for the time being to efforts to establish a national central labor organization.

However, in spite of this obvious governmental hostility, plans went forward to establish at least a federation of unions in the capital city. A meeting to that end finally occurred on October 4, 1921. It set up the Federación Obrera de La Habana, which for the next decade and a half was to play a major role in the Cuban labor movement. Alfredo López, the anarchist leader of the printing trades workers, soon emerged as the leading figure in this federation.

The founding congress of the Federación Obrera de La Habana adopted a number of significant resolutions. These included motions urging the suppression of piecework wage payments, equality of pay for men and women workers, and the limitation of work by minors to six hours a day.

The overall anarchosyndicalist tenor of the founding congress was indicated by its declaration of principles. It proclaimed that the new organization would be open to all "Workers Resistance Societies that have as their principles the class struggle, direct action and collectively reject electoral action."

The Federación Obrera de La Habana had about twenty organizations in its ranks a year after its formation.[63]

THE ECONOMIC CRISIS OF THE EARLY 1920s

The economic boom experienced by Cuba, and particularly its sugar industry, during World War I came to a sudden end in 1920 and 1921. During the conflict, Cuban sugar production had risen from 2,428,732 tons in 1913 to 4,009,734 tons in 1919, and the price of sugar had increased from 1.95 cents a pound in 1913 to 22.00 cents in February 1920. However, by September of the latter year the price had fallen to 3.75 cents a pound.[64]

The upshot of this sudden crisis was that a large proportion of the Cuban-owned sugar firms that had borrowed very heavily from the foreign banks operating in Cuba were unable to pay their debts. As a consequence, these banks, which held mortgages on the sugar haciendas, suddenly became their owners. Many Cuban-owned banks, with fewer resources than the foreign ones, also found themselves bankrupt.

The governments of President Menocal and his successor, President Alfredo Zayas, were helpless to deal with the sudden crisis. A move by Menocal to declare a bank moratorium, whereby they had to pay only 10 percent of their deposits to those holding them, was opposed by the United States government and had to be canceled.

Soon afterward, the U.S. president, Warren Harding, sent a special representative to Cuba, Enoch H. Crowder. In effect, he dictated the economic policy of President Zayas, including negotiation of a loan from the J. P. Morgan Company for $50 million and drastic cutting of the Cuban government budget. Payments on the Morgan loan began to fall due in 1923.[65]

REACTION OF ORGANIZED LABOR TO THE ECONOMIC CRISIS

Inevitably much of the burden of the economic crisis fell on the Cuban workers, particularly upon those in the sugar industry. Employers sought drastically to cut wages and otherwise to reduce labor costs. Understandably, the sugar workers fought back against these measures.

However, the sugar workers were not generally organized. There were apparently only two firmly established sugar workers unions at this time. Hence, when strikes occurred, they were usually more or less spontaneous, and not very well organized.

In November 1922 strikes broke out in two sugar *centrales* in the province of Camaguey. The workers demanded payment of wages that were four months in arrears, as well as wage increases and prompt payment henceforth. The Rural Guard was sent in to occupy both of the plantations, but local support, even among merchants, was such that an agreement was finally reached between the strikers and the owners providing for the return to work of all the strikers without reprisals, wage payments every two weeks, and substantial wage increases.

Then in 1924 and 1925 there were walkouts involving some 3,000 cane cutters in the provinces of Havana and Camaguey. All of these strikes were lost as a result of poor organization and government repression.

Another walkout in 1924 involved thirty *centrales* in an area stretching from Havana province to Oriente. In this case, the walkout had the support of the railroaders, the port workers, and the Federación Obrera de La Habana. We have no information concerning the outcome of this strike.[66]

During the early 1920s there were also important strikes by a wide variety of other workers in various parts of the country. These included railroad men, port workers, chauffeurs, printing trades employees, and several groups of industrial workers.

The railroaders were particularly militant in this period. In February 1924 most of the country's railroad workers were in the Hermandad Ferroviaria. However, the railroad companies were for the most part not willing to recognize the union. Archibald Jack, the manager of Ferroviarios Consolidados, a British-owned company, was particularly adamant about recognizing Local 2 of the Hermandad in Havana, so the workers went on strike on February 23, 1924, and won recognition within twenty-four hours.

However, that strike did not resolve the problems of union recognition on the railroads. On May Day 1924, when a majority of railroad workers refused to go to their jobs on the workers' holiday, the same Archibald Jack dismissed two hundred of them. This action was countered by a general railroad strike called by the Hermandad Ferroviaria, which involved 12,500 workers. The strikers demanded not only general recognition of the Hermandad, but also substantial wage increases. The walkout lasted twenty-one days and was marked by considerable violence. President Zayas finally intervened, naming a three-person arbitration team, which quickly put forward a proposal that acceded to most of the workers' demands; reportedly President Zayas himself convinced Archibald Jack to accept it.[67]

Within the railroad workers' organization, there were two factions. The top leadership was in the hands of reformists, who were willing to allow government conciliation and arbitration procedures in their disputes. This group was led by Juan Arévalo and Otero Busch. The other, more militant, faction was led by

Enrique Varona, head of the union on the Ferrocarril del Norte de Cuba, and was more ready to resort to strikes.

The port workers were also under reformist leadership in this period. With the approval of their unions there was established by the Zayas government in 1923 the *inteligencia portuaria*, an arrangement whereby tripartite boards with union, management and government representatives were established, to seek to mediate conflicts that might arise on the docks. The anarchists, who still represented a substantial part of the port workers, were strongly opposed to these agreements.[68]

One of the most notable labor conflicts of this period involved the Polar Brewery. When the owners of the brewery refused to honor the terms of an existing collective agreement and treated the workers in ways they considered "abusive," the Sindicato General de la Industria Fabril not only called a strike in the brewery in 1921, but organized a widespread boycott of Polar beer. This boycott, supported by the Federación Obrera de La Habana, continued for three years, in the face of strong government opposition. The police not only arrested the union leaders and outlawed the Sindicato General de la Industria Fabril, but also put three leaders of the union on trial on the charge of having poisoned Polar beer. Although the prosecuting attorney demanded the death penalty for the three, they were given amnesty by President Zayas in the face of a general strike declared by the Federación Obrera de La Habana.[69]

CONCLUSION

By the middle of the 1920s, the Cuban labor movement included a substantial number of wage earners in Havana and the island's other cities. Collective bargaining on a regular basis was by no means as yet a characteristic feature of labor relations, and there was still little labor legislation, either protecting the workers against risks or authorizing unions and seeking to regularize their relations with employers.

There had begun to emerge some more or less centralized labor groups, either on an occupational basis, such as the Hermandad Ferroviaria, or on a regional one, such as the Federación Obrera de La Habana. However, there had not yet emerged a national central organization—that would be the next major development within the labor movement.

In these early decades of Cuban organized labor there were three noticeable ideological orientations, the anarchosyndicalists, the Socialists, and the so-called reformists, of which the first was by far the largest. That too would change before very long.

NOTES

1. Mario Riera Hernández, *Historial Obrero Cubano 1574–1965*, Rema Press, Miami, Florida, 1965, page 271.

2. Efrén Córdova, *Clase Trabajadora y Movimiento Sindical en Cuba, Volumen I (1819–1959)*, Ediciones Universal, Miami, 1995, page 150.

3. Riera Hernández, 1965, op. cit., page 17.

4. Córdova, op. cit., pages 24–31.

5. Ibid., page 36.

6. Ibid., page 37.

7. Ibid., pages 40–43. See also Riera Hernández, op. cit., page 18; *Historia del Movimiento Obrero Cubano 1865–1958, Tomo I, 1865–1935*, Instituto de Historia del Movimiento Comunista y de la Revolución Socialista de Cuba anexo al Comité Central del Partido Comunista de Cuba, Editoria Política, La Habana, 1985, pages 22–29; and Carlos del Toro, *El Movimiento Obrero Cubano en 1914*, Instituto del Libro, La Habana, 1969, pages 43–44.

8. del Toro, op. cit., page 45.

9. *Historia del Movimiento Obrero Cubano etc.*, Tomo I, op. cit., page 31.

10. Ibid., page 35; and Córdova, op. cit., page 65.

11. *Historia del Movimiento Obrero Cubano etc.*, Tomo I, op. cit., pages 36–37.

12. Córdova, op. cit., page 44.

13. Interview with José Mandado, President of Sociedad de Dependientes de Hoteles, Restaurantes y Fondas, in Havana, Cuba, September 6, 1949.

14. Córdova, op. cit., page 44.

15. Interview with John Dumoulin, United States anthropologist, in New Brunswick, NJ, October 8, 1973.

16. *Historia del Movimiento Obrero Cubano etc.*, Tomo I, op. cit., page 46.

17. Ibid., page 55. See also del Toro, op. cit., pages 50–51.

18. *Historia del Movimiento Obrero Cubano etc.*, Tomo I, op. cit., pages 47–49; see also del Toro, op. cit., pages 50–51.

19. Córdova, op. cit., pages 73–74; and *Historia del Movimiento Obrero Cubano etc.*, Tomo I, op. cit., pages 61–63.

20. *Historia del Movimiento Obrero Cubano etc.*, Tomo I, op. cit., page 62.

21. Córdova, op. cit., pages 73–74; and *Historia del Movimiento Obrero Cubano etc.*, Tomo I, op. cit., pages 73–84.

22. Córdova, op. cit., pages 74–75; and *Historia del Movimiento Obrero Cubano etc.*, Tomo I, op. cit., pages 71–73.

23. Córdova, op. cit., page 66.

24. *Historia del Movimiento Obrero Cubano, etc.*, Tomo I, op. cit., page 65.

25. Córdova, op. cit., page 66.

26. Ibid., page 68; and *Historia del Movimiento Obrero Cubano etc.*, Tomo I, op. cit., page 64.

27. Córdova, op. cit., page 65.

28. *Historia del Movimiento Obrero Cubano etc.*, *Tomo I*, op. cit., page 126.

29. Ibid., pages 66–67.

30. Ibid., pages 67–69.

31. del Toro, op. cit., page 54.

32. *Historia del Movimiento Obrero Cubano etc.*, *Tomo I*, op. cit., page 126.

33. Ibid., page 126; and Córdova, op. cit., pages 82–83.

34. Córdova, op. cit., pages 82–84; Riera Hernández, op. cit., page 26; and *Historia del Movimiento Obrero Cubano etc.*, *Tomo I*, op. cit., pages 127–132.

35. *Historia del Movimiento Obrero Cubano etc.*, *Tomo I*, op. cit., pages 129–132; and del Toro, op. cit., pages 63–64.

36. Interview with John Dumoulin, op. cit., October 8, 1973.

37. Carlos Fernández R., "Apuntes Para Una Historia del Movimiento Obrero Cubano," (Manuscript), n.d.; *CTC*, magazine of Confederación de Trabajadores de Cuba, Havana, September 1944; Córdova, op. cit., pages 91–95; *Historia del Movimiento Obrero Cubano etc.*, *Tomo I*, op. cit., pages 135–140; Riera Hernández, op. cit., pages 34–35; del Toro, op. cit., pages 66–67.

38. Córdova, op. cit., pages 95–96.

39. *Historia del Movimiento Obrero Cubano etc.*, *Tomo I*, op. cit., page 155.

40. Córdova, op. cit., pages 98–99; and Riera Hernández, op. cit., pages 38–39; *Historia del Movimiento Obrero Cubano etc.*, *Tomo I*, op. cit., pages 157–158.

41. Córdova, op. cit., page 99; *Historia del Movimiento Obrero Cubano etc.*, *Tomo I*, op. cit., page 159.

42. *Historia del Movimiento Obrero Cubano etc.*, *Tomo I*, op. cit., page 159.

43. Ibid., pages 163–164; and Cordova, op. cit., pages 99–100; del Toro, op. cit., page 72.

44. Córdova, op. cit., page 100; and *Historia del Movimiento Obrero Cubano etc.*, *Tomo I*, op. cit., pages 162–163.

45. *Acción Socialista*, Havana, periodical edited by Juan Arévalo, February 1943.

46. Córdova, op. cit., page 107.

47. Ibid., pages 109–110; and *Historia del Movimiento Obrero Cubano etc.*, *Tomo I*, op. cit., pages 173–175.

48. *Historia del Movimiento Obrero Cubano etc.*, *Tomo I*, op. cit., pages 143–146.

49. Ibid., pages 143–152; see also Córdova, op. cit., pages 104–106.

50. *Memoria de los Trabajos Presentados al Congreso Nacional Obrero*, Imprenta y Papelería La Universal, La Habana, 1915, pages 4–5, 11, 147–157.

51. del Toro, op. cit., pages 163–164.

52. Córdova, op. cit., page 110.

53. *Memoria de los Trabajos etc.*, op. cit., pages 161–377; for further information on the 1914 congress see also *Historia del Movimiento Obrero*

Cubano etc., *Tomo I*, op. cit., pages 168–172; Córdova, op. cit., pages 110–114; and del Toro, op. cit., pages 117–126, 130–133.

54. del Toro, op. cit., pages 126–128.

55. Córdova, op. cit., pages 108.

56. Ibid., page 108.

57. Ibid., page 118; see also *Historia del Movimiento Obrero Cubano etc.*, *Tomo I*, op. cit., pages 182–185.

58. Interview with John Dumoulin, op. cit., October 8, 1973.

59. Juan Arévalo, *Problemas de la Unidad Obrera en América*, Havana, 1946, page 55; and Riera Hernández, op. cit., page 47.

60. Córdova, op. cit., page 120.

61. Unless otherwise noted, foregoing from Córdova, op. cit., pages 117–124; and *Historia del Movimiento Obrero Cubano etc.*, *Tomo I*, op. cit., pages 177–185, 198–200.

62. Foregoing from *Historia del Movimiento Obrero Cubano etc.*, *Tomo I*, op. cit., pages 201–203.

63. Ibid., pages 205–208; see also Riera Hernández, op. cit., page 49.

64. *Historia del Movimiento Obrero Cubano etc.*, *Tomo I*, op. cit., page 212.

65. Ibid., pages 213–215.

66. Ibid., pages 217–218.

67. Ibid., pages 220; see also Riera Hernández, op. cit., pages 57–58 and Córdova, op. cit., pages 140–141.

68. *Historia del Movimiento Obrero Cubano etc.*, *Tomo I*, op. cit., pages 220–221

69. Ibid., pages 221–222; see also Riera Hernández, op. cit., page 53; and Córdova, op. cit., pages 139–140.

2

The Confederación Nacional Obrera de Cuba and Its Rivals

In the year 1925 two organizations were established that were to play a major role in Cuban organized labor. One was the Confederación Nacional Obrera de Cuba (CNOC), the country's first national central labor organization, which was for a decade to be the largest element in the labor movement. The second was the Communist Party of Cuba, which was soon to become the most powerful political element working within Cuban organized labor.

FOUNDING OF THE CONFEDERACIÓN NACIONAL OBRERA DE CUBA

The establishment of the Confederación Nacional Obrera de Cuba was the result of two congresses, one held in Cienfuegos in February 1925, the other in Camaguey in August of the same year. The first of these was a preparatory meeting, which drew up a Declaration of Principles for the new organization and named an organizing committee to issue invitations to and prepare for the actual founding meeting of the new central labor body.

What was called the Third National Labor Congress of Cuba then met in August and established the CNOC. That meeting was attended by delegates from eighty-two organizations, while another forty-six sent messages indicating their support for the confederation to be established. It was claimed at the time that there were 200,000 workers represented, in one way or another, at the founding congress of the CNOC. However, this was undoubtedly a considerable exaggeration. For one thing, only two organizations of sugar workers were represented, since that group, the largest single element in the Cuban working class, was still largely unorganized. Also, important groups of workers in Santiago de Cuba, Santa Clara, and Sagua la Grande were not represented. The Hermandad Ferroviaria, the railroaders' national union, which had been founded the year before, was represented only by an observer rather than a full-fledged delegate.

The founding congress of the CNOC laid great stress on the need for the unity of the workers, and there were elements present from all three major ideological tendencies that then existed within the labor movement: the anarchosyndicalists, the reformists, and the Communists. However, the initiative for the formation of the confederation had largely been taken by the Federación Obrera de La Habana, which was still controlled by the anarchosyndicalists, and they were clearly the dominant element in the meeting.

Anarchosyndicalist influence was reflected in many of the resolutions passed at the gathering. The group pledged its support for direct action, the class struggle, general strikes, and rejection of political action. It provided that no one could be elected to its executive "who conducted active propaganda for political parties." The meeting also rejected the idea of asking for government labor reforms.

The meeting dealt with many other problems. It urged equality of treatment of workers of all races. It strongly opposed the policy of succeeding governments of deporting labor leaders who were not native Cubans. It stressed the struggle for the eight-hour day and proclaimed that the ultimate objective of this struggle should be the establishment of the four-hour working day. It was decided that the new confederation would not affiliate with any existing international labor grouping, but resolved that the CNOC should itself call a congress of Latin American union movements to establish a federation among them.

In terms of organization, the founding congress of the CNOC urged formation of industrial unions, which should be grouped together in national federations, as well as regional federations of CNOC affiliates. It declared its opposition to formation of rival organizations where unions already existed.

The Camaguey congress chose a provisional executive committee for the new CNOC. Some months later, representatives of twenty-two unions chose a definitive committee. In both cases, the members of the committees were relative unknowns. Thus, Alfredo López and Antonio Penichet, the anarchosyndicalists who had clearly been the people with greatest influence in the congress, were not among the members of the national committee. Perhaps this was a move to shield the confederation from the persecution of the clearly antilabor government of President Gerardo Machado, which had recently taken office.[1]

Although the anarchosyndicalists clearly were the dominant element in the founding congress of the Confederación Nacional Obrera de Cuba, they soon lost control of it. According to the official history of Cuban organized labor of the Castro Communist Party, the Communists had gained control of the organization by 1927.[2]

ESTABLISHMENT OF THE COMMUNIST PARTY OF CUBA

The triumph of the Bolshevik Revolution in Russia in November 1917, and the subsequent establishment of the Communist International in 1919, aroused considerable interest and enthusiasm in the Cuban labor movement. As elsewhere, there were both anarchists and Socialists among the early Cuban supporters of the Soviet regime. There were proclamations and demonstrations of support for the regime during the Russian civil war (1918–1921). Although there were many in the ranks of both anarchists and Socialists who had become disillusioned with Soviet Russia by the early 1920s, some of the most prominent anarchist labor people, such as Alfredo López, continued to be kindly disposed toward it, although they did not join the Communist Party of Cuba when it was formed.[3]

It was principally from the Socialists, joined by some elements of the newly militant student movement, most notably Julio Antonio Mella, that the ranks of the new Communist Party were drawn. In July 1922, the Agrupación Socialista de La Habana adopted a Declaration of Principles that declared that "it is identified with the revolutionary principles which sustain the Russian Revolution, that it will follow the tactics of the III International which is based in Moscow; and condemns the II International because of its betrayal of socialist principles at the beginning of the European War."[4]

Although he had largely drawn up this Declaration of Principles, Carlos Baliño, the veteran labor leader and Socialist, soon became unhappy about what he regarded as the Agrupación Socialista's failure to put the declaration into practice. He took the lead, therefore, in founding the Agrupación Comunista de La Habana in March 1923. Three months later, a similar group was set up in Guanabacoa, under the leadership of the local tobacco workers union leader, Venancio Rodríguez.

The Agrupación Comunista de La Habana included in its ranks—which amounted to only twenty-seven members—not only

Baliño but also several tobacco union leaders. Julio Antonio
Mella, the student leader, also joined it. The group undertook to distribute several Spanish Communist periodicals, as well as some
pamphlet literature. In March 1924, it began to publish its own
paper, *Lucha de Clases*.[5]

Finally, the founding congress of the Communist Party of Cuba
took place in August 1925. There were not more than twenty people present at this meeting—which to prevent police interference
took place in the homes of several members of the Havana group—
and there were present representatives of only four of the nine
local Communist groups that were known to exist. Enrique Flores
Magón, the Mexican former anarchist who was by then a leader of
the Mexican Communist Party, apparently presided over the sessions of the founding congress of the party of Cuba.

The meeting formally adopted "democratic centralism" as the
guiding principle of its organizational structure. It also voted to
join the Communist International. It did not adopt a document
elaborating in any detail its ideology and philosophy but rather
"adopted a concrete program of demands for the workers and
peasants which would permit the establishment with them of fraternal ties of struggle."

The congress elected a nine-man Central Committee. Most
prominent among them were Carlos Boliño and Julio Antonio
Mella. Five were manual workers and three were important trade
union leaders: Alejandro Barreiro of the Cigar Makers Union and
financial secretary of the Federación Obrera de la Habana; Miguel
Valdés, a leader of the Tobacco Workers Union of San Antonio de
los Baños; and José Peña Vilaboa, leader of the Painters Union of
Havana and first secretary general of the Federación Obrera de la
Habana.[6]

COMMUNIST OPERATIONS IN THE UNIONS

From its establishment, the Communist Party concentrated
heavily on the work within the labor movement. Efrén Córdova
sketched the nature of this activity:

The party put emphasis on the formation of dedicated and competent
leaders, employed full time, who could obtain advantages for the workers, explain the dogmas of Marxism-Leninism and be in a position to
polemicize with their opponents. First they had to train organizers and
then negotiators. The organizers not only served to establish new unions
but also to penetrate the leadership of those already existing. The negotiators bargained for gains or opposed wage reductions with the purpose
of giving prestige to the party among the mass of workers and peasants.
Both groups were trained in the art and practice of debating.[7]

Jorge García Montes and Antonio Alonso Avila, in their history of the Cuban Communist Party, argued that in the beginning the Communists, "Rather than combatting the ideas which prevailed then . . . concerned themselves before anything else, with attaining positions in the trade union organisms which were being created under the impetus of the anarchists and of the reformists. They were more successful in the first than in the second."[8] Given the small size of the party at its inception, this was perhaps the only effective tactic open to them.

Quite early on, the Communists set up cells within unions controlled by their opponents, particularly the reformists. The official history of the Cuban labor movement of the Castro Communist Party commented:

In these sectors was begun the organization of *revolutionary trade union oppositions*, directed against the economist policy or the class collaboration of those leadership . . . which had as essential objectives the raising of the struggle of the workers for their demands and rights against the divisionist action and the submission to Machado of their leaders, for unity with the workers of the whole country in defense of democratic liberties and trade union rights. (Emphasis in the original)

This study noted particularly the groups established in Hermandad Ferroviaria, the tobacco industry, the commercial employees, the trolley car workers, and the hotel and restaurant workers.[9]

As we have noted, the Communists largely took over the leadership of the CNOC in 1927. Their success was achieved largely at the expense of the anarchosyndicalists. Some of the principal anarchist leaders, such as Alfredo López, were assassinated by the Machado regime, but this was not the principal cause of their disappearance as the principal political group within the labor movement. Their long-term failure—in contrast to their counterparts in Argentina or even Mexico—to establish a structured organization, their almost fanatical insistence on the "sovereignty" of each local group or union, as well as their insistence that trade union leaders not be paid full-time officials made them no match for the tight organization, strong discipline, and substantial financial resources of the Communists.[10]

One result of the Communists' capture of control of the CNOC was the affiliation of the confederation with the segment of the international labor movement controlled by the Communist International. Bernardo Lobo of the CNOC attended the celebration of the Tenth Anniversary of the establishment of the Bolshevik regime in Moscow late in 1927 and while there signed a statement which was the first step taken by the Red International of Labor Unions (RILU) to set up its own confederation in Latin America.[11]

Then the CNOC sent José Rego to represent it at the 1929 Montevideo conference that established the Confederación Sindical Latino Americana (CSLA), with which the CNOC became affiliated.[12]

ATTACKS OF THE MACHADO REGIME ON THE LABOR MOVEMENT

Gerardo Machado became president of Cuba at almost the same time that the CNOC and Communist Party were founded. In the 1924 election, he had run against former president, Menocal; according to the reformist union leader Juan Arévalo, Machado's "political campaign was made on the basis of magnificent promises for the improvement of Cuban life; and especially for the working class." On the basis of these promises, some of the reformist labor leaders supported him in the campaign.[13]

However, Machado's own past might well have indicated to those union leaders who supported him in 1924 that he was no friend of organized labor. We have noted earlier his antilabor actions when he was minister of interior of the government of President José Miguel Gómez, when he had violently suppressed strikes, sometimes taking personal charge of such actions.

Machado's antilabor attitude had not changed. During his first visit to the United States after his election he announced that during his administration no strike would be allowed to last more than twenty-four hours. As Efrén Córdova noted, "Machado declared himself from the beginning an adversary of trade unionism and chose as the field of battle the only arm of defense of the workers."[14]

Machado presided over one of the most tyrannical regimes the Republic of Cuba experienced. He organized a formidable secret police that not only jailed, tortured, and killed his opponents inside Cuba, but was also credited with physically eliminating some of those who had fled into exile. In 1928 he insisted on having the constitution changed to permit his reelection, and managed to remain in office for more than eight years.

Machado wasted little time after taking office before he began persecuting the labor movement. In August 1925 there was a strike in three sugar plantations in the province of Camaguey, as the workers demanded that the Yankee managers recognize their union. The railroad workers of the area, whose principal leader was Enrique Varona, one of the more militant leaders of the Hermandad Ferroviaria, declared their backing for the strike. As a consequence, Varona was arrested, accused of planting a bomb on railroad tracks serving one of the plantations involved in the strike. He was released from jail on September 15 but was assassinated four days later by two members of the Guardia Rural.[15]

Varona was only the first of several labor leaders to be killed at the hands of the Machado regime. Efrén Córdova noted that the assassination of Varona "was like a proclamation that the government directed to the country, declaring itself the enemy of the working class in general, and not only of its more radical elements." Three other railroad workers' leaders were killed shortly after the elimination of Varona, and in July 1926, Alfredo López, the country's most outstanding labor leader, was arrested, tortured, and assassinated by the police—his remains were found after the fall of Machado. Another significant victim was José Cuxart Falcón, a leader of the Sindicato General de Obreros de la Industria Fabril (which Machado had outlawed), who was a victim of a favorite procedure of the Machado dictatorship: "shot while trying to escape."[16]

Writing a few months before the overthrow of Machado, Russell Porter summed up the dictator's early drive against the workers' organizations: "President Machado began to crush the organized labor movement in his first year in office. He used the army to break the 1925 railroad strike at Camaguey, and it is charged that the military authorities killed thirty labor leaders at that time. Since then there have been frequent deportations and disappearances of alien and radical labor leaders."[17]

DECLINE AND RECOVERY OF THE CNOC

From 1925 through 1928 the Cuban organized labor movement, particularly the CNOC, was in retreat. The official history of the Castro Communist Party noted the "rachitic" state of the CNOC during this period.[18]

Barry Carr noted the toll that Machado's persecution had taken on the Communist Party, which by this time controlled the CNOC. The party was concentrated mainly in Havana and a few port cities; many of its original cadres had been deported if they were foreigners or had in any case fled abroad, leading the Cuban party to ask for the help of its U.S. counterpart to locate its exiled cadres and help them get back to Cuba.[19]

During the 1920s and afterward there were widely varying estimates of the size of the membership of the CNOC. Early in its existence, it claimed some 200,000 members, a total that undoubtedly was an exaggeration. By 1929, an official Communist source said that there were only 20,000 members.[20] The Chilean historian of Latin American organized labor Moises Poblete Troncoso claimed that in 1930 there were only 4,000 members in the CNOC, and 16,000 in all "revolutionary trade unions."[21]

However, starting in the latter part of 1929, the labor movement began to become more militant. In September, the CNOC published a new program, which included demands for vacations of one month each year, establishment of a minimum wage and of a general social security program, aid to the unemployed, improvement of working conditions of women and children, an end to discrimination based on race and nationality, and the rights of free speech, freedom of assembly, and the strike.

The apparent renewed militancy of the CNOC was met with a decree of the Machado government outlawing it, as well as the Federación Obrera de La Habana and several other union groups. Also, a number of union headquarters were closed down by the government.[22]

However, from its position of illegality, the CNOC launched a call for a nationwide twenty-four-hour general strike in protest against the Machado regime's outlawing of various labor groups, as well as its failure to help the unemployed and its general destruction of civil liberties. The Machado government sought to prevent the strike by arresting more than a score of union leaders, including officials of the CNOC and the Havana Branch #2 of the Hermandad Ferroviaria, on March 18, 1930. The New York Times reported, "While sections of the national police, the secret service and the judicial police were arresting men concerned with the projected strike another group of police were busily engaged in raiding all labor unions and organizations."[23]

Subsequently, the Communists claimed that 200,000 workers had participated in this walkout, although admitting that it was confined largely to Havana and Manzanillo.[24] Jorge García Montes and Antonio Alonso Avila, in their history of the Cuban Communist Party, said that it did not extend beyond Havana.[25] The New York Times reported the day after the walkout: "Street car and omnibus lines were tied up, although some taxicabs, interurban lines and railroads continued to operate. The majority of trade shops were closed, as were coffee shops, cigar factories, sugar mills and sugar cane fields."

The Times also reported on a peculiar aspect of the March 20, 1930, strike. A delegation headed by Rubén Martínez Villena, the head of the CNOC, talked to President Machado, presenting their demands and assuring him that the walkout would be peaceful. For his part, Machado assured them that the illegalization of the CNOC was not yet definitive and could be reversed by the Supreme Court.[26]

The strike was followed by large-scale demonstrations on May 1, when the workers were also urged by the CNOC not to go to work. The May day meeting in Havana received a message from Rubén Martínez Villena, who had been forced to go into exile. When the demonstrators sought to march after their meeting, they were fired by the police, resulting in the death of two workers and the wounding of fourteen others.[27]

There were a number of important economic strikes during the early 1930s. In 1930, these included walkouts of shoemakers, Havana bus drivers, hat workers, bakers, textile workers, and various groups of tobacco workers in Havana and other cities.[28] In 1931, one of the most important strikes was that of the trolley car workers on Havana, which was backed by the tobacco workers, and in support of which the CNOC called a general strike, which failed.

In 1932, the most significant urban walkout was that of 15,000 tobacco workers, which lasted 108 days. When the CNOC suggested that it call a general strike, the tobacco workers' organization, the Federación Nacional de Torcedores, rejected the idea, preferring to deal directly with the employers, rather than to convert their walkout into a general political protest.[29]

Russell Porter noted that after this tobacco strike, "President Machado . . . virtually outlawed strikes. The school teachers threatened to strike last because their salaries were months in arrears, but the government quickly blocked the proposed strike by threatening to use the army. More than 100 labor leaders are said to be held in prison, many of them incommunicado, on charges of communism and terrorism." Porter also noted: "No organized labor movement exists openly today. . . . What labor movement still exists is underground and meetings are held in secret. The military authorities have closed labor headquarters and allow no open meetings without permits from the army."[30]

THE ORGANIZATION OF THE SUGAR WORKERS

Until the early 1930s, labor in the country's most important industry remained largely unorganized. However, in the early 1930s, the Communist Party, and the CNOC, which it controlled, set out with some success to unionize those working in that industry.

In the period following the March 1930 general strike, the Communist Party and the CNOC, to some degree because of directives from the Communist Party of the United States and the Caribbean Bureau of the Communist International (located in New York City), decided to turn their attention chiefly to organizing rural workers. By then the party already had some influence among sugar workers in a few municipalities in the province of Havana, as well as in the town of Banes, where one of the two largest mills of the United Fruit Company was located, and in Jaguey Grande in Matanzas province. It had even established in the last of these places a union, which was quite short-lived.

However, the decision was made to concentrate organizing activities for the time being in Santa Clara province. For this purpose, organizers were called in from outside the province. By September 1930, the party had a branch in the northern Santa Clara town of Encrucijada, and Jesus Menéndez and two other comrades had established a union in the Constancia sugar mill near the town.

In 1931 the party and the CNOC made an intensive study, including a detailed questionnaire, of conditions in three plantations in the province of Havana and two in Santa Clara. After this, the CNOC established a special commission to recruit sugar workers. With the help especially of urban-based Communists from the city of Manzanillo, party cells were established late in 1931 in several sugar plantations in Camaguey and Oriente provinces.

Early in 1932 plans to establish the first national sugar workers' organization began. Since as yet there were few if any formally organized unions, those efforts were perforce concentrated on individuals and small groups of workers who had been recruited by the party and/or the CNOC. These efforts bore fruit in a meeting held clandestinely in Santa Clara in December 1932, attended by workers from thirty-two sugar centrales in all six Cuban provinces. It declared the existence of the Sindicato Nacional de Obreros de la Industria Azucarera (SNOIA).[31]

This conference agreed on a campaign to organize unions, in each case joining the same organization workers in the sugar mills and offices, and the cutters and transporters of cane. It also drew up a manifesto setting forth the generalized demands of the sugar workers and agreed that the first step in organizing unions should be the establishment of "struggle committees."[32]

Efrén Córdova said that this establishment of the first national sugar worker union reflected in part the economic crisis that was facing the sugar industry as a result of the Great Depression. But he added that "it was also the fruit of a long preparatory work of the trade union leaders (principally Communists), as well as the culminating point of a large accumulation of complaints and frictions. It was not possible at this point to continue ignoring the need to put an end to the overweening and dictatorial power of the administrators of the plantations."[33]

The establishment of the SNOIA was followed during the 1932–1933 harvest season by a wave of strikes. They were particularly prevalent in the area around the city of Manzanillo in Oriente Province and throughout the province of Santa Clara, where they were said to have involved 20,000 workers in twenty different *centrales*.[34]

THE REFORMIST UNIONS

The Confederación Obrera Nacional de Cuba was by no means the only central labor group during the Machado period. Although the Communists soon eclipsed the anarchists within the CNOC, the third ideological-political element in the Cuban labor movement, the reformists, continued to be an important factor.

The Hermandad Ferroviaria, established shortly before Machado took power, continued to be principally under reformist leadership, although there was a substantial radical opposition group within the organization. It joined the Pan American Federation of Labor, to which the American Federation of Labor and the Mexican CROM also belonged.[35]

Another important union group that remained predominantly, although not completely, under reformist control during the Machado period was the Maritime Federation. There, too, were segments of the federation that were militantly opposed to the reformist leadership.[36]

In 1925 these two unions, as well as that of the woodworkers and several other smaller ones, joined to form the Federación Cubana del Trabajo, headed by Luis Fabregat, which claimed some 40,000 members in 1929. In 1930, the federation split, and the Unión Federativa Nacional Obrera was formed under the leadership of Juan Arévalo. He maintained that this schism occurred because of the high-handed attitude of Frabregat in not consulting other leaders of the Federación before taking action on important matters.[37] Carleton Beals attributed the split to the rivalry of Arévalo and Fabregat for the favor of President Machado.[38]

Controversy raged during and after the Machado regime concerning the activities of Arévalo, Fabregat, and some of the other reformist leaders. Arévalo in particular was the target of allegations that he had collaborated with the dictatorship. However, he subsequently pointed out that he was tried by a court after the fall of Machado on charges of having collaborated with the dictator and was acquitted by a jury made up of active trade unionists, opponents of Machado.[39]

Arévalo wrote an extensive defense of his actions during the Machado dictatorship:

The Hermandad Ferroviaria de Cuba proposed a general strike. President Machado issued a strong threat against the promoters of the strike. At this time the entire country was on the side of the president, with the sole exception of Mendieta and a few friends. . . . No one dared to stand up to him in those moments. And the Hermandad did dare to do so. Until that time we were friends of the president, but we were at the service of the Hermandad; we had to obey the orders of the Central Committee of Camaguey, whose representative in Havana I was, and we did obey the Committee and defied Machado, along with the Hermandad. At this time I was slated to leave to attend the I.L.O. conference in Geneva. I had been named to the Cuban delegation. The government gave us the money necessary for the voyage as well as our passport. The time to embark came, but the strike was starting and we could not absent ourselves at this hour. . . . The Central Committee of the Hermandad was jailed and I, in place of going to Geneva, was put in the Santa Clara prison.

Arévalo went on to say that after being released, be became active once again in the Central Committee of the Hermandad, was a delegate of the Woodworkers Federation and the Unión Marítima, and was a leader of the Federacón Cubana and the Unión Federativa. After some time, Machado agreed once more to treat with the Hermandad, which offered assurances that the violence of the 1926 strike would not be repeated. Arévalo claimed that until the summer of 1933 the reformist labor movement attempted to stay strictly within the law and in so doing won some favorable legislation and was instrumental in having many of the more radical labor leaders released from jail.[40]

In conversation with me, Arévalo claimed that the reformist leaders guided their part of the labor movement on strictly non-political lines, refusing either to support or to oppose Machado, and it was for this reason that Machado left them more or less alone.[41]

Finally, Arévalo pointed to the different attitudes that his group and the CNOC leaders adopted at the time of the 1933 revolutionary general strike that resulted in Machado's overthrow, when the CNOC backed the dictator and Arévalo claimed that his group had refused to do so.

The left-wing Cuban unionists then and later charged that the Arévalo group was in the service of Machado. Thus, the official history of Cuban organized labor of the Castro Communist Party said half a century later:

The FCT was not a serious force in the labor movement. . . . But its leader enjoyed in addition to monetary aid, support of the police apparatus of the dictatorship. Furthermore, after the defeat of the railroad strike in 1926, the new leadership of the Hermandad, in close union with

Arévalo, converted that organization into another bulwark of Machadoism in the labor movement.[42]

Some commentators outside Cuba made the same argument. Thus Carleton Beals, writing shortly after the fall of Machado, called the Federación Cubana del Trabajo a "fake Machado organization" and said that Arévalo published in his periodical *Acción Socialista* pictures of Machado with captions such as "The true friend of labor." He also noted an exchange between Arévalo and Fabregat at the time they fell out in which the former accused the latter of being in the pay of the police, and Fabregat put out manifestos and leaflets with photographs of alleged letters written by Arévalo to the police, with lists of workers to be expelled or arrested.[43]

Arévalo's exoneration after the fall of Machado, together with the fact that he continued to have some appreciable influence within the labor movement, enough that the Communists found it convenient to work with him in the Confederación de Trabajadores de Cuba in the late 1930s and early 1940s, would seem to indicate that he and some of those associated with him were not guilty of much of what they were charged with. They headed two of the largest of the country's unions in the Machado period—the railroaders and maritime and port workers—and perhaps they felt that a nonconfrontational posture vis-à-vis the Machado regime was the best way to prevent an all-out attempt by the dictatorship to destroy these unions.

THE CRISIS OF THE MACHADO DICTATORSHIP

By the beginning of 1933 the economic and political situation of Cuba was in a state of major crisis. The Great Depression had struck the Cuban economy with particular severity, and the patience of the island's populace for the tyranny of Gerardo Machado was being exhausted.

The long-enduring difficulty of the sugar industry, dating from right after World War I, had been greatly aggravated by the depression. In an attempt to cut the world supply of sugar and keep up the price, Machado had decreed a 40 percent decline in the Cuban harvest of 1932–1933. This had intensified the economic crisis.

The workers and peasants of Cuba bore the greatest burden of the impact of the Great Depression on Cuba. Russell Porter reported in the *New York Times* in February 1933 on the economic situation at that time:

Reports from reliable sources in the provinces outside of Havana tell of even greater sacrifices by the people in the rural districts than in the capital. Although the agricultural populace in Cuba can sustain life on a small wage, it must have a few months' work in a year to obtain rare necessaries. . . . In the present emergency the sugar planters are unable, because of their own financial troubles, to supply anything like a normal amount of employment, and are unable to pay those they do employ a sufficient living wage, with the result that the workers, being underpaid, are underfed and underclothed and their vitality is being reduced.

But the urban population did little better than those in the countryside. Porter wrote that "the President, finding that new foreign loans were impossible to obtain, had to stop most of his public works building program, which to a large extent had offset the effects of the depression that began in Cuba with the fall of sugar prices in 1925. Thousands of men were thrown out of work by this cessation of building."

Porter continued:

These dismissals were followed in 1931 and 1932 by the dismissals of thousands of government employees in every department except the army and the national police, causing more discontent. Many of these employees had not received their pay for months, and have still not received it. . . . All these contractions in government payments diminished the purchasing power of the population and, added to the fall in sugar prices and tax and customs increases, led to lower wages in private business, reduction in business activity, decreased imports from the United States and a lower standard in general social conditions.[44]

However, not only the economic situation had turned against Machado: so had domestic politics, and the international situation. Many old-line politicians had joined the opposition and some at least were certainly plotting against the regime.

Perhaps most significantly, the new government of the United States led by Franklin D. Roosevelt, which came to power on March 4, 1933, quickly decided that something would have to be done to force Gerardo Machado out of power in Cuba. Roosevelt sent Sumner Welles as the U.S. ambassador to Havana to bring his removal to pass.

THE AUGUST 1933 GENERAL STRIKE AND THE CNOC-CP DEAL WITH MACHADO

The final crisis of the Machado regime began with what at first appeared to be a relatively innocuous strike on July 25, 1933, of the bus drivers of Havana, provoked by a threatened wage decrease. On July 29, however, the walkout was joined by the trolley car workers and taxi drivers, followed soon afterward by the port workers and railroaders. On August 4, the capital's newspapers were closed down. The strike had also begun to spread all over the island, as a revolutionary walkout against the Machado regime.

Meanwhile, on August 3, the Communist Party had issued a call for a general strike, calling for the overthrow of Machado and the establishment of a "Soviet government of Workers and Peasants." This document was as vitriolic in its denunciation of Machado's opponents as of him. While praising the "United Front of the masses against the economic offensive, the terror and imperialist war," it also cried, "Down with the reformist, anarchist and police leaders who sell out and sabotage the struggle! Down with Machado and the leaders of the bourgeois-landlord opposition!"[45]

President Machado finally understood the gravity of the strike crisis and on August 5 declared martial law throughout the country. A strike committee composed of delegates from the principal unions that had walked out then decided to declare a nationwide general strike. Machado responded to this by sending troops from Camp Columbia into the center of Havana. There were clashes with the demonstrators, which resulted in both deaths and injuries to those demonstrating. Efrén Córdova quotes the American writer Huden Strode as saying that the "strike spread like a trail of powder from one pueblo to another until it reached the smallest villages of the island."[46]

On August 6, President Machado summoned a Communist Party delegation to the Presidential Palace. Rubén Martínez Villena, Joaquín Ordoqui, and Jorge Vivo went to confer with the dictator. They reached an agreement with him whereby he would ensure that all the economic demands raised by the groups that had started the walkout would be met, and promised that the CNOC and the Communist Party would be legalized; in return, the Communist Party and the CNOC would call off the general strike. Apparently none of this accord was actually put into writing.[47]

On the same day that the Communist leaders met with Machado, the Party issued the "Manifesto of the Communist Party of Cuba Analyzing the Development of the Strike Movement," which denied the political nature of the general strike:

The P.C. and the C.N.O.C. declare openly to the masses that this strike is not the final strike for seizing power. It is possible that that final struggle is approaching, but the present general strike has not itself, nor can it have the objective of bringing down the feudal-bourgeois-imperialist regime, or even the government of Machado; Machado will not be brought down by strikes, but by the insurrection of the well armed masses, with rifles, with machine guns which the proletariat lacks in this moment.[48]

Following a bit further on this same line of argument, the Communist Party Manifesto said:

We make this of the general strike and of the subsequent struggles, the means by which we overcome the obstacles and produce the conditions, not present today, that impede us from carrying out, for the moment, the definitively victorious insurrection of the masses against the bourgeois-feudal-imperialist power and for the establishment of a firm Worker and Peasant Soviet Government.[49]

In conformity with the agreement with Machado, César Vilar, then secretary general of the Confederación Nacional Obrera de Cuba, called a meeting of the CNOC Executive. That officially called off the general strike.

This move by the Cuban Communists had only been taken after consultation with the Caribbean Bureau of the Comintern, located in New York. It had given its approval for the Cuban Communists to make overtures to Machado and had sent a young Cuban, Felipe González, who had just returned from studying in Moscow, to participate in discussions of the issue with the Cuban party leadership. In that discussion most of the top party leaders supported the idea, although apparently Felipe González himself and César Vilar were opposed—although Vilar went along with the decision once it was made.[50]

Of course, since the Communists and the CNOC had not been responsible for what had started as an economic strike of a particular group of workers and ballooned into a nationwide revolutionary general strike against the Machado dictatorship, they were not in a position effectively to call off the walkout. It continued in full force. Finally, on August 11, two colonels—perhaps at the instigation of Ambassador Sumner Welles and certainly with his approval—demanded that President Machado resign. The deposed president then fled into exile. Thus was consummated the first successful military coup d'etat in the Republic of Cuba.

Shortly afterward, on August 13, the Communist-CNOC periodical El Trabajador, in the article "In the Face of the Great Combat," after noting the victories of a few workers' groups, said: "Workers: Maintain until triumph the strike firm in those places where demands have not been met. . . . Maintain the struggle until victory, and once that is achieved, organize the return to work in an organized form, creating unions, strengthening the existing ones and preparing yourselves for new and victorious struggles."[51]

The efforts of the Communists and the CNOC to save the dictator Machado at the last minute had obviously failed. At the time their deal with the dictator was made, Sandalio Junco and other opponents of the Communists within the labor movement denounced the Communist deal with Machado as a betrayal, and even a half a century later, the Communists were still explaining what had impelled them to act as they had in early August 1933.

Fourteen years after the overthrow of Machado, one of the principal Communist trade union leaders, Carlos Fernandez R., admitted to me that the move had been a "political mistake" but insisted that it had been made "in good faith," and that there was no question of a "deal" that with Machado being involved. He said that the Americans were at that moment threatening to intervene, having warships mobilized for that purpose, and were suggesting that Machado quit. As a consequence, the Communist union leaders figured that it was better that a weakened Machado stay in power than that the Americans intervene. He added that the reason why the CNOC leaders fell into this political error was that they were still much influenced by anarchist ideas.[52]

Juan Marinello, the longtime titular president of the Communist Party, and Carlos Rafael Rodríguez, a leader of both the original Communist Party and that of Fidel Castro, gave somewhat different, although not conflicting, explanations of the party's pact with Machado in August 1933. Marinello said, "The immaturity of the Party and the inexperience and youth of its leaders, made it commit the error of supporting President Machado, in opposition to the striking workers." Rodríguez wrote that "the Communist Party supported at the last moment the regime of Machado because of the vertical anti-Yankee position of the ruler, who personally insulted Welles and urged his immediate exit from Cuba."[53]

Finally, the official history of the Cuban labor movement of the Castro Communist Party, published in 1985, explained the Communists' and CNOC's action by saying that they had not understood that what had started as series of localized economic walkouts had become a revolutionary strike against Machado:

This new character of the strike was not understood immediately by the leaders of the party and of the CNOC. For them, the general strike continued being the sum of isolated economic and solidarity strikes, and consequently, they believed that, if their demands were met, the strikers must return to work. They did not understand that the strike against Machado had entered into its decisive phase, or the firm disposition of the hundreds of thousands of workers not to return to work so long as Machado continued in power.

The Castro Communist writer added:

This myopia was reflected also in an erroneous conclusion that the leaders of the party reached concerning the just recognition that the substitution of Machado by a government of the bourgeois-landlord opposition would mean leaving Cuba in the state of a semi-colony and the popular masses in the same misery and slavery. Their conclusion was that, faced with the impossibility that Machado would be immediately replaced by a revolutionary government of workers, the struggle of the working class would only serve to help precisely that opposition to seize power.

This account went on.

This conclusion was profoundly false, being mechanical, not being based on a correct analysis of the dialectical development of the situation, and essentially, not taking into account that the revolutionary masses, aroused by the victory over Machado and oriented in their action by a correct policy of their Marxist-Leninist vanguard, could have assured profound changes, that is to say, the carrying out of the agrarian and anti-imperialist program for which the Communist Party had agitated and struggled since its foundation.[54]

ESTABLISHMENT OF "SOVIETS" AFTER THE FALL OF MACHADO

During the sugar harvest of the spring of 1933, as we have seen, there had been a considerable number of strikes over wage and other issues. A few of those were marked by violence and even the taking over of mills and other property by the workers. However, so long as Machado remained in power, local government, the police, and nearby military units were hostile to this strike movement.

The situation changed with the overthrow of the dictatorship. In many cases, local municipal officials disappeared or were forcibly ousted by elements who had been opposed to the dictatorship of Machado. In a few incidents, the Communists participated in or even organized such local seizures of power.

With the overthrow, on September 4, of the government that had succeeded that of Machado, as the result of a coup by noncommissioned officers of the army, together with student elements, local and provincial government broke down further, and, in a number of cases, local military units, led by noncommissioned officers, sided with striking workers and with more radical political elements in the towns and even in a few cities.

It was against this breakdown of law and order that the establishment of "soviets" was undertaken by the Communists.[55] At the end of August, the Fifth Plenum of the Central Committee of the Communist Party met. It issued a call for formation of local soviets. It defined a *soviet* as "an organization formed by delegates of the Strike and Struggle Committee and of revolutionary organizations and other mass organizations which accept the United Front." However, it warned, "No elements which exploit the labor of the workers can be elected to the soviets."

The Communist Party document then provided that

in areas where under the impulse of the masses the authorities and the groups which until yesterday constituted the bourgeois-landlord opposition have not succeeded in forming a new government, or where the control of the people was carried out under the direction of the Party . . . there must be organized immediately a Council of Workers, Peasants, Soldiers and Sailors (soviets), under the hegemony of the proletariat and the direction of the Communist Party and take power in its hands.

The document mentioned nine places in which this situation was considered to exist.[56]

The official history of the Cuban labor movement of the Castro Communist Party said that such soviets were established in thirty-six sugar *centrales*, accounting for about 30 percent of Cuban sugar production. It noted, "In many of these places they took the railroads, the sugar companies, and extended this control to the subports, to the neighboring villages and agricultural zones."[57]

This study took the soviet established at the Mabay *central* near Manzanillo in the province of Oriente as an example of the way the soviets functioned. That soviet took a number of steps. First, it declared the strike then in progress as settled on terms favorable to the strikers. It seized control of the warehouses, the refinery, and the cattle of the *central*, which provided it with funds to pay the workers who returned to their jobs and to get food for everyone in the *central*. It divided up 250 *caballerias* (8,250 acres) of land among the agricultural workers and peasants. It also established a "self defense force," which had "a modest armaments: rifles and revolvers."

The Mabay soviet also carried out cultural tasks. It established schools, and "in the union headquarters there were talks on political and social themes in which provincial and national leaders of the Communist Party participated." It likewise carried the message of the soviets to other sugar plantations.

Finally, in October, the soviet succeeded in reaching an agreement with the owners of the plantation. That accord provided for the eight-hour workday, recognition of the union, a minimum wage and payment in cash, as well as "the right of the trade union organization to designate all necessary personnel except the administrator."

Once this agreement had been reached, the Mabay soviet dissolved. The Castro Communist Party report noted that "like the soviet of Mabay, that of central Nazabal and all of the others that had their origin in the strikes for the eight hour day, wage increases and other demands, and with the termination of the strikes, the soviets ceased to exist."[58]

The Castro party study raised the question as to whether the slogan of soviets had been justified. It concluded, "Neither the objective nor subjective conditions of Cuba, nor the international conditions in which the revolution developed in the period of August 1933 to March 1935, favored establishment in Cuba of a worker and peasant government in the soviet or any other form."[59] It added:

Like the international Communist movement in general—of which the PCC formed a part—the Communist Party had not freed itself yet from Lenin called "the infantile illness of leftism," common to the young Communist parties. It overestimated the rate of maturing of the revolutionary situation, overrated in an exaggerated way the objective and subjective premises of the socialist revolution and underestimated the forces of the class enemy.[60]

Of course, this report at most hints at the fact that the Cuban Communists were following the policies of the Communist International that were in effect at the time and had been imposed by Stalin. The "youth" of the Cuban Communist Party had little to do with the matter.

STRIKES DURING CESPEDES INTERREGNUM

After the overthrow of Machado, a new government headed by Carlos Manuel de Céspedes, descendant of the president of the First Cuban Republic (1868–1878), took office. With strong support from the United States ambassador, Sumner Welles, it was composed of traditional more or less conservative politicians. However, it was destined to remain in office only a little more than three weeks. That period was marked by widespread labor unrest.

Strikes were by no means confined to the sugar industry, which we have already noted. The Céspedes government spent considerable time and energy in trying to bring a peaceful end to walkouts in other segments of the economy.

The New York Times reported on August 22 that a strike of three thousand dock workers in Havana had been settled the previous day. The shipping companies had agreed not only to recognize the union, but also to establish a closed shop and accept a system whereby the dock workers were employed on a rotating list instead of competing for jobs every day. However, port workers in several other towns on the north coast of the island remained out on strike.

The *Times* also reported that there were numerous other strikes in progress. These included stoppages by bakers, shoe workers, and streetcar operators in Havana, as well as the employees of the railroads in Oriente and Camaguey provinces.[61]

The prevalence of strikes during this period was a reflection of the generally militant attitude not only of workers and peasants, but also of students and middle-class elements as well. This effervescence created a quick end to the Cespedes regime, which had been so carefully crafted by Ambassador Welles.

LABOR POLICIES OF THE FIRST GRAU SAN MARTÍN REGIME

On September 4, 1933, the government of President Carlos Manuel de Céspedes was overthrown by a military revolt of noncommissioned officers, led by Sergeant Fulgencio Batista. The rebellious enlisted men first installed a five-person government, known as the Pentarquia, made up of university students and Professor Ramón Grau San Martín of the Medical School of the University of Havana. However, after a few days it was decided to name Grau San Martín as provisional president. He governed with a cabinet, the most important members of which were the student Antonio Guiteras, who was minister of government (interior), and former Sergeant Batista, by then a colonel, as minister of defense.

The program of the Grau San Martín government was socially oriented and nationalist. Efrén Córdova noted the prolabor policies of the regime, which

established the eight-hour day maximum "for all kinds of occupations," recognized the legitimacy and functions of the unions, provided for a minimum wage for sugar workers, created the Secretariat of Labor, extended the application of the law on labor accidents, recognized the right to strike, including solidarity strikes, revalidated and made effective the prohibition of payment of wages in vouchers or tickets, and promulgated the "law of 50" to 80 percent.

This last law provided that at least 50 percent of all employees of all firms had to be native Cubans.[62]

The "50 percent law" was the most controversial of the labor measures of the Grau San Martín revolutionary government. We have noted the long-standing tendency of employers in the tobacco industry to name young Spaniards as apprentices, thus opening the way for them to the best paid positions in that industry. We have also seen the massive importation of Jamaicans and Haitians to work in the sugar industry during World War I. Both of these practices had stimulated large-scale discontent in native Cuban workers, which the Grau government measure was designed to assuage. However, it also met strong criticism from the ranks of the immigrant workers, and during the Grau regime and for some years thereafter, the Communist Party and the CNOC were particularly vocal in their opposition to the 50 percent law. Half a decade was to pass before the Communist-controlled trade unions came around to support the measure.[63]

The nationalist orientation of the Grau San Martín regime was shown not only in the 50 percent law but in its "intervention" in the United States–owned Cuban Electric Company, the suspension of payment on a debt that the Machado regime had contracted with the National City Bank, and the temporary seizure of the holdings of the Cuban American Sugar Company.[64]

Minister of Government Antonio Guiteras was particularly friendly to the labor movement. Typical of his actions was his intervention in a strike of the employees of the Cuban Telephone Company at the end of November. On his insistence, the company signed an agreement with the union that provided for "recognition of the union, the establishment of a forty-five hour week and fifteen-day vacations with pay." According to the *New York Times*, Guiteras had told the employers that "they would be compelled to recognize the union."[65]

THE CNOC AND THE GRAU SAN MARTÍN REVOLUTIONARY GOVERNMENT

In spite of the prolabor attitude and actions of the Grau San Martín revolutionary government, the Communist Party and the segment of the Cuban organized labor movement that it controlled did not support that regime. The official history of Cuban organized labor of the Castro Communist Party noted:

With the simplistic judgment on the government of Grau, and particularly of Guiteras, not only was it not possible for the party to have an attitude of support of that government while combating at the same time its vacillations toward imperialism and its repressive actions against the workers, but it was also not possible to bring about a national anti-imperialist front in which would participate figures such as Guiteras, and even less, like Grau. The Party understood that the policy of the united anti-imperialist front was realizable, essentially, only on the base of the masses. With the *leftist* policy it became, naturally, very difficult for such a wide front to be created in the year 1933.[66] (Emphasis in the original)

What this does not say is that the policy followed by the Cuban Communist Party (and the unions it controlled) was in strict conformity with the "line" of the Communist International at that time. According to that "Third Period" position, groups such as those determining the policies of the Grau regime were "social fascists" and therefore were to be violently attacked.

A more or less typical attack of the Communists and the CNOC on the Grau san Martín regime was a Manifesto of the CNOC on September 10, 1933. It proclaimed that

the so-called Revolutionary Junta is a bourgeois-latifundist government which at the same time that it employs its demagogic "revolutionary" language, employs machine guns against worker demonstrations and detains workers because they distribute manifestos of the Confederación Nacional Obrera de Cuba, and is a government serving Yankee imperialism, before which it has bowed from the first moment of its existence, recognizing the enormous and heavy debt of the bankers of Wall Street.[67]

In the closing days of the Grau regime, the Communist-controlled faction of the Cuban labor movement held two important congresses. One of these was the Fourth Congress of the Confederación Nacional Obrera de Cuba; the other was the Third National Conference of the CNOC's sugar workers organization, the SNOIA.

The CNOC Congress began on January 12, 1934, and continued through January 16. There were some 2,400 delegates, who claimed to represent more than 400,000 members. The session reviewed the history and accomplishments since the CNOC's foundation in 1925. According to the Castro Communist Party's account, the Congress

underscored the experience and lessons of the struggle of the CNOC for the consolidation and the unity of its revolutionary unions; against the anarchosyndicalist leftovers and the corrupting and paralyzing action of the reformists; for the organization of the unemployed and the solution of the problem of unemployment; for the rights of youth, of women and the discriminated-against Negro masses; for the improvement of conditions of life and labor of the workers; against the offensive of the exploiting classes, of the Machado tyranny and North American imperialism; against the effects of the capitalist economic crisis started in 1929; against the imperialist war in gestation and for the defense of the USSR, etcetera.[68]

Several of the resolutions and decisions of the CNOC Congress are particularly worthy of mention. In terms of organization, the meeting went on record as in favor of establishment of single unions in each factory and the merger of existing craft unions. It also resolved to establish twenty-seven national industrial unions and fifty-one regional federations.[69]

The congress adopted new statutes for the CNOC. These discarded the provision in the original statutes that had forbidden anyone from holding office in the organization who "carries on active propaganda in political parties." The resolution on the new statutes proclaimed: "The 'apoliticism' preached by the anarchosyndicalists leads the proletariat to inaction and its submission to other bourgeois-latifundist parties. The Confederación Nacional Obrera de Cuba has replaced its old principles of 'Apoliticism' with the politics of the proletarian class."[70]

The congress adopted two apparently contradictory motions with regard to the unity of the labor movement. On the one hand, it declared that "all our organizational work must be based on the application of the widest united front, that unites in struggle all those workers, in their place of work, organized and unorganized, without discrimination of trade union or political ideology to defend their immediate interests." On the other hand, "the congress ratified the line carried out by the CNOC of strengthening the work of Revolutionary Opposition in reformist unions, attempting to attract to those groups the largest possible number of workers of different political currents and affiliation, to guarantee the united front from below."[71]

The Communist orientation and control of the CNOC were clear at the Fourth Congress, which declared that "the Confederación Nacional Obrera de Cuba must not hide the fact that it has a close relationship with the Communist Party, as the most advanced part of the proletarian class."[72]

The congress also

expressed the firm position of the labor movement against imperialist war and in defense of the USSR. . . . With the objective of aiding the development of revolutionary and internationalist consciousness among the worker masses, the congress agreed to carry on a systematic campaign of popularization of the great successes of the Soviet Union in socialist construction, in the constant improvement of the conditions of life and labor of the workers and its unbreakable policy of peace.[73]

It also ratified affiliation of the CNOC with the Red International of Labor Unions and the Confederación Sindical Latino Americana.[74]

The Third Conference of the Sindicato Nacional de Obreros de la Industria Azucarera met on January 15–16, 1934. There were reported to be delegates from 103 sugar mills as well as from "numerous" plantations and other centers associated with the sugar industry.

This conference passed in review the sugar strikes that had taken place during 1933. It estimated that something like 200,000 workers had taken part in these walkouts, and that they included not only mill workers but also those involved in harvesting and transporting the cane. Emphasis was placed on the necessity of recruiting the latter type of workers into the unions and paying special attention to their problems.

The conference also dealt at length with the problems created by the government restriction of the size of the sugar harvest and launched a call for "a free harvest" in the 1934 season. It was argued that crop restriction was mainly in the interest of "Yankee imperialism."[75]

THE NON-COMMUNIST LABOR MOVEMENT IN THE GRAU SAN MARTÍN PERIOD

The Communists and the CNOC by no means had monopoly control of the Cuban labor movement during the Grau San Martín revolutionary government. This was the case not only in Havana, but in some provincial cities as well, and even among the sugar workers.

In Havana, the Federación Obrera de La Habana, which had been founded just after World War I and had taken the lead in establishing the CNOC, was by this time under the leadership of a combination of Trotskyists and some Socialists and members of the Partido Aprista. Its principal leader was Sandalio Junco, who had been one of the CNOC delegates to the founding congress of the Confederación Sindical Latino Americana in Montevideo in 1925. He had subsequently gone to Europe, including the Soviet Union, and had been won over to Trotskyism by the Spanish Trotskyist leader Andrés Nin. On returning home, he had been expelled from the Communist Party in 1932, whereupon he had led in the establishment of a Trotskyist party, the Partido Bolchevique-Leninista.[76]

The Federación Obrera de La Habana (FOH) still had a majority of Havana trade unions in its ranks, and the Communists had taken those that they controlled out of the organization, to establish the Federación Regional Obrera de La Habana, which was officially recognized as the Havana branch of the CNOC at its Fourth Congress.[77]

There was a counterpart of the FOH in Santiago de Cuba, also under Trotskyist control.[78] These two groups supported the government of President Grau.[79]

The reformist elements that had existed since the birth of the labor movement in Cuba also continued to control a substantial part of the labor movement. This included Hermandad Ferroviaria, as well as well as most of the craft unions, which Efrén Córdova estimated numbered between 450 and 500.[80]

Some important unions in this period were reportedly controlled by the ABC, a revolutionary group that had used terror tactics against the Machado dictatorship and had emerged for a while after the tyrant's fall as an important political group. The Communists accused it of being "fascist," although its influence in organized labor would seem to cast doubt on that categorization. In 1933–1934 it was said to control the electrical and telephone workers' unions.[81]

Finally, the anarchists still had some influence in the labor movement. Of them, Efrén Córdova said, "There were before any others, the anarchosyndicalist groups whose importance had diminished but were not to be disdained in spite of the fact that documents of the CNOC were accustomed to refer to the 'remainders' of this tendency."[82]

Some of the non-Communist unions were particularly favored by the Grau government and particularly by Antonio Guiteras. Such was the case of the union of workers in the United States–owned Compañía de Electricidad. When the government "intervened" against that company, taking control (for the time being at least) from its owners, a committee of union members was set up to help administer it. That committee recommended substantial reductions in electric rates, a recommendation that was accepted by Guiteras. Mario Riera Hernández said that it was that development that gave rise to the Federation of Electrical Workers, which was to become one of the country's most important unions.[83]

Non-Communist unions were not confined to the major cities. Barry Carr has noted of the sugar workers:

Numbers of unions at mills in Oriente province, especially those who were members of the Unión Obrera de Oriente and Sindicato Regional de Obreros de la Industria Azucarera de la Region de Guantánamo, were opposed to the SNOLA/CNOC. Libertarian and anarchist sentiment was substantial enough in the centrales and sugar field to support a meeting in Ciego de Avila on December 31, 1933 and plans to establish a national sugar workers' union opposed to the CNOC/SNOLA.[84]

Events during the Grau San Martín revolutionary regime were significant for the future of the labor movement because they saw the beginnings of elements that were to be the principal contenders with the Communists for control of the labor movement in the late 1930s and the two following decades. After the fall of the Grau regime, the elements controlling the Federación Obrera de

La Habana were to join the political party Joven Cuba, which was founded by Antonio Guiteras, and after his death in 1935 joined the Partido Revolucionario Cubana (Auténtico), the new party established by the former President, Ramón Grau San Martín. By the late 1930s, the Auténticos were the largest group within organized labor that opposed the Communists. Eusebio Mujal, who was to become the leader of the Auténtico labor faction, was already emerging in 1933 as Sandalio Junco's principal lieutenant.[85]

The second element in the later opposition to the Communists were the so-called independents, that is, those not affiliated with any particular party. One of the principal leaders of that group was Angel Cofiño. Mario Riera Hernández has said that Cofiño got his start as a principal leader of the Federation of Electrical Workers during the Grau San Martín government of 1933–1934.[86]

LABOR STRUGGLES AFTER THE FALL OF GRAU SAN MARTÍN

The Communists and CNOC were not the only enemies of the Grau San Martín revolutionary government. The U.S. administration was its sworn foe. Ambassador Sumner Welles and his successor, Jefferson Caffery, made little secret of their opposition to and disdain for the revolutionary regime and finally convinced Colonel Fulgencio Batista to get rid of it. On January 15, 1934, he carried out a coup d'etat that overthrew President Grau; after a very short interregnum in which Carlos Hevía and Carlos Márquez Sterling each served as president for little more than a day, on January 18 Batista installed Carlos Mendieta as provisional president. Mendieta, onetime colonel in the Second War for Independence, was a traditionalist politician who had joined the opposition to the Machado regime in the late 1920s. With the overthrow of Grau San Martín, effective power was in the hands of Colonel Batista, where it remained for more than a decade.

In the months after taking office, President Mendieta issued a number of decrees concerning organized labor. One legalized collective bargaining and provided procedures of conciliation and arbitration for such negotiations. Another specified that strikes could de declared illegal if those procedures had not been used. A third prohibited unionization of government employees and denied them the right to strike. There was also enacted a sweeping "Law in Defense of the Republic," which, among other things, forbade agitation to change the existing form of government, provided severe penalties for unions that did not adhere to the government's collective bargaining processes, and banned presentation of new demands for six months after conclusion of a strike.

The government was authorized to deport foreigners who advocated a change in the form of Cuban government or who acted so as to "curb the right to work of employers and workers."

Other legislation dealt with working conditions. Three decree laws provided a certain degree of stability of employment for workers and the right to fifteen days' vacation a year and regulated the work of women and children. The Mendieta government also ratified several International Labor Organization accords.[87]

In spite of the mixed nature of the Mendieta government's labor legislation, most of the labor movement regarded that regime as hostile to organized labor. In any case, the economic crisis continued, providing the same reasons for strikes as had existed in 1933.

Strikes were numerous. The Communist leader Joaquín Ordoqui claimed that between the overthrow of Grau and the general walkout of March 1935, there were some eighteen hundred strikes.[88] At the inception of the Mendieta regime these were especially prevalent among the sugar workers, and United States–owned enterprises were particularly involved. In the case of a walkout at the Preston installation of the United Fruit Company, the strikers were attacked by two hundred soldiers, and there were severe casualties. In that case, too, United States Marines were landed "to protect American property."[89]

By the middle of 1934 there were a considerable number of trade union leaders who were in jail as the result of strike activities. In July some 10,000 workers of various groups, including textile, cigarette, petroleum, and printing trades workers, were on strike demanding release of these prisoners.[90]

On two occasions, the CNOC called for a general strike. The first of these instances was on February 7, when the Federación Regional Obrera de La Habana, the Havana affiliate of the CNOC, called such a walkout. In that case, there was strong opposition from the older Federación Obrera de La Habana, controlled by Trotskyists and other non-Stalinist or anti-Stalinist elements, as well as from the Hermandad Ferroviaria, and the walkout was far from being general.[91] The second general strike call by the CNOC was issued for October 8, 1934, with demands for unemployment insurance and an end to the "terror," and in solidarity with several partial strikes that were then under way.[92]

However, although the FOH and other groups opposed the efforts of the Communist Party and the CNOC to launch general strikes, they also had a considerable role in the wave of walkout that did take place in 1934. One of the most publicized strikes of the Federación Obrera de La Habana was sometimes called the "Ten Cent Strike." This was a walkout in August 1934 of employ-

ees of commercial establishments in Havana, including the Woolworth's "Five and Ten Cent Stores." This was the first time these
workers had been generally organized.[93]

In spite of the limited success of the CNOC's attempt in February 1934 to launch a general strike, a major labor crisis
developed in the following month. The U.S. magazine *Current History* noted, "strike conditions in Cuba, which bordered on civil
war at the beginning of March." The Mendieta government responded to the situation by arresting eighty "labor agitators" on
March 5 and on March 9 decreed the legal dissolution of all unions "that were then defying the 'special emergency' law of
February 10, which authorized the government to terminate all
strikes 'endangering the nation.' The government also suspended
all constitutional guarantees for a period of ninety days. By the
middle of the month this particular crisis had passed with the
return to work of many of the striking groups."[94]

One strike in 1934 was of particular significance. This was the
walkout of 6,000 employees of the Ministry of Communications,
which lasted from August 11 to August 29. This was important
for at least two reasons: because it occurred among government
workers even though they had been forbidden by the Mendieta
government to organize, let alone go on strike; and because it received backing from a wide range of other workers. There were
sympathy strikes by various worker groups, transport workers
gave strikers free passage on their vehicles, barbers gave them
free haircuts. The strikers were demanding job security, seniority
pay, reestablishment of wages at 1929 levels, and several other
improvements in working conditions. They also demanded removal of administrative employees who had been too closely
associated with the Machado regime and the freeing of some
workers who had been arrested for trade union activities.

The government did its utmost to break the strike. They used
civilian strikebreakers, as well as some army telegraphists, arrested strike leaders, and took other measures of reprisal against
the workers. However, because of the skills of many of those on
strike, which made them hard to replace, and because of the wide
popular support for the walkout, the government finally gave in.
An agreement between the ministry and the strike committee acceded to most of the workers' demands, including de facto union
recognition.[95]

One characteristic of the labor situation of 1934 was the bitter
rivalry between the Communists and CNOC, on the one hand,
and their opponents in the trade union movement on the other.
This conflict sometimes became violent. Thus, on August 27, an
armed group emerged from the headquarters of the CNOC and

went to attack the headquarters of the Federación Obrera de La Habana, resulting in one death and injury of several people.[96]

In spite of the continuing economic crisis and the political and labor turbulence, collective bargaining and the signing of labor-management agreements made some headway in this period. One of the most important of these was a collective contract signed in May 1934 between the Federación Sindical de Plantas Eléctricas and the United States–owned Compañía Cubana Electricidad. It contained forty clauses dealing with union recognition and the union shop, promotion procedures, seniority provisions in case of layoffs, vacations, sick pay, a minimum wage of sixty pesos a month, and provisions concerning the length of the workweek. Efrén Córdova noted, "It is probable, however, that this agreement was not representative of what it was then possible to obtain from less wealthy firms."[97]

THE GENERAL STRIKE OF MARCH 1935

What developed into the revolutionary general strike of March 1935 began with a walkout of both teachers and students in the nation's public schools in February, demanding not only the greater financial support for the schools, but also resumption of democracy. By February 25, the *New York Times* reported that 4,000 teachers and 100,000 students had abandoned the classrooms. They were joined by students of the University of Havana, who began a campaign to convert the movement into a general strike.[98]

Efrén Córdova described the spread of the walkout across the island:

Like the case of the strike of August 1933, the movement thus started served as the trigger for people to express their opposition to the government, this time that of Mendieta. . . . One after another, unions and masses of workers were joining the protest without the need for slogans or exhortations. It was an unrestrainable impulse from the bottom to the top that forced the adhesion of the most diverse organizations and was taking on the characteristic of popular uprising.[99]

Finally, on March 9, the CNOC called for a general strike. However, this occurred only after the movement had become one in fact. Both the CNOC and the Communist Party had felt that the movement was "premature" and certainly could not lead to the "workers and peasants government" that they were seeking. They also undoubtedly were hesitant to join a movement that was getting its principal political impetus from the ABC revolutionary organization.[100]

The reaction of the Mendieta government and particularly Colonel Batista, the army commander, was ferocious, substantially more drastic than had been President Machado's response to the general strike two years before. The constitution was suspended and martial law was declared in Havana; soldiers occupied the University of Havana, which was closed, as it would remain for almost three years. Colonel José E. Pedraza was named military governor of Havana under the martial law regime there.

Efrén Córdova described the government's reaction to this strike:

Pedraza began immediately a bloody campaign of repression that had no precedents in the agitated history of the country. Well-known leaders of the strike were taken from their homes and assassinated. A great number of union headquarters were assaulted and the archives destroyed. Many public employees were jailed or dismisses in summary form. The special courts did not cease dictating condemnatory sentences against the strikers. The armed forces occupied all the vital sectors of the economy and once in control of them proceeded to operate them directly, using strikebreakers and forcing the employees to work.[101]

The U.S. magazine *Current History* said after the strike was over that "sober estimates" placed the number of workers who had participated in the work stoppage at 500,000 and added that "included in this number were practically all the school teachers of the island, about 50,000 government employees, all varieties of labor unions from the most respectable to those of the extreme left, the bulk of the ABC, the leaders of the Auténtico group and the various groups of radicals on the Left fringe."

Current History's report on the March 1935 strike concluded: "The record is clear. The Cuban Government won by an appeal to force and by measures as violent as any used by Machado. Labor unions have been broken up and their funds confiscated. Many of the ablest and most patriotic leaders of the island have been jailed or forced to flee. It does not augur well for peaceful elections in the near future."[102]

AFTERMATH OF THE MARCH 1935 GENERAL STRIKE

The suppression of the March 1935 general strike underscored the fact that Cuba was being governed by a military dictatorship headed by Colonel Fulgencio Batista. Although at the end of the year "elections" were held and subsequently Miguel Mariano Gómez was installed as "constitutional president," he was ousted by Batista a few months later when he had the audacity to veto a bill backed by the dictator providing for establishment in rural areas of schools run by members of the armed forces. He was succeeded by Federico Laredo Bru.

A December 1936 article in the *New York Times* described the nature of this regime: "The Cuban army, built up from 5,000 to 22,000 during the past three years, must be reckoned with not merely as an instrument of force but also as a powerful political force. Added to this is the military reserve of about 40,000 men and women reservists who, with relatives and friends, constitute a political nucleus of considerable importance."

The article continued:

Shrewdly realizing that it is difficult to control the people indefinitely through the sheer force of arms, Colonel Fulgencio Batista, the army chief has set about to popularize himself and the armed forces by the greatest publicity campaign ever staged in Cuba. A special department in the army pours out an unending stream of propaganda through movies, books and pamphlets to the soldiers. The propaganda condemns all forms of radicalism and eulogizes the efficiency of a military-controlled government and the duty of the army to regiment the people for the good of the nation. More propaganda extolling the army's activities is loosed through the controlled press.[103]

The Cuban workers were a particular target of both repression and propaganda. Large numbers of trade unionists were jailed, and a considerable number lost their lives. Also, as the official labor history of the Castro Communist Party recorded:

Many trade union headquarters were destroyed, robbed of their funds, and possessions by the police and the army; others occupied by members of the "reserve," establishing military control of the workers' organizations. The railroads were militarized; in firms, factories and public offices there were placed military supervisors who spread terror and with whose approval there were reductions in personnel. . . . Thousands of workers, teachers and public employees who had been distinguished in past struggles were thrown out of work.

This study noted that this persecution was not confined to the CNOC and its affiliates but was leveled against all factions of the labor movement, including tobacco workers, the Hermandad Ferroviaria, and the electric workers federation, which were not Communist-controlled.[104]

In January 1936, a "labor exchange law" was decreed, providing that all workers must register with a labor exchange, providing their photograph, fingerprints, list of employers, and reasons for discharge in the previous five years. Those failing to do so were to be subject to imprisonment.[105]

As late as February 1937, the *New York Herald Tribune* reported:

Cuba's military rulers are sifting the country for agitators in an anti-radical drive that may not be halted until the ranks of organized labor have knuckled under the control of the Army. For the first time in the republican history of the island, officers of general staff headquarters have been assigned to the Labor Department. . . . The two officers are . . . expected to speed up the Army's relentless campaign against radicals, a campaign begun with what is tantamount to a demand for the cooperation of commercial and industrial leaders through a military circular letter marked "confidential. "

That letter said:

I request that as soon as possible you provide this office (staff headquarters) with a confidential report of all employees at your disposition, including therein: full names, age, nationality, civil state, race, profession, home address and names of parents; as well as any available information concerning their antecedents; and, if possible, photographs of workers who have shown themselves to be agitators.[106]

An important event also took place outside Cuba that was soon to have a very significant impact on Cuban politics and the Cuban organized labor movement. This was the drastic change in the "line" of the Communist International, which was formally ratified at the Seventh Congress of the Comintern in August 1935. This change abandoned the Third Period policy of Communist isolation from and bitter enmity toward all other left-wing political groups and union movements controlled by them, in favor of the so-called popular front policy of alignment with them, and even with more conservative elements that proclaimed themselves "antifascist."

A curious result of this change, insofar as Cuba was concerned, was an article by César Vilar, head of the CNOC, who had gone into exile in the United States, that appeared in a New York Socialist newspaper in December 1936. It recorded that "the ` `-tional Cuban Federation of Labor issued and distributed widely a special bulletin containing all resolutions sent by the Executive Council of the A.F.L., many of its International and National Unions, the British Unions and others in favor of Cuban labor, to the President, Dr. Gómez, and to Colonel Fulgencio Batista. Many brothers were jailed for distributing this bulletin." The article added, "Today, stimulated with the valuable support of the A.F.L. we shall increase our resistance and tenacity in spite of greater sacrifices."[107]

In spite of the considerable persecution to which it was sub-
jected, the Cuban labor movement continued to exist, and even
grew somewhat between 1937 and 1938. Efrén Córdova noted
that the number of legally registered unions grew from 558 in the
former year to 621 in the latter, and membership increased from
170,000 to 220,000. Córdova also noted that "little by little some
of the dissolved federations were beginning to be reconstituted,
beginning in 1937 with the Federación de Trabajadores Mariti-
mos, the next year with that of transport and a little later four
industrial federations and various regional ones."[108]

The CNOC continued to function illegally to some degree. As
early as July 1935 it held a plenum meeting, attended by delegates from five regional federations "and some confederated
unions." The Communist tobacco workers' leader, Lázaro Peña,
was chosen as the new secretary general of the CNOC.[109]

There were also some efforts to reunite the labor movement on
a regional and national scale. Thus, in September 1935 a Comité
de Enlace de Colectividades Obreras was organized in the city of
Havana, and in 1937 a Comité de Unificación Obrera de la
Provincia de La Habana was organized with a view to establishing
a united labor group in that province, with the possibility later of
setting up a united national labor group.

Efrén Córdova noted:

In spite of the modest objectives and limited jurisdiction, the committees
mentioned had the important distinction of having been constituted
jointly by reformists and revolutionaries. Such coexistence of trade unionists that previously had been generally situated in opposing positions
was a positive signal for the reunification of the labor movement.[110]

CONCLUSION

The decade from 1925 to 1935 had seen the development of a
militant Cuban national labor movement. For the first time, there
existed a nationwide central labor organization, the Confederación
Nacional Obrera de Cuba, as well as a number of important national
industrial unions and regional federations. For the first time, too,
the workers of the country's largest economic sector, the sugar
workers, had been unionized to a substantial degree.

During most of this period, the Communist Party had been
the most powerful single political element active in the labor
movement. However, there remained substantial remnants of anarchosyndicalist influence, as well as that of the so-called reformist
elements. Near the end of the period there appeared what, in the
form of the Auténticos, was to become the major competitor of the

Communists for influence in organized labor in the subsequent period.

During this decade, the labor movement was confronted with two ferocious dictatorships, those of President Machado and Colonel Batista. Organized labor was largely responsible, finally, for bringing down the first of these, but failed in its efforts to dethrone the second. However, both dictators became aware of the dangers of trying to destroy the labor movement—Machado learning the lesson too late, Batista, as events in the next decade would show, being more successful in learning the lesson that more was to be gained by efforts to domesticate organized labor than by attempts to destroy it.

Efrén Córdova has well summed up the situation or organized labor after the 1925–1935 decade:

A certain languor overtook the large nuclei of workers, some exhausted and others disheartened after various years of almost continued agitation. . . . The physical elimination of some leaders and the jailing of many trade unionists also generated fear and the inclination of many to abstain. But the decapitation of trade unionism and the disheartening of some workers did not in any way signify the extinction of the labor movement. For one thing, the conditions of life and work of the working population continued being critical in 1935. . . . For another, the trade union spirit remained latent in large groups of workers who were conscious of the need for an organization and remembered the great tradition of solidarity that had been manifest in Cuba during more than sixty years.[111]

NOTES

1. Efrén Córdova, *Clase Trabajadora y Movimiento Sindical en Cuba, Volumen I (1819–1959)*, Ediciones Universal, Miami, 1995, pages 142–145; *Historia del Movimiento Obrero Cubano 1865–1958, Tomo I, 1865–1935*, Instituto de Historia del Movimiento Comunista y de la Revolución Socialista de Cuba anexo al Comité Central del Partido Comunista de Cuba, Editoria Política, La Habana, 1985, pages 225–228; Evelio Tellería, *Los Congresos Obreros en Cuba*, Editorial de Ciencias Sociales, La Habana, 1984, pages 146–198.

2. *Historia del Movimiento Obrero Cubano etc.*, Tomo I, op. cit., pages 248–249.

3. Ibid., pages 190–194.

4. Ibid., pages 194–195.

5. Ibid., pages 228–229.

6.Ibid., pages 230–233; see also Córdova, op. cit., pages 130–132.

7. Córdova, op. cit., page 132.

8. Jorge García Montes and Antonio Alonso Avila, *Historia del Partido Comunista de Cuba*, Ediciones Universal, Miami, 1970, page 65.

9. *Historia del Movimiento Obrero Cubano etc.*, Tomo I, op. cit., page

249.

10. Córdova, op. cit., pages 151–153.

11. *International Press Correspondence*, periodical of Communist International, December 22, 1927.

12. *CTC*, magazine of Confederación de Trabajadores de Cuba, Havana, September 1944, interview with José Rego.

13. Juan Arévalo, *Nuestras Actividades Sindicales en Relación con el General Machado y Su Gobierno*, Ediciones de Acción Socialista, Havana, 1947, page 3.

14. Córdova, op. cit., page 150.

15. Ibid., page 150; and *Historia del Movimiento Obrero Cubano etc.*, *Tomo I*, op. cit., page 242.

16. Córdova, op. cit., page 151; and *Historia del Movimiento Obrero Cubano etc.*, *Tomo I*, op. cit., page 243.

17. *New York Times*, February 6, 1933.

18. *Historia del Movimiento Obrero Cubano etc.*, *Tomo I*, op. cit., page 257.

19. Barry Carr, "Sugar and Soviets: The Mobilization of Sugar Workers in Cuba-1933," paper prepared for the Tenth Latin American Labor History Conference, Duke University, April 23–24, 1993, page 16.

20. *El Movimiento Revolucionario Latino Americano*, Report of the First Conference of Latin American Communist Parties, Buenos Aires, 1929, page 229.

21. Moisés Poblete Troncoso, *El Movimiento Obreo Latinoamericano*, Fondo de Cultura Mexico, D.F., 1946, page 195.

22. *Historia del Movimiento Obrero Cubano etc.*, *Tomo I*, op. cit., pages 256–258.

23. *New York Times*, March 19, 1930.

24. *Historia del Movimiento Obrero Cubano etc.*, *Tomo I*, op. cit., page 259.

25. García Montes and Alonso Avila, op. cit., page 107.

26. *New York Times*, March 21, 1930.

27. *Historia del Movimiento Obrero Cubano etc.*, *Tomo I*, op. cit., pages 260–261.

28. Córdova, op. cit., page 168.

29. Ibid., page 170.

30. *New York Times*, February 6, 1933.

31. Carr, op. cit., pages 16–17.

32. *Historia del Movimiento Obrero Cubano etc.*, *Tomo I*, op. cit., pages 271–273.

33. Córdova, op. cit., 171.

34. Carr, op. cit., page 18.

35. Interview with Juan Arévalo, reformist union leader and sometime Socialist, in Havana, August 8, 1947.

36. Poblete Troncoso, 1946, op. cit., page 193.

37. Interview with Juan Arévalo, op. cit., August 8, 1947.

38. Carleton Beals, *The Crime of Cuba*, J. P. Lippincott Co., Philadelphia, 1934, page 249.

39. *Acción Socialista*, magazine of Juan Arévalo, Havana, May 1941.

40. Arévalo, op. cit., page 3.

41. Interview with Juan Arévalo, op. cit., August 8, 1947.

42. *Historia del Movimiento Obrero Cubano etc., Tomo I,* op. cit., pages 256–257.

43. Beals, op. cit., page 249.

44. *New York Times,* February 6, 1933.

45. *Mundo Obrero,* Communist labor periodical, Havana, August–September 1933, pages 3–4.

46. Córdova, op. cit., page 176.

47. Interview with Carlos Fernández R., sub-delegado before Official and Employers' Organizations of Confederación de Trabajadores de Cuba headed by Lázaro Peña, member of Communist Party, in Havana, August 11, 1947; see also García Montes and Alonso Avila, op. cit., pages 124–125.

48. *El Movimiento Obreo Cubano Documentos y Artículos, Tomo II, 1925–1935,* published by Instituto de Historia del Movimiento Comunista y de la Revolución Socialista de Cuba, Adjunto al Comité Central del Partido Comunista de Cuba Editorial de Ciencias Sociales, La Habana, 1977, pages 382–383.

49. Ibid., pages 385.

50. Interview with Carlos Fernández R., op. cit., August 11, 1947; and García Montes and Alonso Avila, op. cit., pages 124–125.

51. *El Movimiento Obrero Cubano Documentos y Artículos etc., Tomo II,* op. cit., pages 388–389.

52. Interview with Carlos Fernández R., op. cit., August 11, 1947.

53. Mario Riera Hernández, *Historial Obrero Cubano 1574–1965,* Rema Press, Miami, 1965, page 84.

54. *Historia del Movimiento Obrero Cubano etc., Tomo I,* op. cit., pages 283–284.

55. Carr, op. cit., pages 19–20; see also *Historia del Movimiento Obrero Cubano etc., Tomo I,* op. cit., pages 288–290.

56. *Historia del Movimiento Obrero Cubano etc., Tomo I,* op. cit., pages 290–291.

57. Ibid., page 292.

58. Ibid., pages 293–295.

59. Ibid., page 295.

60. Ibid., page 297.

61. *New York Times,* August 22, 1933.

62. Córdova, op. cit., page 186; see also Tellería, op. cit., page 204.

63. Córdova, op. cit., page 187.

64. Ibid., page 186.

65. *New York Times,* December 1, 1933.

66. *Historia del Movimiento Obrero Cubano etc., Tomo I,* op. cit., page 302; see also Tellería, op. cit., pages 208–209.

67. *El Movimiento Obrero Cubano Documentos y Artículos etc., Tomo II,* op. cit., page 246.

68. *Historia del Movimiento Obrero Cubano etc.,* op. cit., *Tomo I,* page 303.

69. Ibid., page 309, 311.

70. Ibid., page 310.

71. Ibid., page 309.

72. Ibid., page 310.

73. Ibid., page 306.

74. Ibid., page 311; see also Córdova, op. cit., pages 197–203 for discussion of this CNOC Congress, and for documents of this Congress see *El Movimiento Obrero Cubano Documentos y Articulos* etc., *Tomo II*, op. cit., pages 469–624, and Tellería, op. cit., pages 209–226.

75. *Historia del Movimiento Obrero Cubano* etc., *Tomo I*, op. cit., pages 313–314; see also Córdova, op. cit., pages 203–205.

76. See Robert J. Alexander, *Internationalism Trotskyism 1929–1985: A Documented Analysis of the Movement*, Duke University Press, Durham, NC, 1991, page 228.

77. *Historia del Movimiento Obrero Cubano* etc., *Tomo I*, op. cit., page 311.

78. Alexander, op. cit., page 228

79. *International Press Correspondence*, December 8, 1933.

80. Córdova, op. cit., pages 201–202.

81. García Montes and Alonso Avila, op. cit., page 164.

82. Córdova, op. cit., page 201.

83. Riera Hernández, op. cit., pages 93–94.

84. Carr, op. cit., pages 18–19.

85. Córdova, op. cit., page 201.

86. Riera Hernández, op. cit., page 94.

87. Córdova, op. cit., pages 189–90; *Historia del Movimiento Obrero Cubano* etc., *Tomo I*, op. cit., pages 315–316.

88. Cited in Córdova, op. cit., page 191.

89. *Historia del Movimiento Obrero Cubano* etc., *Tomo I*, op. cit., pages 317–318

90. Ibid., page 318.

91. Ibid., page 319; Cordova, op. cit., page 211.

92. Córdova, op. cit., page 312.

93. García Montes and Alonso Avila, op. cit., page 164; see also Riera Hernández, op. cit., page 98.

94. *Current History*, May 1934, pages 214–215.

95. Córdova, op. cit., pages 213–214; *Historia del Movimiento del Movimiento Obrero Cubano* etc., *Tomo I*, op. cit., pages 320–321.

96. García Montes and Alonso Avila, op. cit., pages 164–165.

97. Córdova, op. cit., page 193.

98. *New York Times*, February 26, 1935.

99. Córdova, op. cit., page 214.

100. Ibid., pages 214–215; *Historia del Movimiento Obrero Cubano* etc., *Tomo I*, op. cit., page 337.

101. Córdova, op. cit., page 215.

102. *Current History*, May 1935, page 192.

103. *New York Times*, December 25, 1936.

104. *Historia del Movimiento Obrero Cubano 1865–1958, Tomo II, 1935–1958*, Instituto de Historia del Movimiento Comunista y de la Revolución Socialista de Cuba anexo al Comité Central del Partido Comunista de Cuba, Editoria Política, La Habana, 1985, pages 4–5.

105. *The Challenge of Youth*, newspaper of Young People's Socialist League, Chicago, November 1936, page 2.

106. *New York Herald Tribune*, February 7, 1937.

107. *New Leader*, newspaper of Social Democratic Federation, New York, December 19, 1936.

108. Córdova, op. cit., page 220.

109. *Historia del Movimiento Obrero Cubano etc., Tomo II*, op. cit., pages 14–15.

110. Córdova, op. cit., pages 220–221.

111. Ibid., page 219.

3

The Early Years of the CTC

The crisis in the Cuban labor movement provoked by the failure of the revolutionary general strike of March 1935 lasted for something more than a year. During that period many of the leaders of the outlawed Confederación Nacional Obrera Cubana and other important union groups remained in jail, in hiding, or in exile, although the CNOC was able to hold a clandestine Fourth Plenum meeting in July 1935.[1] Many union headquarters were closed down by the authorities, and collective bargaining was virtually at a standstill.

Two factors brought about a change in this situation, starting in 1936. One of these was a drastic change in the line of the Communist Party, and consequently of the part of the labor movement under its control. The other was an alteration in the attitude and policies of Colonel Fulgencio Batista, and hence of the government he dominated.

Of course, the change in the position of the Communist Party did not originate in Cuba; it was part of the worldwide policy shift of the Communist International, which began to appear in 1934 with the establishment of a "united front" between the French Communist Party and the Socialist Party, whom the Stalinists had until a few weeks before denounced as "social fascists." This profound alteration in outlook and action found formal ratification at the Seventh Congress of the Communist International in August–September 1935, which endorsed the establishment of "popular fronts" by each national Communist Party, that is, electoral and other alliances with all parties proclaiming themselves antifascist. The Seventh Congress also endorsed abandonment of the "Third Period" policy whereby each national Communist Party had a trade union movement it dominated, urging instead the merger of the Communist-run union groups with others of different political orientation, a process that in fact the Comintern had already started to put into practice.

One can only speculate on the causes of the change in policy of Colonel Batista. It seems likely that, at least that early in his career, he did not want to go down in Cuban history as "another Machado." Of humble origins, and himself a mulatto, he undoubtedly had a belief in the need for social and economic change in Cuba, as well as a desire to gain support, if not popularity, among his humbler fellow citizens.

Whatever his motives, Batista began to modify his dictatorship. Elections were held in December 1935, as a result of which Miguel Mariano Gómez became president and Federico Laredo Bru vice president. Although a few months later Batista forced Gómez's resignation when he vetoed a law providing for establishment of a network of rural schools under control of the army, Laredo Bru filled out the rest of the term, until 1940.

The Laredo Bru government made a number of reforms, particularly in the education and health fields. But its most important measure was the Ley de Coordinación Azucarera, which created profound changes in the country's most important economic sector.

There were three different groups involved in the sugar industry. One consisted of large landowners (many of them still foreign firms) who, in addition to cultivating cane, controlled the sugar mills where the first phase of processing took place. The second was made up of the renters (virtually all of them Cubans), known as *colonos*, who used land belonging to the larger firms and who until 1937 were subject to losing their leases at the whim of the landowners. The third group were the wage workers, employed both in cultivating and cutting cane and in the sugar mills.

Efrén Córdova summarized the change brought about by the Ley de Coordinación Azucarera:

This law conferred first of all on those who cultivated the land and planted the cane the right to permanence on the fincas that they occupied, thus inflicting a severe blow on the latifundio system and the absentee owners. The law provided in addition a new method of paying wages in cutting, transport and processing of the cane, making them depend on the price of sugar. For the agricultural phase and during the harvest, the minimum wage was fixed in accordance with the official price of sugar in the fifteen days before work began. For the industrial workers, the minimum was also fixed in accordance with the price of sugar, beginning with one peso (1.00) when the price was not higher than 1.56 [cents] per pound of crude sugar on shipboard. Although the price of sugar was not yet high, that system established the basis for an impressive increase in wages in the 1940s and 1950s. This provided, in effect, an indirect but efficacious form for participation in the profits that would open new horizons in the level of living of those who worked in the sugar sector.[2]

BATISTA-COMMUNIST NEGOTIATIONS

The first reaction of the Communists (and hence of the underground CNOC) to the change in Batista's policies was negative. As the official history of the Cuban labor movement of the Castro Communist Party noted:

Both the CNOC and the PC denounced Batista, saying that Batista's objective with all these promises was to change the image which our people had of Batista and his military clique, to limit the protests and growing militancy against the dictatorship and reinforce the role of the armed forces in the administration of the country, in the face of the aspirations for power of civil sectors of the dominant classes.[3]

The Communists and the CNOC pushed demands for their legalization, as well as for a general political amnesty and the calling of elections for a constitutional assembly. They also carried on campaigns for support of the Republican side in the Spanish Civil War and in support of the radical policies of Mexican President Lázaro Cárdenas.[4]

In this period of 1936–1937, the Communists, in pursuance of the new popular front line of the Comintern, sought to establish an alliance of all the parties and groups of the opposition to the Batista-controlled regime. One step in this direction was the establishment in March 1937 of a legal "front party" for the Partido Comunista, that is, the Partido Unión Revolucionario (PUR), headed by Juan Marinello and Salvador García Aguero and consisting principally of intellectuals and others not publicly associated with the Communist Party. The PUR then took the lead in trying to fuse some factions of the Auténtico Party of the former President, Ramón Grau San Martín, the local Aprista Party, and others, an effort that gave rise to the Bloque Revolucionario Popular. However, as the Communists themselves admitted, this organization "did not succeed in consolidating itself."[5]

However, further changes in Batista's policies and resistance of other opposition groups to overly close association with the Communists caused drastic alterations in the line of the Communists. They were converted from the most violent opponents of Batista, as they had been in 1935–1936, to his close allies, a transformation that became clear in 1938.

Late in 1937, President Laredo Bru decreed a general political amnesty, which covered some 4,000 people, including those who had been jailed during and after the March 1935 strike.[6] In May 1938, the government announced its intention to call general elections for a constitutional assembly. In that same month, the government permitted the legal appearance of the "unofficial" Communist Party daily paper, *Hoy*, which at its inception had a circulation of some 80,000 copies.[7] The government also legalized the hitherto clandestine opposition parties.[8]

During this period, there were undoubtedly negotiations in progress between the Communist Party and Batista. With the re-turn to electoral politics, Batista certainly had set his eye on being elected president, and for this purpose he had begun to put together what came to be known as the Coalición Socialista De-mocrática. Perhaps overestimating the influence of the Communists among the voters, Batista was undoubtedly eager to gain their support for the 1940 election.

Efrén Córdova outlined the nature of the Batista-Communist negotiations: "What Batista offered the Communists was precisely what they wanted, the same things they had asked of Machado: the opportunity to participate in the political process and freedom of action to control the trade union movement."[9]

Fausto Waterman, one of the principal Auténtico labor leaders in the 1940s, claimed that the two most important concessions Batista made to the Communists in the 1937–1938 negotiations were legalization of their party and control of the Ministry of La-bor, through which they could control the trade union movement, in part by guaranteeing legal recognition of Communist-controlled unions, including a number that were largely "paper" organiza-tions, with little or no membership. Waterman maintained that until the exit of Batista from the presidency in 1944, the real power of the ministry was exercised by a Communist who served as "trade union delegate" there.[10]

As a consequence of these negotiations, the Communists' atti-tude toward Batista changed markedly. For instance, in the Tenth Plenum of the Central Committee of the party in July 1938, Sec-retary General Blas Roca claimed that "there is taking place a process within the reaction bloc, in which Batista has com-menced to carry out actions which do not correspond entirely to what the fascistic elements are demanding of him."[11] In that same meeting, a resolution was adopted that Batista "is no longer the focal point of reaction but the defender of democracy."[12]

A week after this Plenum, the Communist leaders Blas Roca and Joaquín Ordoqui met with Colonel Batista in the Camp Co-lumbia barracks outside Havana. There, according to Efrén Córdova, they reached an agreement that led to the legalization of the Communist Party two months later.[13]

UNIFICATION OF THE CUBAN LABOR MOVEMENT

While these political trends were operating, the process of rebuilding the labor movement was making marked progress. Not only were new unions being organized and recognized by the Ministry of Labor, but all of the political tendencies within the labor movement were working toward unification of organized labor and the eventual establishment of a new central labor organization that would include virtually all of the country's organized workers.

The official labor history of the Castro era Communist Party sketched this process of recuperation and reunification of the labor movement, noting

The orientation to fuse the dual unions in the clothing, shoe, manufacturing industry, food workers, tobacco and transport sectors, to struggle for the unification of different trade union organizations of chauffeurs of trucks, taxis, etc., as well as the unions of trolleycar workers of Havana, Matanzas, Camaguey and Santiago de Cuba. In this unifying effort some members of unions of the CNOC and some reformist leaders were establishing contacts, which after much effort, expanded and played a positive role.

One of the earliest and most notable examples of the Communists' abandonment of dual unionism was the decision of the Federación Sindical Regional de La Habana (of the CNOC) to enter into contact with the Federación Obrera de La Habana (controlled by ex-Trotskyites) "with a view to uniting in a single federation." At a meeting of representatives of both groups on July 19, 1935, the Committee for Free Trade Union Organization was established.[14]

By early 1937 the movement toward unification of the labor movement had made considerable progress. The Castro era Communist Party's official labor history noted that by then

there was a large number of unions organized in Havana as in the interior of the country, including in fields as important as transportation and the sugar industry . . . it had passed to the reorganization or organization of trade union sections in firms and industrial unions, the fusion of dual unions, and even successful work for other higher forms of organization, such as the national federations of transport, the food sector, that of textiles and clothing; in the maritime, port, tobacco and sugar sectors.

By the beginning of 1937, the Secretariat of Labor reported that there were 558 legalized unions, with 168,232 members.[15]

The first unification of the labor movement on a provincial basis took place in the province of Oriente. At a conference in March 1937, attended by delegates of seventy-five unions from throughout the province—both CNOC affiliates and "independent" unions—the Federación General de Trabajadores de Oriente was established.[16]

A year later, in March 1938, a unity congress of the organized workers of the Province of Havana was held. According to the Castro era Communist Party's official labor history, "This was the first time in the history of the Cuban labor movement that there had been joined in a single congress leaders of organizations of such ideological diversity." The 130 unions represented at the meeting claimed 90,000 members. There was a fraternal delegate present from the National Maritime Union of the United States, and a message was read from Vincente Lombardo Toledano, secretary general of the Confederación de Trabajadores de Mexico. The congress established the Federación de Trabajadores de la Provincia de La Habana.[17]

Efrén Córdova stressed the importance of the establishment of a unified labor federation in the Havana region:

The reconstitution in March of 1938 of the Federación de Trabajadores de la Provincia de La Habana served as a double "test" of the possibility of giving life to a unified central labor group authorized by the government. It was, in the first place, the result of the joint action of reformist and Communist leaders who at least on the regional level succeeded in reaching an accord. In the second place, there was no visible opposition from the government. With the way prepared shortly before by the Batista-PCC agreement, it was the turn of the national labor leaders to carry forward the moves for unification and organization necessary for giving life to a wide based central labor group that could include the various tendencies in conflict.[18]

THE CUBANS AT THE FOUNDING CONGRESS OF CTAL

An important step toward establishment of a new Cuban central labor organization was the participation of Cuban trade union leaders in the founding conference in Mexico City of the Confederación de Trabajadores de América Latina (CTAL) in September 1938. This conference, called by the Confederación de Trabajadores de Mexico, with the support of the government of President Lázaro Cárdenas, assembled labor leaders from most of the Latin American countries.

A Cuban delegation consisting of Communist, Auténtico, and "independent" labor leaders was present at this hemisphere meeting. They participated actively in the affairs of the Mexico City meeting. Lázaro Peña was the most important of the Communist leaders present in Mexico. Among the Auténticos were Sandalio Junco and Eusebio Mujal.[19]

Among its other objectives, the founding congress of the CTAL sought to encourage establishment of national central labor groups in those countries in which they did not yet exist. Among its resolutions was one pledging the new organization "to orient the constitution of wide committees which will direct the struggle for a common platform of workers demands in each country and achieve the complete unity of the working class on the national level, overcoming internal struggles." The Declaration of Principles of the CTAL stressed the need "to achieve the unification of the working class within each country."[20]

In the spirit of these statements of the CTAL, the Cuban delegates signed what came to be called the Pact of Mexico, which proclaimed:

formally and solemnly before the representatives of the Confederación de Trabajadores de Mexico it is our firm decision to work energetically, under the banner of the class struggle, to establish as soon as possible a national central labor group in the Republic of Cuba, pledging our word of honor as worker combatants to shortly organize and carry out in our country a National Workers Congress of Unification, as the indispensable basis to achieve the structuring of a national trade union organism, to bind together more and more the fraternal and class relations among the workers organizations of the American continent, in accordance with the postulates which we have accepted as the basis for the Confederación de Trabajadores de América Latina, but of the entire world, combating with decision and energy all menaces to the democratic system of government and all efforts to establish, from whatever part of the world, a fascist regime, implacable enemy of the popular classes.[21]

ESTABLISHMENT OF THE CONFEDERACIÓN DE TRABAJADORES DE CUBA

On their return home, the Cuban delegates to the CTAL founding congress set to work to establish a new central labor organization. In this effort, they had at least the passive support of the Laredo Bru–Batista government.

This acceptance of the establishment of a new national labor confederation that would be more or less independent of the government undoubtedly reflected an evolution in the thinking and policy of Colonel Fulgencio Batista, perhaps influenced by the forthcoming elections for a constitutional assembly, and subsequently for president, as well as by the agreement he had reached with the Communist Party. A bit less than a year before, in November 1937, the Secretariat of Labor had sought to establish a central group under its own control. A congress to that end had been held, at which the delegates had been carefully selected, and those who were clearly not willing to be unconditional supporters of the government were either denied credentials or not allowed to speak at the meeting. However, in spite of the care taken by the Secretariat, the delegates finally decided not to establish a commission to organize a central labor group, "alleging that they lacked the authority to reach such an agreement."[22]

With the return of the Cuban delegates to the CTAL congress, there was formed the Comité Organizador del Congreso Obrero Nacional, to undertake the establishment of a new national central labor organization. It finally issued invitations to union groups throughout the country to send delegates to a congress in Havana from January 25 to 28, 1939. There were present 1,500 delegates representing 789 organizations. The opening session of the congress was addressed, by among others, Minister of Labor Juan M. Portuondo Domenech, CTAL President Vicente Lombardo Toledano, Mexican CTM leader Fidel Velázquez, and Joseph Kowner, representing the Congress of Industrial Organizations of the United States.

The congress performed its most important function by officially declaring the dissolution of the Confederación Nacional Obrera de Cuba and the formation in its place of the Confederación de Trabajadores de Cuba (CTC). The new confederation was made up of industrial federations covering various segments of the economy, and geographical federations in each province. These federations in turn would consist of unions of individual firms, of particular trades, or of whole industries.

The CTC, as originally structured, had annual or biennial congresses as its highest authority and a national council of fifty-five people, with an executive of fifteen secretaries, each with a vice secretary, to conduct the day-to-day business of the organization. The relatively large size of the national council and national executive was necessary to give adequate representation in those bodies to the three principal ideological-political elements within the new confederation, that is, the old Communist-controlled CNOC, the onetime Trotskyist (by 1939 Auténtico Party) Federación Obrera de La Habana, and the "reformist" Federación Cubana del Trabajo.

The founding congress of the CTC passed a wide range of resolutions in addition to those creating the new organization.

These included demands for a daily minimum wage of $1.50 for industrial workers and $1.20 for those in agriculture; the policy that parts of the Ley de Coordinación Azucarera favoring the sugar workers be put fully into practice; the establishment of social security funds for workers in all branches of the economy; elimination of decrees and laws of the 1934–1936 period that limited the free functioning of unions, collective bargaining, and the right to strike. There was also a resolution calling for election of a constitutional assembly "with free and sovereign character."[23]

There was undoubtedly an effort to obtain certain political balance within the leadership of the CTC, although Communist influence was certainly most pronounced. In each of the fifteen secretariats making up the executive committee, a Communist was either secretary or vice secretary, and the other person was drawn from the Auténticos, the former Federación del Trabajo de Cuba (FTH) or new "independent" elements which had appeared in the mid-1930s.[24]

The first secretary general of the CTC, chosen at its founding congress, was Lázaro Peña, a Communist tobacco workers leader and last secretary general of the CNOC. Efrén Córdova stressed the importance of Peña in cementing unity at the inception of the CTC:

The work of unification was made more possible by the personality of Lázaro Peña who from the first moment demonstrated a special ability to cultivate good relations with other leaders. Peña . . . was blessed with clear intelligence and possessed the political tact, capacity for dialogue and other qualities necessary to be a great trade union leader. Formed by the party, Peña was totally imbued with Marxist doctrine and knew well its objectives, but knew how to pursue them with tact and suaveness, which provided a great advantage for Communist control of the CTC.[25]

THE CONSTITUTION OF 1940

The enactment of the Constitution of 1940 was a significant event in Cuban labor history. Following the model of the Mexican Constitution of 1917, it included a number of labor and social provisions that were of importance to the organized workers. Although some of these required further legislation, which was not always enacted, it constituted a significant advance so far as the labor movement was concerned.

The CTC played an active role before and during the constitutional assembly. It presented to that body an "exposition of the rights of the workers, which brought together the basic demands of the national proletariat which it wanted to become constitutional principles, as a guarantee of their social, political and economic rights." During the four months that the Constitutional Assembly was functioning, the CTC mobilized public demonstrations in favor of its demands, as well as organizing letter writing campaigns for the same purpose.[26]

Efrén Córdova sketched the importance of the new constitution for organized labor:

The programmatic precepts announced the new worker orientation of labor legislation, pointed to the goal of full employment and established the principle of social justice as a possible source of law. However, for the Cuban workers and their organizations what most interested them were the concrete accomplishments, rights and tangible benefits and not interpretations of long-term developments. And it was on that plane of immediate aspirations that the Constitution provided the greatest successes, since in addition to elevating to the rank of a constitutional principle provisions as important as the eight hour day *maximum*, it introduced other measures of effective protection of the worker, as for example: a) the 44 hour week with 48 hours' pay; b) one month of rest for every eleven of work within a normal year, a prescription which was very advanced for the period and which almost no other country of the world had yet enacted; c) paid maternity leave of six weeks preceding birth and six afterwards; d) the right of the pregnant woman to not have to do work requiring physical effort during the three months before birth; and e) the reduction of the maximum work day to six hours for minors between 14 and 18. (Emphasis in the original)

Córdova also noted other important labor provisions of the constitution: a minimum wage, exemption from legal seizure of the workers' minimum wage and working tools, equal pay for men and women and without regard to race, wages and salaries as an employer's preferential financial obligation, and weekly payment of wages and salaries.

The Constitution of 1940 also provided for the workers' right to form unions and to bargain collectively with their employers. It also recognized the workers' right to strike, as well as the employers' right to declare a lockout—the latter a provision that the unionists among the constitutional assembly delegates opposed. It likewise provided that there be adequate inspection personnel to enforce labor protective legislation.[27]

Even the official labor history of the Castro era Communist Party recognized that the 1940 Constitution "had progressive and democratic content, expressed in articles which consecrated the principle of national sovereignty, as well as numerous social rights and political liberties."[28] However, it complained that "many important conquests in the constitutional text depend on complementary laws which had to be approved by the Chamber of

Representatives and by the Senate, composed in their majority of politicians corrupted in the service of the oligarchy."[29]

On the other hand, Efrén Córdova tended to downplay the failure of Congress to act after 1940 to put into effect some pro-labor parts of the constitution:

Even though the Legislative Power was afterwards negligent in adopting the complementary laws foreseen in the Constitution, it is not true as claimed by followers of Castro and some writers in the U.S., that the advances and reforms of the Constitution existed only on paper. Apart from the norms which went immediately in effect, many others were put into effect through decree-laws, presidential decrees, agreements-laws and resolutions of general application, while for others there was no need for a new law, since there already existed adequate provisions before the Constitution.[30]

THE CTC AND WORLD WAR II

Only a few months after establishment of the Confederación de Trabajadores de Cuba, World War II commenced. Perhaps the clearest indication of the preponderant influence of the Communists in the CTC in this period were the positions taken by the confederation with regard to that conflict.

The Second World War began on September 1, 1939, with the German invasion of Poland. Less than two weeks before that, the Stalin regime reached an accord with the Nazi government that went far beyond the "nonaggression pact" announced on August 22, including an agreement for division of Eastern Europe by the Stalin and Hitler regimes, and assured Hitler of the benevolent neutrality of the Soviet Union in whatever conflict with the Western powers might be generated by the attack on Poland.

Of course, the Stalin-Nazi Pact rendered totally inoperative the policies that the Communist International had been following for half a decade. On a national level in each country, gone was the policy of "popular front," that is, a broad alliance of all parties and groups professing opposition to fascism. Internationally, there was no more support for a political and military alliance against the Rome-Berlin-Tokyo Axis, which the Comintern had been urging at least since 1935.

In place of popular frontism and antifascist unity on a national and an international level, the "line" of the Communist International was that the war that broke out on September 1, 1939, was an "imperialist war," a conflict to cover division of the spoils among the warring powers, the outcome of which made absolutely no difference to the workers of the world. That position was maintained until June 22, 1941, when the Hitler regime invaded the Soviet Union.

With the Nazi attack on the Soviet Union, the Communist International's position changed once again, by 180 degrees. From being a conflict on June 20, 1941, in which the international working class had absolutely no interest, World War II became on June 22, 1941, a holy crusade against the Axis powers and in defense of the Soviet Union and its allies.

The Communist Party of Cuba followed totally the various shifts in Soviet and Comintern policy. The degree of Communist control of the CTC (at least on issues that were important to the Stalinists) was demonstrated by the way in which the leading organs of the Confederación endorsed the varying Communist positions on the questions involving the Second World War.

The "imperialist" nature of the war between 1939 and 1941 was spelled out in a resolution of the Third National Council meeting of the CTC in September 1940:

On the first anniversary of the war, the imperialist character of this conflict is confirmed with greater clarity as each belligerent disputes a new division of the world, the redivision of zones of influence and the subjugation of the colonial peoples. . . . Neither Germany nor Italy defends any just cause, nor does England—with the support of the United States—fight for freedom or for democracy of any people of the world. This is an unjust war, anti-popular and reactionary, as much on one side as on the other, in which the peoples are being sacrificed criminally for the benefit of their oppressors.

The resolution went on: "This is a war which is carried on by the English and Nazi-fascist imperialists for the benefit of the rich, of the arms manufacturers, the great merchants and bankers, who enrich themselves fabulously with it, while the workers suffer the greatest exploitation and are assassinated on the battle fronts or the bombings of the rear guard."

Insofar as Cuba was concerned, the September 1940 resolution proclaimed, "The Cuban workers, who are already suffering the consequences of this war without taking part in it, with the closing of factories, the paralyzation of ports, low wages, hunger and misery, do not wish our country to be involved in the inferno of barbarism, destruction and death."

The operative parts of the resolution pledged the CTC "to struggle against the imperialist war, denounce its character and the ends which are sought as much by one belligerent as the other, developing powerful national movement to assure that our country keeps out of the criminal conflict." To this end, it opposed the measure pending in Congress to establish compulsory military service and pledged "to combat all propaganda in favor of the war."[31]

The position of the CTC experienced a 180-degree turnabout with the Nazi attack on the Soviet Union. In an amplified meeting of its executive committee soon after that event, a resolution that was passed proclaimed:

The war which the Nazi imperialists have launched against its people and against all peoples, with their aggression now against the Soviet Union, obliges all workers to manifest not only their sympathies with the land of socialism, but also their disposition to struggle with enthusiasm and decision for the cause that we all embrace—feeling it a duty of all men of the world—to support it in becoming victorious in the defense of its territory, for the progress and future of humanity which that symbolizes, in the face of the invasion of slavery, retrogression and barbarism which fascism signifies.[32]

The CTC, in conformity with this change in attitude toward the war, changed its position with regard to obligatory military service. As the official labor history of the Castro period Communist Party stated, "The CTC also issued a warm exhortation for inscription in Obligatory Military Service and the incorporation of women in the Feminine Service for Civil Defense."[33]

In conformity with this change of policy toward the war, the CTC put great emphasis on doing everything possible to prevent interference with production for the war effort. Lázaro Peña expressed this position at the Fifth National Council meeting of the CTC:

We proclaim the duty of the working class to struggle to avoid interruptions of the production necessary to win the war. The CTC, which defends resolutely the demands of the workers, which is constituted to struggle for their demands, the reason for existence of which is the need to struggle with organized and decided force against the abuses and exploitation of the employers, the CTC—in these moments of national life—proclaims the necessity of avoiding conflicts in the patriotic interest of winning the battle of production.

Peña went on:

The workers of Cuba—conscious of what the present struggle signifies—will know how to find means of defending their demands, their rights and their conquests, while avoiding at the same time conflicts which signify interruptions in production, but without that signifying for a moment, that they adopt legal measures which suppress or restrict the right to strike and other instruments of defense of the workers. . . . Only in extreme cases . . . will the workers accept to go on strike.[34]

EXPANSION OF THE LABOR MOVEMENT

The period 1937–1947 was one of the relative calm for the Cuban organized labor movement. This was due to several factors. One was the improved economic situation during much of this period. The increased demand for and improvement in the price of Cuban sugar as a result of recovery from the Great Depression and then from World War II, as well as the system of regulation of the United States sugar market, which somewhat favored Cuban producers, tended to stimulate the whole Cuban economy. Greater income from sugar stimulated other sectors of the Cuban economy, including manufacturing, commerce, and government expenditure on capital investments and other programs.

Another factor of significance insofar as the labor movement was concerned was the continuing alliance between Fulgencio Batista and the Communist Party, which largely dominated organized labor during this period. The Communists joined Batista's Coalición Socialista Democrática, both in the election of the 1940 constitutional assembly and in the general election for president and congress after the adoption of the new constitution, supporting the election of Batista as president in the 1940 election. Communist collaboration with Batista reached a high point when President Batista named the Communist Party president, Juan Marinello, and later Carlos Rafael Rodríguez, as "ministers without portfolio" in his cabinet."[35]

This alliance served the Communist Party well during these years, by giving them preferred access to the Secretariat of Labor. Efrén Córdova noted "the sympathetic view of the functionaries of that ministry . . . had for Communist leaders"[36] and "the easy access" the Communist union leaders had "to key functionaries of the Ministry of Labor."[37]

Thus, both the economic and political situation of the 1937–1947 period led to a very substantial increase in the membership and influence of he labor movement. The official labor history of the Castro period Communist Party noted:

In this period the organization of the masses of the workers, especially the labor unions, grew and developed without interruption and with a more accelerated rhythm than in the past. Thousands of workers who had been separated from all social and organized life decided to join together in labor unions—bank employees, those of air transport, etc.—in peasant associations, youth, feminine and black organizations.

This same source cited the period March–July 1943 as an example of this growth of the labor movement and related organizations. In that period, forty-five new unions were established by workers in 1,134 "new centers of productions," nineteen dual unions were united, and about five thousand peasants organized and established peasant associations in forty different localities.[38]

This growth of the labor movement was reflected in the expansion of the Confederación de Trabajadores de Cuba. Whereas, in the CTC founding congress in 1939 there were 567 unions with 220,666 members, those numbers had increased to 595 and 410,000 by the time of the Second Congress. There were 961 unions with 406,000 members at the time of the Third Congress in 1942.

Between the third and fourth congresses of the CTC, the leadership changed the basis of calculating "membership," substituting dues payers for the rather vaguer concepts of "affiliates" or "followers." As a result, the figures for the confederation at the time of its Fourth Congress in 1944 showed a decline in membership to 163,184, although the number of unions affiliated had grown to 1,183.[39]

In addition to increase in the number of unions and union members, the CTC organizational structure was considerably strengthened during this period. Generally, the CTC leadership sought to establish industrial unions, including within their ranks all of the workers of a particular factory or other enterprise. However, in some cases old unions organized on a craft basis persisted. This was particularly the case among the tobacco, transport and port workers. In Havana, for instance, there were still sixteen craft organizations among the port workers, eleven such tobacco unions, seven in the transport field.[40]

However, in many cases wider types of unions were established. Thus, in Havana there was founded the Union of Non-Alcoholic Cafes, bringing together the workers of many such small enterprises. Generally, in the sugar industry, single unions including both agricultural workers and those in the mills, were established; all of the workers in the Polar Brewery formed a single union, and the Sindicato de Trabajadores del Petroleo de la Provincia de la Habana included the workers of the Sinclair and Shell Refineries, although those of Standard Oil maintained a separate organization.[41]

There was relatively little effort by employees to curb the growth and power of the labor movement by establishing organizations of their workers under employer control. Efrén Córdova wrote: "Except in some rural zones, and even there very rarely, there was little effort of employers to deal with yellow unions. The Cuban employers were not prone to organize and finance unions under their control, and the workers were not inclined to join spurious unions or ones inspired by the boss."[42]

However, there were a few such cases. One of these was the union in the Ariguanabo textile plant in Bauta in the province of Havana, the largest firm in the textile industry. Until 1944 it was dominated by the employer, but in that year both the Communists and the Auténticos worked successfully to destroy the firm's domination of the union, which then joined the Textile Workers Federation.[43]

Individual unions were increasingly joined in federations. In October 1939, some sixty-eight unions of sugar workers established the Federación Nacional de Trabajadores Azucareros. In 1940, the Federación Nacional de la Industria Textil y de la Aguja was formed by unions of textile and clothing workers. In that same year the Federación Nacional de Trabajadores Gastronómicos united workers in the hotel and restaurant industry, and a federation was established by the musicians. In 1944, the Federación Nacional de Trabajadores Telefónicos collected all of the telephone workers unions. Of course, even before establishment of the CTC there had existed the electrical and maritime workers federations, as well as Hermandad Ferroviaria, which was the federation of railroaders.

There were also regional labor federations for each province. Before the establishment of the CTC such groups had existed in four of the six provinces, and in 1940 new ones were organized in the two remaining provinces of Pinar del Río and Matanzas.[44]

An important step in terms of the organization of the labor movement was the legal recognition that was finally granted to the Confederación de Trabajadores de Cuba, the first time that a central labor organization had gained such status since the outlawing of the CNOC in March 1935. The CTC was legalized by a presidential decree on April 7, 1943.[45]

Efrén Córdova noted the transformation of the labor movement's general role in Cuban society during the period under discussion:

Trade unionism evolved from a challenging posture that it had maintained in previous decades to an attitude of greater moderation, which induced it to act within the established institutional framework. In a certain sense, one could say that it effected a transformation that brought it from a generally extreme position in the social system to being an important sector of civil society, and even a power factor in the Cuban *establishment.* (Emphasis in the original)

As evidence of this new role, Córdova cited CTC participation in the price control mechanism established by the government during World War II, the fact that President Grau San Martín addressed the Fourth Congress of the CTC, and the close relations established under both President Batista and President Grau with the Ministry of Labor. He also cited labor participation in government bodies such as the National Minimum Wage Commission and the Labor Maternity Junta. Córdova observed, "A spirit of tripartite cooperation began to appear, at least at the national level."[46]

The official labor history of the Castro era Communist Party also recognized these changes in the role of organized labor:

In the new conditions and in the face of new tasks, the organization and trade union leaders were required to raise their ideological and political capacity to be able to defend in correct and firm ways, among others, the positions of the CTC in support of national unity against fascism, and in defense of the national economy. This required the collaboration of the working class with the other social classes, including their exploiters, in the common effort to defeat fascism and defend the national economy, even though this, for certain, was in the hands of the bourgeoisie and directed by it.[47]

EXTENSION OF COLLECTIVE BARGAINING

By the early 1940s, collective bargaining and the resulting agreements became virtually the rule. As Efrén Córdova wrote, "Gradually the idea was generalized that negotiation was one of the principal functions of the union, and it should dedicate to that a good part of its human and financial resources."[48]

Generally, collective bargaining was at the level of the individual firm. However, in some instances, it was conducted on an industrywide basis, particularly in the sugar industry and in the tobacco sector, where there were negotiations concerning the problem of mechanization.

Frequently, the government intervened in the collective bargaining process. Usually, government representatives were mediators or conciliators. However, in some instances, government officials served as arbitrators, handing down ultimate decisions. But in some cases, as in negotiations in the Polar Brewery, they were never called upon to intervene.

Córdova summed up the situation thus: "In most of the cases of negotiations they went forward in a relatively normal form, with accords reached in days or weeks, depending on the lengthiness of the list of demands. Particularly in middle-sized firms, where labor relations were more personal, negotiations were frequently conducted harmoniously." However, Córdova also noted that in a number of firms, particularly in the sugar industry, there was frequent need for the government to intervene to reach—or force—agreements.

Sometimes the government felt forced to go so far as to take temporary control of firms to impose agreements. Among other cases, this happened in the Havana Electric Railway, the Coca Cola Company, Ferrocarrileros Unidos, and the Omnibus Aliados Bus Cooperative in Havana during the 1940s.

The issues dealt with in collective bargaining agreements evolved from what they had been in previous decades, when they had often dealt mainly with employer recognition of unions, and with fulfillment of terms provided for in legislation. Córdova indicated that in the 1940s agreements dealt with

the specific aspirations and needs of each firm and group of workers. The contract . . . began to have the objective of going beyond the minimum standards of legislation . . . in the 1940s . . . negotiation ceased being a matter of solving conflicts and was converted into a normal and periodic exercise with its own reason for existence. No longer was union recognition, which had caused too many strikes, discussed. Its existence accepted, there were negotiations over the facilities that would be conceded to it (headquarters, bulletin board, shop stewards' access to the administration, dues checkoff) as well as substantive questions concerning control of promotions and transfers, procedures for layoffs, creation of internal health and safety commissions, and grievance procedure. However, from the beginning of this period the largest number of sectors . . . continued giving priority to the wage question.[49]

Sometimes the collective agreements reached during this period were quite extensive and covered a wide range of subjects. For instance, the 1950 contract between the Federación Sindical de Trabajadores Telefónicos de Cuba and the Cuban Telephone Company was a document of 100 pages, which dealt not only with union recognition and wages and hours, but with procedures for promotion and layoffs, a grievance procedure, checkoff of union dues, conditions for receiving leaves of absence, office space for local unions and the federation, and various other issues. It was printed so that those on both sides could know its provisions.[50]

By 1943, government figures indicated that there were 2,537 collective agreements in effect. That number increased to 4,152 by 1951.[51]

However, although regular collective bargaining became more or less the rule, this did not mean that there were no conflicts. Although, as we have noted, the policy of the CTC after the Nazi attack on the Soviet Union was to prevent strikes whenever possible, some walkouts did in fact occur.

On the one hand, there were segments of the labor movement, including the printing trades, construction, and transport, in which there was still influence of anarchosyndicalists who did not accept the "class collaboration" policies of the CTC leadership. They sometimes undertook strikes such as a walkout of the Unión Nacional de Artes Graficas that closed down the major printing firms of Havana for a month.

In addition, as Efrén Córdova noted, "It was not always easy to put aside old customs and the essence of labor-management relations often led to confrontation. Wage increases, reductions of personnel, and the fulfillment of the large range of dispositions that conferred social benefits continued to be the most frequent causes of conflict."[52]

One of the most significant strikes in this period was that of the henequen workers of Matanzas against a company that had tried to close its factory to prevent the unionization of its workers, and had reduced its workers' wages by 10 percent. According to the official labor history of the Castro period Communist Party: "The firm resistance of the workers and general mobilization in solidarity brought a favorable solution to this conflict. There were also conflicts with several textile factories, the owners of which threatened to close down their enterprises to prevent organization of their workers."[53]

There is no doubt that during World War II and for some time thereafter, collective bargaining—whether through direct union-employer negotiations or by government intervention when direct discussions reached an impasse—generated very substantial gains for Cuban workers. The official labor history of the Castro period Communist Party sketched some of these: In the case of the sugar workers, largely because of presidential decrees, wage increases ranging from 10 percent to 20 percent were received in 1941, amounting to 57 million pesos; a general raise of 50 percent in 1942; as well as a provision for workers to receive the same wage in the "dead" season as during harvesting, were obtained. Port and maritime workers established the system of rotating employment for their members, thus eliminating favoritism by the employers. Railroaders obtained wage increases ranging from 10 percent to 20 percent in 1941, and 4–8 percent in 1943, and maintenance-of-way employees gained a minimum wage of 45 pesos a month.

The electrical workers won not only wage increases, but the reemployment of union members dismissed during the March 1935 general strike and indemnity to those same workers amounting to about 300,000 pesos. Also, between 1942 and 1944, the tobacco workers received wage increases amounting to 10,504,202 pesos.

This same Castro era source noted: "To these successes of sectors united in federations there must be added those achieved by other groups of workers throughout the island in struggle with their respective employers. Among these were miners, henequen workers, textile workers, musicians and other sectors." It summed up the accomplishments of the unions in terms of wage increases: "In four years—1940 to 1944—the CTC and the united struggle of the workers whom it represented, under the maximum leadership of Lázaro Peña, won for the workers in industries, commerce, transport and similar activities, 264 million pesos in wage increases."[54]

These gains of organized labor undoubtedly reflected a general improvement of the economic situation of the island and the levels of living of its inhabitants. Efrén Córdova noted:

The statistics of the United Nations showed that from 1945, Cuba was one of the three leading countries of Latin America in such significant indicators of modernization and development as the number of calories in the diet of the ordinary citizen, the number of periodicals, radio stations and other means of diffusion, the number of houses in relation to the population, the level of hygiene in the cities, and in educational facilities. . . . The progress registered in living conditions was not only experienced by the upper and middle classes, but also by a high percent of the working class.[55]

However, Córdova also noted that there were elements of the working class who were largely unaffected, as well as rural workers who had moved to the cities in the hope of improving their lot but had been unable to find employment in the "formal" economy and had become part of a growing "informal" economy.[56]

FIRST FOUR CONGRESSES OF THE CTC

We have noted the spirit of cooperation and compromise among various ideological tendencies that characterized the founding congress of the Confederación de Trabajadores de Cuba in January 1939. In the next three congresses of the confederation this spirit was less evident, but the unity of the organization was maintained.

The Second Congress of the CTC met between December 12 and 16, 1940. There were 713 delegates representing some 410,000 workers. Eleven national federations were represented "as well as organizations of other sectors: metallurgy, chemical and food industries, construction, graphic arts, the petroleum industry, the theater and related activities, various industries and agricultural workers."[57] As we have already noted, this CTC congress followed the Communist line on World War II during the period of tacit alliance of the Soviet regime with the Nazi government—proclaiming the war to be "imperialist" and insisting on Cuban neutrality in the conflict.

The Third Congress of the CTC met almost exactly two years after the preceding one, on December 9–12, 1942. There were 1,336 delegates representing 961 unions and 24 industrial, provincial, and regional federations. At that meeting, relations between the Communist trade unionists and their ideological and political opponents were particularly difficult.[58]

Finally, the Confederación de Trabajadores de Cuba held its Fourth Congress in December 1944, with 1,063 delegates present, representing virtually all of the country's local unions and trade union federations. This was the first national CTC meeting held after Fulgencio Batista had lost control of the government. His successor, Ramón Grau San Martín, addressed the opening session.[59] Relations between the Communists and their opponents were somewhat less fractious than they had been two years before, although this situation was obviously "the calm before the storm."

Efrén Córdova noted the generally moderate tone of the resolutions adopted during these first four congresses of the CTC:

It was a language that was positive and developmentalist, which was in conformity with the text of various resolutions favoring a greater institutionalization of labor relations. The Second and Fourth Congresses took particular interest in pronouncing in favor of approval of laws complementary to the Constitution; there were also references to the elaboration of a labor code and in place of advocating as in the past the unrestricted right to strike, various proposals alluded to the establishment of systems of conciliation and arbitration. . . . All the congresses also advocated the creation of social security, including insurance for infirmities not associated with work, and maternity insurance, but it was only the IV Congress that proposed an ample program of social security for all sectors, including agricultural and domestic workers.

Córdova also stressed the preoccupation of these congresses with such issues of immediate concern to the workers as unjustified dismissals from work, collective contracts, paid vacations, and the work of apprentices and women. They also dealt with economic problems arising from the war, calling for price controls, subsidies for workers adversely affected by the conflict, and the provision of adequate housing at affordable prices.

As Córdova also noted, the early CTC congresses likewise dealt with a wide range of national economic problems not directly associated with labor-management relations. These included development of electric power, promotion of the Cuban merchant marine, the creation of a central bank, and stimulation of development of manufacturing.[60]

IDEOLOGICAL CONFLICTS WITHIN THE CTC

From its inception, of course, the CTC had within it unions and federations controlled by several different ideological tendencies. Although the Communist Party was the predominant political group within the confederation during its first eight years, and Lázaro Peña remained CTC secretary general, there were from the beginning elements more or less hostile to the Stalinists.

By the end of World War II there existed three major political factions within the CTC, and at least two less significant ones. The largest opponent of the predominant Communists were the unionists of the party headed by former President, Ramón Grau San Martín; the Partido Revolucionario Cubano (Auténtico), popularly referred to as the "Auténticos." The second major non-Communist element was the group generally known as "independents," which included some old-line "reformist" leaders and newer figures who tended to be "pure and simple" trade unionists without clear political affiliations. The two groups of less significance were the anarchosyndicalists, who, as we have noted earlier, continued to have influence in a limited number of industrial sectors, and the Trotskyists, whose base of support was by the late 1940s limited largely to the eastern region and city of Guantánamo.

The Communists continued to be the dominant political element in the CTC until 1947. This dominance was undoubtedly due in part to their longstanding leadership in organizing the workers in such key fields as the sugar industry, as well as the ability of Communist-led unions (as well as others that were not under Communist control) to win substantial gains for their unions' members during the period of relative economic prosperity that started in the late 1930s. Their alliance with Batista, which after 1937 assured them of predominant influence in the Ministry of Labor, was also a major factor in assuring the Communists a dominant position in the CTC and many of its affiliated unions.

However, anti-Communist union leaders also claimed that the Communists used "gangster methods" to keep control of at least some unions. An Auténtico maritime workers leader claimed that this was particularly true, for instance, in the case of the port workers of Havana.[61]

Auténtico union leaders also accused the Communists of "milking" the unions for the benefit of the Communist Party. One leading Auténtico unionist, for instance, claimed that as many as 80 percent of the members of the party were on the payrolls of unions under the party's control.[62] The Auténtico maritime leader whom we have already cited recounted an incident in which the government issued a decree claiming an increase of the price of cigars from nine to ten cents, and when the Auténtico union leaders Francisco Aguirre, Eusebio Mujal, and Goliat himself went to see the prime minister to ask that all of the price increase be passed on to the tobacco workers, they found Lázaro Peña there before them, together with some employer representatives, to argue that the price increase not specify any set increase in workers' wages, because, Goliat claimed, an agreement had been made for the employers to pass on part of their increased income to the Communist Party.

Goliat also cited the case of the largest sugar plantations where the workers were supposed to receive 10 cents a bag of a government subsidy, but the Communist leaders of that union had agreed that the amount be reduced to 6 cents, with 2 cents going to the Communist Party, and the employers keeping the final 2 cents.[63]

One of the principal anarchist trade union leaders made somewhat similar charges. He said that the Communists in control of the CTC spent about $11,000 a month on salaries for their followers who held posts in the Confederación, and that the party also raised considerable funds through a kind of blackmail of employers, threatening them with attacks in the party-controlled press and from Communist-controlled unions if they did not pay something into the party's coffers. One way such payments were made was through taking "advertisements" in the Communists' radio station 1010, advertisements that in fact were never broadcast because the employers involved felt that they would be bad publicity for their firms if they were in fact put on the air.

This same anarchist leader felt that for a long time one of the advantages of the Communists was the fact that their principal rivals, the Auténticos, worked "very sporadically" against them in the unions.[64]

The non-Communist factions in the labor movement were by no means united in their opposition to Stalinist control of the CTC and various unions. The most consistent opponents of the Communists were the Auténticos, whose general support in the labor movement grew substantially in the years after the founding of the CTC. Other groups did not have consistent positions, sometimes collaborating with the Communists, sometimes with the Auténticos.

THE COMISIÓN OBRERA NACIONAL AUTÉNTICA (CON)

The Auténtico trade unionists originated in several sources. One was the Trotskyites, who in the early 1930s had controlled the Federación Obrera de La Habana, one of the principal labor groups that later cooperated in the process of labor movement unification which led to the formation of the CTC. After the downfall of the government of President Ramón Grau San Martín in January 1934, his former minister of interior, Antonio Guiteras, established his own political party, Joven Cuba, which most of the Trotskyist trade unionists soon joined. After Guiteras's murder in 1935, Joven Cuba joined the Auténticos.[65]

Another element among the Auténticos trade unionists undoubtedly consisted of workers who had not previously had any particular political affiliation but were attracted by the pro-labor positions of the 1933–1934 Grau San Martín administration and who, when the deposed president established the Partido Revolucionario Cubano (Auténtico) some months after his overthrow, joined the new party. Finally, the small Cuban Aprista Party also joined the Auténticos in the later 1930s.

The role of the Auténtico trade unionists, within their own party as well as within the labor movement, was formalized at the end of 1940 with the establishment of first the "workers section" and then of the Comisión Obrera Nacional (CON).[66] Efrén Córdova indicated, "The section was part of the internal structure of the party (as were the feminine section and that of youth), whereas, the commission had greater autonomy and permitted its members therefore to occasionally have discrepancies with the policy of the party and to define goals and strategies which were convenient for it."[67]

The CON was headed in the beginning by Sandalio Junco, a black trade unionist who had been the founder of Cuban Trotskyism and head of the FOH. When he was assassinated late in 1942 at a meeting called to commemorate the anniversary of Antonio Guiteras's death, which the Communists had called on their supporters to prevent, he was succeeded by Eusebio Mujal, also an ex-Trotskyist. Fausto Waterman, a leading figure in the CON, claimed subsequently that the murder of Junco was part of a deliberate campaign of the Communists to liquidate the Auténtico labor leaders, citing a number of other assassinations of the party's trade unionists that had allegedly been carried out by the Communists.[68]

The CON organized a national labor congress at the end of 1942 at which Junco was memorialized. Those participating reaffirmed the nationalist and anti-Communist objectives of the CON. The congress also included various anti-imperialist pronouncements and elements of Auténtico "social doctrine."[69]

One of the functions of the CON was to organize throughout the country "Auténtico fractions" in all of the unions in which the Partido Auténtico had members or followers. In this, of course, they were following the pattern long set by the Communists. Ironically, the Communists in this same period gave up—at least temporarily—the "Communist fractions" that they had long had in the trade union movement.[70]

The CON made its first appearance as an organized group at the Second Congress of the CTC in December 1940. The official labor history of the Castro era Communist Party noted: "In the congress there were reflected the efforts of the Comisión Obrera Nacional of the PRC to undermine and divide the trade union movement. Eusebio Mujal, Junco and others attempted to win over, with intrigues and underhanded means a part of the delegates."[71]

The struggle between the Auténticos and the Communists intensified in the Third Congress of the CTC in December 1942. The Castro Communist labor history claimed:

The Mujalistas who headed the Comisión Obrera Nacional of the PRC traveled around the country, organized meetings and used their peons in the local labor commissions—in large part declassed elements—to try to impose in the assemblies of the unions the election of antiunitarian delegates. In this work, they went so far as to employ the procedure of fabricating paper unions, that is, inexistent ones, or to revive unions that had no connection with the CTC, nor registration with the Ministry of Labor.[72]

At the Third Congress, the CON leaders refused to allow any of their people to take posts in the new Executive Committee of the CTC. When four Auténticos did so, they were thrown out of the party.[73]

By the time of the Fourth Congress of the CTC in 1944, two months after the newly elected President Ramón Grau San Martín took office, a kind of truce was reached between the CON and the Communist leaders in the CTC. For the first time, CON trade unionists were officially elected to the leadership of the CTC,. with the approval of both the Communists and the Auténticos. Four

CON members were named to the Executive Committee of the confederation (of a total of thirty-one).[74]

Throughout the wartime period, the Communists in the CTC leadership tended to favor the "independents" among the non-Communist leaders, apparently seeking to use them to counterbalance the Auténticos and the CON. In 1944, for instance, nine independents were elected to the CTC Executive Committee. Efrén Córdova wrote: "During the period of the first four congresses, the Communists worked to preserve unity, giving places in the Executive Committees to the representatives of other tendencies. They succeeded always, however, in giving a larger role to the independents and reformists in detriment of the group of Junco and Mujal."[75]

THE LABOR MOVEMENT AND GRAU SAN MARTÍN'S ELECTION

In 1944, the Auténtico presidential candidate, Ramón Grau San Martín, defeated the nominee backed by the outgoing President Fulgencio Batista, Carlos Saladrigas. The Communist Party continued to form part of Batista's Coalición Socialista Democrática, which, although losing the presidency, continued to have majorities in both houses of Congress. The Communists increased their vote substantially over what they had received four years before, electing four members of the Chamber of Deputies and for the first time electing three senators.[76]

NOTES

1. *Historia del Movimiento Obrero Cubano 1865–1958, Tomo II, 1935–1958*, Instituto de Historia del Movimiento Comunista y de la Revolución Socialista de Cuba anexo al Comité Central del Partido Comunista de Cuba, Editoria Política, La Habana, 1985, pages 14–15.

2. Efrén Córdova, *Clase Trabajadora y Movimiento Sindical en Cuba* Volumen I *(1819–1959)*, Ediciones Universal, Miami, 1995, page 224.

3. *Historia del Movimiento Obrero Cubano etc., Tomo II*, 1985, op. cit., page 26.

4. Córdova, op. cit., page 224.

5. *Historia del Movimiento Obrero Cubano etc., Tomo II*, op. cit., pages 33–35.

6. Córdova, op. cit., page 224.

7. *Historia del Movimiento Obrero Cubano etc., Tomo II*, op. cit., page 42.

8. Ibid., page 43.

9. Córdova, op. cit., page 228.

10. Interview with Fausto A. Waterman, a leader of Comisión Obrera

Nacional of Partido Auténtico, subsequently secretary of Youth and Sports Affairs of Confederación de Trabajadores de Cuba, in Havana, August 9, 1947.

11. *Historia del Movimiento Obrero Cubano etc.*, Tomo II, op. cit., page 42.

12. Córdova, op. cit., page 229.

13. Ibid., pages 229; see also *Historia del Movimiento Obrero Cubano etc.*, Tomo II, op. cit., page 143.

14. *Historia del Movimiento Obrero Cubano etc.*, Tomo II, op. cit., page 16; see also Evelio Tellería, *Los Congresos en Cuba*, Editorial de Ciencias Sociales, La Habana, 1984, pages 288–289.

15. *Historia del Movimiento Obrero Cubano etc.*, Tomo II, op. cit., page 28.

16. Ibid., pages 28–29.

17. Ibid., pages 36–37; see also Tellería, op. cit., pages 290–293.

18. Córdova, op. cit., page 230.

19. Interview with Fausto A. Waterman, op. cit., August 9, 1947.

20. Córdova, op. cit., page 231.

21. *Historia del Movimiento Obrero Cubano etc.*, Tomo II, op. cit., pages 49–50; see also Tellería, op. cit., pages 293–298.

22. *Historia del Movimiento Obrero Cubano etc.*, Tomo II, op. cit., pages 32–33.

23. Ibid., pages 50–57; see also Córdova, op. cit., pages 231–235.

24. *Historia del Movimiento Obrero Cubano etc.*, Tomo II, op. cit., pages 55–56; see also Tellería, op. cit., pages 299–305

25. Córdova, op. cit., pages 233–234.

26. *Historia del Movimiento Obrero Cubano etc.*, Tomo II, op. cit., page 76.

27. Córdova, op. cit., pages 254–257.

28. *Historia del Movimiento Obrero Cubano etc.*, Tomo II, op. cit., page 76.

29. Ibid., page 77.

30. Córdova, op. cit., page 257.

31. *Historia del Movimiento Obrero Cubano etc.*, Tomo II, op. cit., pages 68–70.

32. Ibid., page 104.

33. Ibid., page 107.

34. Ibid., page 108.

35. Ibid., page 122.

36. Córdova, op. cit., page 296.

37. Ibid., page 294.

38. *Historia del Movimiento Obrero Cubano etc.*, Tomo II, op. cit., page 134.

39. Córdova, op. cit., page 265.

40. *Historia del Movimiento Obrero Cubano etc.*, Tomo II, op. cit., page 135.

41. Córdova, op. cit., pages 267–268.

42. Ibid., page 289.

43. Interview with Pascasio Lineras, secretario de propaganda of Sindicato Textil Ariguanabo, subsequently textile workers' leader of Organización

Auténtica, in Havana, August 4, 1947.

44. Córdova, op. cit., pages 267–268; see also *Historia del Movimiento Obrero Cubano, Tomo II*, op. cit., pages 87–88.

45. *Historia del Movimiento Obrero Cubano, Tomo II*, op. cit., page 129; see also Tellería, op. cit., pages 311–318.

46. Córdova, op. cit., page 278.

47. *Historia del Movimiento Obrero Cubano etc., Tomo II*, op. cit., page 136.

48. Córdova, op. cit., page 284.

49. Ibid., pages 284–289.

50. *Contracto Colectivo de Trabajo Concertado Entre la Federación Sindical de Trabajadores Telefónicos de Cuba y la Cuban Telephone Company*, Havana, May 27, 1950.

51. Córdova, op. cit., page 289.

52. Ibid., page 280.

53. *Historia del Movimiento Obrero Cubano etc., Tomo II*, op. cit., pages 93–94.

54. Ibid., pages 127–129.

55. Córdova, op. cit., page 247.

56. Ibid., page 248.

57. *Historia del Movimiento Obrero Cubano etc., Tomo II*, op. cit., page 91; see also Tellería, op. cit., pages 319–326.

58. *Historia del Movimiento Obrero Cubano etc., Tomo II*, op. cit., pages 122–126; see also Tellería, op. cit., pages 327–336.

59. *Historia del Movimiento Obreo Cubano etc., Tomo II*, op. cit., pages 148–149; see also Tellería, op. cit., pages 327–349.

60. Córdova, op. cit., pages 271–272.

61. Interview with Gilberto Goliat, member of Executive Committee of Confederación de Trabajadores de Cuba (Cofiño faction), subsequently secretary general of Federación Obrera Marítima, in Havana, August 10, 1947.

62. Interview with Fausto A. Waterman, op. cit., August 9, 1947.

63. Interview with Gilberto Goliat, op. cit., August 10, 1947.

64. Interview with Modesto Barbeito, secretario Sindical de la Asociación Libertaria de Cuba, subsequently official of Federación de Trabajadores de Plantas Eléctricas, in Havana, August 6, 1947.

65. For information on Cuban Trotskyists, see Robert J. Alexander, *International Trotskyism 1929–1985: A Documented Analysis of the Movement*, Duke University Press, Durham, NC, 1991, pages 228–230.

66. *Historia del Movimiento Obrero Cubano etc., Tomo II*, 1985, op. cit., page 112.

67. Córdova, *Volumen I*, 1995, op. cit., page 292.

68. Interview with Fausto Waterman, op. cit., August 9, 1947

69. Córdova, *Volumen I*, 1995, op. cit., page 293.

70. Ibid., page 292; see also *Historia del Movimiento Obrero Cubano etc., Tomo II*, op. cit., page 136.

71. *Historia del Movimiento Obrero Cubano etc., Tomo II*, op. cit., page 92.

72. Ibid., page 125.

73. Ibid., page 126; see also Córdova, op. cit., pages 292–293.

74. *Historia del Movimiento Obrero Cubano etc.*, *Tomo II*, op. cit., page 152; see also Córdova, op. cit., page 293.

75. Ibid., page 293.

76. *Historia del Movimiento Obrero Cubano etc.*, *Tomo II*, op. cit., page 141.

4

The CTC Split and Its Aftermath

The changed political situation after the June 1944 election clearly had its influence on the labor movement, and particularly on the Confederación de Trabajadores de Cuba. Communist control of the CTC had been based, at least in part, on the alliance between the party and Fulgencio Batista. It was hardly conceivable that such friendly relations could be maintained by the Communist CTC leaders with the new Auténtico president.

However, in spite of his opposition to the Communists, President Ramón Grau San Martín was faced with major problems if he should decide to help to deprive the Stalinists of control of the CTC. He lacked a majority in Congress, and the army was still largely in the hands of officers who owed a greater or less degree of loyalty to General Batista. Furthermore, World War II was still in progress, and both the Communists and the Auténticos were committed to helping the Allied war effort.

The upshot of this situation was a certain spirit of compromise between the Auténticos—their party, the CON, and the president—and the Communists during the first two years of Grau San Martín's government. This compromise was clear in the labor movement. It was also reflected in the pronouncements of both President Grau and the Communist leaders of the CTC.

Grau San Martín seemed immediately after his election to indicate the intention of challenging Communist control of the CTC. In an interview with the conservative newspaper *Diario de la Marina* only two days after his election, the president-elect indicated his belief that the CTC was "subordinate to a political party which is contrary precisely to the ideals and interests of the great majority of the Cuban workers."

However, the Communist leaders of the CTC did not reply in kind to what might have been judged a provocative statement by the president-elect. In fact, three weeks after his election, Grau San Martín received a delegation from the CTC, headed by Lázaro Peña, its secretary general. On this occasion, Grau told his visitors: "The visit of the Cuban workers pleases me very much, since our triumph in the elections was the triumph of all the people of Cuba. In the PRC we fight for the improvement of the conditions of life of the workers. This interview is testimony of the possibility of consolidating unity so as to be able to continue on the road of progress and to make our major contribution to the war effort."

For his part, Lázaro Peña told the president-elect, "We want to take this opportunity to express to you the sympathy with which your pronouncements in favor of collaboration of all national forces has been received in the workers' sectors, because we feel that it is our obligation to have close collaboration with your government in the work that it proposes to carry out on behalf of the community."

Peña also commented: "The workers are satisfied to hear your words with respect to maintenance of labor policy. We are in agreement with you that we workers must cooperate with capital to increase production. We are interested in harmonic solutions and we promise to aid with all our force the victory of the allied countries."[1]

The spirit of compromise existed not only between the president and the CTC Communist leaders, but within the Confederación de Trabajadores de Cuba itself. As the official labor history of the Castro era Communist Party said: There predominated immediately the tendency toward collaboration and mutual respect, and as a consequence, there were conversations between leaders of the CTC and members of the Comisión Obrera Nacional of the PRC (A)."

The same source noted:

The unity between the CON and the leaders of the CTC on the eve of the celebration of the IV Congress, was based on a program of struggle for the most urgent demands of the workers, among them the promulgation of a labor code, the issuance of real regulations of the social rights established in the Constitution, and the adoption of a general social security law. In addition, there was insistence on points such as the struggle against racial discrimination and aid to the peasants, etc., which had been strongly supported by the CTC since its establishment. . . . Furthermore, accords were reached to strengthen the labor movement through organization of nonunion workers, consolidation of discipline in the unions, and strengthening of the CTC finances through punctual payment of dues by the unions to the Confederación.[2]

As a consequence of this agreement, the Fourth Congress of the CTC was the calmest and least controversial such meeting since the one that established the confederation.

This cooperative spirit among the various political elements within the CTC continued for some time after the Fourth Congress. On May Day 1945 when, as had become customary, the CTC presented a series of demands to the president of the Republic; the Executive Committee of the CTC prefaced the list of demands with a statement to the effect that "the CTC declares that the Cuban workers appear before the President of the Republic not only to present demands but also to make clear their sincere and respectful support and to reiterate to him their decision to do everything in their power to contribute to the success of his progressive Government."

For his part, President Grau also maintained a more or less friendly attitude toward the CTC in spite of its being Communist controlled. He appointed representatives of the Confederación, including Communists, on a commission he appointed to draw up a labor code. He also named the Communist sugar workers' leader Jesús Menéndez as a member of the official delegation sent to the United States in March 1945 to negotiate the terms of sale of Cuban sugar in the United States. Finally, in March 1945 President Grau ordered the payment of $750,000 to the CTC to complete construction of a large new headquarters in Havana, a project that until then had been severely underfunded.[3]

BACKGROUND OF 1947 SPLIT IN THE CTC

There were at least two developments that finally produced a split in the Confederación de Trabajadores de Cuba. One was the improvement in the political situation of the Auténtico government. The other was a change in the line of the Communists.

In 1946, two years after the election of President Grau San Martín, the Auténticos and their allies won control of both houses of Congress. By that time, too, Grau had been able to retire most of the higher military officers who were loyal to Batista, substituting for them more "professional men."[4] The Grau administration was thus in a position after mid–1946 to move against Communist control of the national labor movement without the political risks that would have been involved when Congress and the military were not under the control of the Auténticos and their allies.

In the 1944–1946 period there was also a major change in the orientation and policies of the Communist Party, as a result of the onset of the Cold War. As Efrén Córdova noted:

The Communists ceased having the cooperative nature of the war and renewed their attacks against those whom they considered allies of Yankee imperialism. A pamphlet of Blas Roca entitled *Al Combate!* published in 1946 reflected the new line of attack on Yankee imperialism and the American Federation of Labor (AFL), denunciations of the Government of Grau and calls for labor unity in Latin America.[5]

This change in Communist line in the immediate postwar period was reflected in the official labor history of the Castro period Communist Party, which characterized this change as a struggle against "Browderism."[6]

Earl Browder was between 1930 and 1945 the secretary general of the Communist Party of the United States. In that role, he had close contacts with the Cuban party, giving them advice, as well as aid, in the struggle against Machado. In 1935, at the Seventh Comintern Congress, it was decided that Browder and the United States Communist Party would constitute a "clearinghouse," where advice and help would be provided, in coordination with the Comintern headquarters in Moscow, for the Latin American Communist Parties, particularly those in and around the Caribbean. Browder gave his (and Comintern's) approval to the Cuban party's development of an alliance with Batista in the late 1930s and thereafter.[7]

During the latter part of the World War II, Browder developed a thesis to the effect that the wartime alliance between the Soviet Union and the capitalist nations of Britain and the United States could continue indefinitely. Fabio Grobart, the eminence grise of the Cuban party, subsequently described this theory; Browder had

a false perspective of the world situation considering that after the victory a modified capitalism could coexist harmoniously and without contradictions with socialism; that the imperialist countries would be capable of resolving through harmonious accord, their sharp contradictions; that the imperialists themselves within each country would be capable of participating in national unity and directing it to the complete destruction of fascism and guarantee peace; that the imperialists themselves would be able to cooperate to avoid the postwar economic crisis and unemployment, promoting the development of our dependent peoples and the welfare of the laboring masses.[8]

One obvious result of the Cuban party's endorsement of Browderism, according to the Castro era Communist Party's official labor history, was the January 1944 decision to change its name from Partido Unión Revolucionaria Comunista to Partido Socialista Popular,[9] a decision taken after consultation with

Browder.[10] Several other Caribbean Communist Parties made similar name changes about the same time, while the U.S. party became the American Communist Political Association.

Luis Serrano Tomayo, a onetime Communist trade union leader in Oriente Province, who after 1940 became an Auténtico and ultimately became secretary general of the Tobacco Workers Federation, claimed that the change in name did not change the nature of the Cuban Communist Party. He argued that the Popular Socialist Party existed for "electoral purposes" and that "anyone could join it," while there continued to exist a clandestine Partido Comunista de Cuba, headed like the PSP by Blas Roca as secretary general, in which Fabio Grobart, a European who did not become a Cuban citizen, played a major role. It was the clandestine party that in fact determined the policies of the legal one.[11]

During the early months of 1945, Browder's wartime theory was strongly attacked from Moscow and he was removed as secretary general; before the end of the year he was expelled from the Communist Party of the United States (CPUSA). Phillip Jaffe has argued that Browder's removal as head of the CPUSA was Stalin's signal of the outbreak of the Cold War.[12]

With the denunciation of Browder by Moscow, the Cuban Communists had to repudiate their association with him, and with the line that he had been following during the latter part of World War II. This was done at the Third National Assembly of the Party in January 1946.[13]

As a result of these developments affecting both the Auténticos and the Communists, the truce between them worked out in the labor movement in 1944 ended by mid–1946. The Comisión Obrera Nacional of the Partido Auténtico set about a campaign to oust the Communists from control of the Confederación de Trabajadores de Cuba and its affiliates. Typical perhaps was the experience of the Auténtico tobacco worker union leader who was sent by the CON to the Las Villas region, to try to gain Auténtico control of the labor movement in that area. Several years later, he claimed to me that when he arrived there were only 11 unions of 400 in the region that were Auténtico-controlled, but within fourteen months the Auténtico dominated 230 unions in the area. He admitted that "in some cases this change was done by outright violence," but that in most cases the control was taken away from the Communists "by legitimate means."[14]

THE SPLIT IN THE CONFEDERACIÓN DE
TRABAJADORES DE CUBA

The organic split of the Confederación de Trabajadores de Cuba into two competing organizations took place in the middle months of 1947. One important causative factor was the formation of the Comisión Obrera Nacional Independiente (CONI).

The CONI was established in January under the leadership of Angel Cofiño, head of the Federation of Electrical Workers, who became its secretary general, together with Vicente Rubiera of the Telephone Workers and Ignacio González Tellechea of the Maritime Federation. Efrén Córdova noted that "the three leaders enjoyed a good reputation, had solid support in their federations and could figure as independent candidates."[15]

According to Cofiño himself, who by his own admission had long been "very close" to the Communists although never a party member, the CONI was not established as an anti-Communist group, but rather for the purpose of enhancing independents' influence in the Communist-Auténtico struggle within the CTC. However, the Communists interpreted it as aimed against them and began a violent campaign against Cofiño in their press and elsewhere.[16] Understandably, this campaign drove the CONI into an alliance with the Auténticos' CON.

Meanwhile, Minister of Labor Francisco Benitez, and Carlos Prío Socarrás, who succeeded Benitez in May 1947, sought to persuade the Communists to agree to have Lázaro Peña retire as secretary general at the forthcoming Fifth Congress of the CTC. But Peña made it clear that he would under no circumstances give way for an Auténtico, whereupon the minister suggested the name of Angel Cofiño. However, the Communist leaders refused to consider Cofiño's taking over the secretary generalship.[17]

The Fifth Congress of the CTC was scheduled to take place between April 7 and 10, 1947. However, this meeting never took place, because of serious incidents that resulted from the decisions of the credentials committee concerning which delegates were eligible to be seated.

There were challenges of delegates by both sides, which the credentials committee, composed of one representative each of the Communists, the CON of the Auténticos, and the CONI, found it very hard to resolve. Francisco Aguirre, the Auténtico member of the committee, challenged the credentials of 183 delegates, and the other members also challenged others.

There was also considerable violence by both sides. On April 4, shots were fired on the national headquarters of the Partido Socialista Popular. On the next day occurred the act of violence that provided a reason (or excuse) for the minister of labor to intervene in the situation.

The explanation of the incident of April 5 varied depending on who was telling the story. According to the official history of the Castro period Communist Party

an armed group, headed by Emilio Surí Castillo, assaulted the headquarters of the Sindicato Textil y de la Aguja, where the Credentials Commission was functioning, for the purpose of seizing the documentation; something which they were unable to do, since the workers repelled the aggression with gunfire and the attackers were forced to retire after one of their own was killed.[18]

A very different version was given by Fausto A. Waterman, a leader of the CON, a few months afterward. According to him, Surí Castillo had gone to where he had been told he could obtain his credentials but was told that he had to go to the Textile Union headquarters. Sensing trouble, he had first gone to the CON office, where he was joined by Francisco Aguirre, Fausto A. Waterman, and several others, one of whom was Félix Palú. When they arrived at the Textile Union building an armed guard at the entryway sought to bar them from entering, but they pushed him aside and went in. Upstairs, they were told that there were no credentials for Surí Castillo, and so he and his companions seized the credential by force, and as they were returning downstairs, they were fired at by people at the head of the stairs and down below, and Felix Palú was killed.[19]

After this incident, Minister of Labor Prío Socarrás decreed the indefinite postponement of the opening of the CTC Congress. He also named a new Credentials Commission to decide on which delegates had the right to attend the CTC Fifth Congress. President Grau promised that the congress would soon meet. As the Castro period Communist labor history commented, "The leaders of the CTC had no alternative but to accept the government decision, although they protested against it."[20] The minister said that the congress would meet in July and suggested at the same time that the two sides name an ad hoc committee to check on the work of the Credentials Commission, a proposal accepted by the Auténticos, but rejected by the Communists.[21]

A deadlock was thus created. It was finally broken when the Communist majority in the outgoing CTC leadership set May 4–9 as the dates for the Fifth Congress to meet. The Communists claimed that that meeting was attended by representatives of about 900 of the 1,200 unions then legally existing. The unions under Auténtico and CONI control were not represented.

The Communist version of the CTC Fifth Congress passed nearly 250 different resolutions during the five days it met. These included protests against possible reduction of the Cuban sugar quota in the United States market, demands that the government curb speculation and price gauging, calls for establishment of a central bank and a special agricultural development bank, demands that Congress pass the laws required to put into practice the social segments of the 1940 constitution, and a variety of other matters.

The May CTC Congress also chose a new leadership. Lázaro Peña was reelected secretary general. It was claimed that the new Executive Committee included Auténticos as well as Communists and members of several other parties and people who were political independents. Three months after the May Congress, Carlos Fernández R., a Communist member of the Executive Committee elected there, told me that there were twenty-four Communists, twelve Auténticos, two members of the Partido Ortodoxo, six Liberals, and one member of the Partido Democrático. There were also ten independents.[22]

However, Auténtico CON leaders rejected the claim that members of their party had participated in the May CTC Congress and had been elected to the Communist-controlled CTC's Executive. Emilio Surí Castillo, Auténtico leader among the sugar workers and secretary general of the CON in 1947, claimed that Rogelio García Hagranit, who the Communists claimed was an Auténtico, had actually been elected to the city council of Camaguey as a Communist, and José Luis Amigo, who had been chosen as CTC correspondence secretary, was not an Auténtico as the Communists claimed, but rather a member of the Orthodoxo Party, which had recently broken away from the Partido Auténtico. Surí Castillo added that all of the Auténticos who had pro-Communist leanings had become Ortodoxos.[23]

In any case, the faction of the Confederación de Trabajadores de Cuba that was dominated by the CON and the CONI was established at their version of the Fifth Congress of the CTC, which met on June 6–8, 1947, in conformity with a call issued by the Ministry of Labor. This congress, too, adopted a wide variety of resolutions, dealing with national economic problems, the demand for agrarian reform, and various other matters. Reflecting the alliance between the CON and the CONI, Angel Cofiño was elected secretary general, and the other six most important positions on the new Executive Committee were divided equally between representatives of the CON and CONI, Francisco Aguirre, Pablo Balbuena, and Emilio Surí Castillo, representing the former, and Vicente Rubiera of the Telephone Workers, Ignacio González

Tellechea of the Maritime Workers, and Arturo Aguero representing the CONI.[24]

THE STRUGGLE BETWEEN THE TWO CTCs

In the months after the splitting up of the Confederación de Trabajadores de Cuba there were bitter struggles within many of the industrial and regional federations between adherents of the Communist CTC and the Auténtico-Independent confederation. The latter group was aided by the Grau San Martín government, which first ousted the Communist CTC from the Palacio de los Trabajadores, the still uncompleted confederation headquarters, and turned the building over to the rival group. Then, in November 1947, it extended legal recognition to the CTC headed by Angel Cofiño. Under existing law, there could only be one legally recognized national central labor organization.

When I visited Havana in early August 1947, the principal anarchist union leader, Modesto Barbeito, who was aligned with the Cofiño CTC, admitted that he thought that the Communists still controlled the majority of the country's unions.[25] At the same time, Carlos Fernández R., a leading member of the Executive Committee of the Lázaro Peña CTC, claimed that it still controlled the maritime, tobacco transport, and sugar workers' federations, as well as those of airline workers, musicians, and meat packers. He said that the bank workers and railroaders were split and claimed that the only industrial federations clearly affiliated with the Cofiño CTC were those of electrical workers, telephone employees, and hotel and restaurant workers, in addition to three new small federations that had been established since the split.[26]

However, Fausto A. Waterman, a leading official of the Auténticos' Comisión Obrera Nacional, told me a quite different story. According to him, supporters of the Cofiño CTC controlled a majority of the unions in all of the fifteen industrial federations except those of land transport workers, airline employees, tobacco workers, and maritime laborers.[27]

The electrical and telephone workers federations were clearly in the hands of the Cofiño CTC. According to Cofiño at that time, there was no Communist influence in the electrical workers organization.[28] According to Vicente Rubiera, secretary general of the Federación Telefónica, although a few leaders of his federation had attended the May CTC Congress that reelected Lázaro Peña, they were subsequently deprived of their posts and banned from holding office in the Federación Telefónica for four years.[29]

Some of the smaller federations were also firmly in the hands of anti-Communist elements. These included the Federación Nacional de Vendidores y Auxiliares, an organization of salesmen that had been established a few months before the split in the CTC. Its Executive Committee consisted of sixteen Auténticos, two Liberals, and two Communists. Its secretary general was elected Secretary of Correspondence of the Cofiño CTC.[30]

In the case of the commercial workers' organizations, two new federations were formed during the CTC crisis. One, the Federación Nacional de los Trabajadores del Comercio (FNTC), was controlled by the Auténticos and was immediately given legal recognition by the Ministry of Labor. In view of the law forbidding dual unions, that action meant that the Communist-controlled federation of commercial workers, founded about the same time, could not get such recognition. The secretary general of the FNTC was given a position on the Executive Committee of the Cofiño CTC.[31]

Similarly, the Federación Nacional de Trabajadores de la Medicina was established early in April 1947. It claimed to have fourteen of the existing nineteen unions of health workers in its ranks, was controlled by the Auténticos, and was granted by the Ministry of Labor legal recognition, which was denied to a Communist-controlled federation established about the same time.[32]

In the case of the Graphic Arts Workers, a congress to form a national federation met at the same time as the April CTC Congress was scheduled but was suspended by the Ministry of Labor at the same time that the CTC Fifth Congress was suspended. Leaders of the Communist-controlled unions in the field called a new congress to meet simultaneously with the Communist-controlled CTC Fifth Congress in May. It established the Federación Nacional de Artes Graficas, but the Ministry of Labor, in the face of objections by Auténtico printing trades leaders to its recognition, had not legalized the new federation by August 1947.[33]

Particularly bitter struggles took place among the sugar and maritime workers. In the former case, although the top figures in the federation continued to be Communists and it continued for some time to be officially part of the Lázaro Peña CTC, the federation was very much split in the period that followed the two rival CTC Congresses. However, Emilio Surí Castillo, the principal Auténtico leader among the sugar workers, claimed in August 1947 that of the 220 unions in the Sugar Workers Federation, only 100 were under Communist control, the Auténticos had 115 and independents 5. Surí Castillo added that anti-Communist forces represented a substantial majority of the 220,000 organized sugar workers, since they controlled most of the largest local unions.[34] After the two rival CTC Congresses, there was reportedly a meeting of representatives of 111 local sugar unions that repudiated the alignment of the federation with the Lázaro Peña CTC and voted to affiliate with that headed by Angel Cofiño.[35]

Professor Harold Dana Sims described his view of what happened in the Sugar Workers Federation (FNTA):

During 1947 Labor Minister Carlos Prío had begun to name labor leaders, sending soldiers and Auténtico CON members to seize locals. In November, Menéndez called for sugar workers to elect delegates to the Sixth FNTA Congress. . . . Prío's order to suspend the Congress was ignored and the gathering took place. Jesús was unanimously reelected secretary general. . . . The "official" FNTA Congress met and elected Surí secretary general. Police seized FNTA offices for Surí, expelling the Menéndez leadership. Jesús visited Oriente Province to hold rallies, some of which were blocked by the Rural Guard and Auténtico CON toughs.[36]

For several months there was a somewhat confused situation in the Maritime Workers Federation. The national leadership of that federation had traditionally been in the hands of independents, rather than of either Communists or Auténticos. The independents controlled the ports of Camaguey, Matanzas, the Oriente, and Pinar del Río, but the Communists dominated the port of Havana, the country's largest.[37]

However, in the face of the split in the CTC, the independents in the Maritime Workers Federation also split. As we have noted, Ignacio González Tellechea was a founder of the Comisión Obrera Nacional Independiente and as such supported the Angel Cofiño CTC. However, two other principal Independent maritime leaders, Ramón León Rentería and Antonio R. López Castillo, were elected to the Executive Committee of the Lázaro Peña CTC and at least for a while supported it.[38]

The Council of the Federación Obrera Marítima Nacional had voted to send delegates to the Fifth Congress called by Lázaro Peña, and then to affiliate with the CTC, headed by him. However, subsequently (it was claimed by anti-Communist maritime leaders), 87 of the federation's 162 unions voted to repudiate this and send delegates to the Fifth Congress, which elected Angel Cofiño as secretary general.[39]

There was considerable violence, some of it fatal, during this struggle for control of the Cuban labor movement. The deaths of two Communist trade union leaders, Jesús Menéndez of the Sugar Workers Federation and Arcelio Iglesias of the port workers, drew particular attention.

The struggle for union control was particularly violent among the sugar workers. Jesús Menéndez, a Communist member of the Chamber of Deputies and secretary general of the Federación Nacional de Trabajadores Azucareros (and of its Communist-controlled version after the split), had continued to rally support for his federation after the Auténticos established a rival FNTA in November 1947. The Menéndez federation also carried on a long battle to maintain the system, first established after Grau San Martín took office as president, whereby the workers received a substantial part of any increase in the price Cuba received for its sugar.

On January 22, 1948, in the provincial town of Yara, a local military commander, Captain Joaquín Casillas, attempted to arrest Jesús Menéndez on unstated charges. In the encounter that ensued, Menéndez was shot to death by the captain. Menéndez's friends asserted that he was shot in the back; the captain's associates claimed that Menéndez had fired the first shot at Casillas, who returned fire, face to face. In any case, Menéndez was dead.[40]

Arcelio Iglesias had for years been secretary general of the Stevedores Union in the port of Havana. He had led a struggle to prevent the shipment of sugar "in grain," that is, not in bags, and in sea ferries. Among his opponents he had a reputation for using strong-arm methods to maintain his party's control of his union. In any case, he was assassinated on October 17, 1948.[41]

By 1949 the struggle for control of the labor movement had been won, at least for the time being, by the opponents of the Communists. Eusebio Mujal, who had recently become secretary general of the legal Confederación de Trabajadores de Cuba, claimed that it had "the vast majority" of the organized workers in its ranks, with about 1,100 unions compared to the 50 to 60 that the Communists still controlled. He said that of the thirty-one industrial unions in the country, twenty-nine belonged to the Auténtico-controlled CTC, which also had a regional federation in every province.[42]

Mujal claimed that there were some 800,000 workers in his CTC, each of whom paid between $1.00 and $1.50 a month to his or her union. The local unions paid a per capita to the CTC of $0.05 a month, providing a total of about $40,000 a month to the confederación. However, CTC expenses were about $60,000 a month; the difference was made up by levies on the salaries of the labor leaders who were deputies or senators. He cited his own case: as a senator, he received $4,000 a month and paid $2,000 to the CTC.[43]

The legal CTC also controlled most of the sugar workers unions by 1949. José Luis Martínez, a member of the Executive of the legal Sugar Workers Federation, claimed that of the 210 sugar unions on the island, the legal FNTA had all but 12 in its ranks, although the Communists maintained their own version of the FNTA.[44]

The Communist themselves recognized that they had lost control of the great majority of the country's unions. Referring to the legal CTC as the CTK (Strike Breakers Labor Confederation), the official labor history of the Castro period Communist Party noted that "in spite of the loss of prestige of the CTK leaders and the lack of agreement of the workers with them, the fact is that the CTK had succeeded in bringing into their organization an important part of the worker masses."[45]

As a result of this situation, the Communists, at the beginning of 1951, "oriented workers of certain sectors to enter the official unions, as occurred for example, in Omnibus Aliados. A few months later numerous other unions were dissolved to enter their respective official organizations."[46]

However, the official labor history of the Castro Communist Party commented that "it was not easy to put this line into practice." There were workers in the Communist-controlled CTC who would not agree to return under any terms to the unions of the rival confederation. Others thought that the maneuver was useless, that they would be "lost" in the unions controlled by the anti-Communists. In addition, resistance to such Communist penetration of the unions of the legal CTC was often offered by those unions themselves.[47]

Efrén Córdova claimed:

On a national scale, the Communist protests were weakening an the official CTC continued to displace them, reducing them to minimal influence. The Cuban labor movement thus got rid of Marxist control without major upsets. Neither the Government of Grau nor that of Prío had to use violence or use drastic methods to consolidate the CON. The new CTC had recognition of the employing class and it was establishing itself everywhere as the recognized representative of the workers.[48]

Córdova speculated on the reasons for the relatively easy victory of the CON-dominated CTC. One was that "the new central continued operating with the same militant and demanding style of its predecessor"; another was that "the Partido Auténtico in spite of its great weaknesses still was popular." Finally, the easy victory of the anti-Communist CTC could be explained, according to Córdova, because

the Marxist influence was more of a bureaucratic and directing nature than being concerned with the masses. A large part of the latter always remained indifferent toward the struggles for power that took place at the top of the movement. Another part thought that the Auténtico Government had done exactly the same thing to help its group as that of Batista had done to consolidate the Communists in control of the CTC.[49]

To some extent, the Communists agreed with the analysis of Efrén Córdova of the causes for their defeat in the labor movement. Although stressing the importance of the use of force by the anti-Communist elements, and the fact that the Lázaro Peña CTC and its affiliates were deprived of legal recognition, the official history of the Castro period Communist Party laid particular emphasis on another factor. The Communist and CTC press, while carrying on

a vast propaganda about the immediate demands of the workers, the economic and social problems which particularly affected the working class and the nation . . . did not pay attention to the systematic task of raising the class consciousness and Patriotism of the workers. They denounced the Mujalistas and their allies as agents of imperialism, but did not go further in that direction; did not efficaciously explain the character of imperialism and of the oligarchy and its service as principal causes of all the ills of Cuba and of the suffering of the people, and the historic role of the working class in the struggle for a free country and a regime based on social justice.[50]

CTC CONGRESSES AFTER THE SPLIT

The Communist-controlled Confederación de Trabajadores de Cuba held only one congress after the division of the CTC. The other CTC held two such national meetings, one in 1949, the other in 1951.

The Lázaro Peña CTC held its Sixth Congress in Havana on April 8–10, 1949. It claimed that the 1,113 delegates represented "517 worker organizations of all the country and all the industries." It adopted resolutions calling on units of the CTC, and the "Committees of Struggle and Unity" that had been established within the legal CTC, to stress the need for unity in the labor movement and to win over the workers by leading the struggle against the employers and the supposedly antilabor actions of the Auténtico government. It also reiterated the importance of the organization's affiliation with the Communist-controlled international labor groups, the World Federation of Trade Unions and the Confederación de Trabajadores de America Latina in the Western Hemisphere.[51]

In his report to the Congress, Lázaro Peña insisted on the "independence" of the CTC, which he headed. Although asserting that he was proud of being a Communist, he added:

I must declare with the same frankness that the CTC is not and has never been a Communist organization, is not and has never been at the service of the Partido Socialista Popular or of any party, as it is not and had never been at the service of the Government or of any government. The CTC has been, is, and always will be, the organization of all of the workers. At the service of all workers, without distinction of races or colors, of ideologies or political affiliations.[52]

The Sixth Congress of the legal CTC was held April 27–29, 1949. It was concerned to a considerable extent with a new split in the organization, which led to the foundation of the Confederación General del Trabajo (which we shall discuss later). It also marked the assumption of full control by the Auténticos' CON and the election of Eusebio Mujal, until then head of the CON, as secretary general of the CTC.

The Sixth Congress was also concerned with tightening the function of the organization, which had become lax to a considerable degree as a result of the dissensions that gave rise to the CGT. Francisco Aguirre, who reported to the Congress as secretary general, noted in his report:

In the last period of the Executive Committee of the Confederación dissensions were deepened as were the lack of unity and work of the labor movement. National Council meetings were not held and meetings of the Executive of the CTC were held only with difficulty. Its meetings were not characterized by responsible sessions of orientation, and as a result our labor movement declined.[53]

The Sixth Congress of the legal CTC was attended by 3,552 delegates, representing twenty-eight national industrial labor federations. Its opening session was addressed by President Carlos Prío Socarrás and his minister of labor, Dr. Edgardo Butteri, among others.[54]

The Seventh Congress of the legal CTC presented an entirely different picture. It met on May 28–30, 1951. There were 3,222 delegates from 33 industrial federations and 1,860 unions. There were also 340 fraternal delegates from a number of foreign groups.

As usual, the Seventh Congress passed numerous resolutions dealing with wage increases, limitations of the length of the working day, price controls, and other bread-and-butter Cuban issues. There were also a number of resolutions on international questions, demanding the end of the remainders of colonialism in America, opposition to all forces of imperialism, and specific issues such as expression of solidarity with the workers of Yugoslavia and the demand that the Peruvian dictatorship of

General Manuel Odría give a safe conduct to Víctor Raúl Haya de la Torre, the Aprista Party leader, to leave the foreign embassy in Lima where he had been forced to stay for more than two years. The CTC also ratified its affiliations with the new world labor group, the International Confederation of Free Trade Unions.[55]

THE CONFEDERACIÓN GENERAL DEL TRABAJO

The alliance between the Comisión Obrera Nacional of the Auténtico Party and the Comisión Obrera Nacional Independiente, which had been formed in 1947, soon began to unravel. In 1949 it broke apart, as a result of which a third central labor group, the Confederación General del Trabajo, was established.

Actually, at least four different ideological groups had participated in establishment of the anti-Communist Confederación de Trabajadores de Cuba. The overwhelmingly largest of these was the CON of the Auténtico Party, which adhered to the social and nationalist philosophy of that party.

The second element were the independents, of whom Angel Cofiño of the Electrical Workers Federation and Vicente Rubiera of the Telephone Workers Federation were the principal figures. They were not associated with any political party and in earlier years had often collaborated with the Communists. In the period after the schism in the CTC, Rubiera, at least, showed some interest in association with the hemispheric labor group that the Perón regime in Argentina was trying to piece together, although he never made any firm commitment to the Peronistas.[56]

A third element within the anti-Communist coalition was the anarchists. At the time of the split in the CTC in 1947, the anarchists of the Federación de Grupos Anarquistas still had control of unions in the port of Nuevitas in Camaguey Province and had some strength in the gastronomic, shoemakers, medicine, and tobacco federations. They claimed to have nuclei "in almost all labor centers."[57] Subsequently, they also gained some influence in the Electrical Workers Federation.[58]

Finally, there was the Acción Revolucionaria Guiteras (ARG). This was one of several terrorist organizations that had grown up in the aftermath of the Revolution of 1933. It had been formally established in 1939 by former members of Joven Cuba, the party originally established by Antonio Guiteras, minister of interior in the 1933 revolutionary government of Grau San Martín. It professed to have abandoned terrorism after the Auténtico victory in 1944 and had become "a legal political organization," although not a political party. They defined themselves as being "revolutionary socialists" and, unlike other terrorists or former terrorist groups, had sought some influence in the labor movement. In 1947 the ARG claimed to have major influence among the trolley car workers of Havana and some following among railroad workers.[59]

In the months after the 1947 split in the CTC, tension developed between the CON and the independents, particularly Angel Cofiño and Vicente Rubiera. Undoubtedly, among the causes were the desire of the Auténtico CON people to have effective control of the Confederación and Angel Cofiño's wish to be effectively the secretary general of the CTC.

An open break between the two factions of the legal CTC occurred when Pablo Balbuena, the secretary of organization of the CTC, an Auténtico, called a meeting of the National Council to plan for the next congress of the CTC, thus assuming the role of the secretary general. When Cofiño protested this move to the Ministry of Labor, he found no support. As a consequence, he and his supporters decided to withdraw from the CTC and establish their own federation.[60]

When this break occurred, the Cofiño-Rubiera group had the support of the anarchists. The Acción Revolucionario Guiteras stayed with the Auténticos and the CTC, for which they were rewarded with three seats on the CTC Executive.[61]

The upshot of this situation was the holding of two separate congresses in April 1949, one the Sixth Congress of the CTC, the other the founding congress of the Confederación General del Trabajo. The latter claimed to have 1,118 delegates representing 531 unions. Among the groups represented, aside from the electrical and telephone federations, were the "Ten Cents" union (Woolworth's), the Omnibus Aliados, some Havana port workers, the American Steel metallurgical union, and unions from two sugar centrales.[62] The invitation to attend the founding congress of the CGT had been issued by Angel Cofiño and Vicente Rubiera of the CONI and Helio Nardo and Modesto Barbeito, secretary general of organization of the Asociación Libertaria de Cuba.[63]

The CGT had a number of significant leaders. Aside from Cofiño and Rubiera, there were the maritime union leader González Tellechea, and the anarchist Lauro Blanco. However, as Efrén Córdova noted, "It was not in fact a rival capable of competing with the twenty some federations . . . which Mujal had aligned in his support." Furthermore, the Ministry of Labor, in conformity with the law, refused to grant legal recognition to the CGT.[64]

The CGT did not last long. In March 1950, Vicente Rubiera withdrew the Telephone Workers Federation from the CGT. This proved to be fatal to the new confederation. All the elements in the CGT soon sought reentry into the legal CTC, and their overtures were accepted. As a result, the Nineteenth National Council of the CTC, which formally called the Seventh Congress of the Confederación, delegated "all its functions to a Commission of Direction made up of Angel Cofiño, Vicente Rubiera, Ramón León Renterría, Marcos A. Hirigoyen, Francisco Aguirre, Emilio Surí Castillo, and Eusebio Mujal Barniol."[65] Only three of these seven men—Aguirre, Surí Castillo and Mujal—were members of the CON of the Auténtico Party.

In the name of the CTC this Commission of Direction issued a reply to an attack on the labor movement recently made by the Asociación de Industriales. This document noted that it had been "approved" by the National Executive Committee of the CTC.[66]

The Comisión de Dirección also organized the traditional CTC May Day parade in front of the presidential palace. Among those reviewing the parade (in which the telephone and electrical workers had a particularly noticeable role), along with President Prío Socarras, were Eusebio Mujal and Angel Cofiño.[67]

INTERNATIONAL ROLE OF LEGAL CTC

A significant aspect of the activities of the legal Confederación de Trabajadores de Cuba in the 1947–1952 period was in the international field, on both a hemispheric and a world level. Under Lázaro Peña, the CTC had been a leading affiliate of the Confederación de Trabajadores de America Latina (CTAL), which after 1944 was Communist-dominated. One of the decisions of the July 1947 Fifth Congress of the CTC that elected Angel Cofiño as secretary general was to withdraw from the CTAL. Eusebio Mujal and Francisco Aguirre of the CON had earlier promised Serafino Romualdi, the Latin representative of the American Federation of Labor, that once the Communists had been ousted from control of the CTC, relations with the CTAL would be broken off.[68]

The leaders of the legal CTC also participated actively in plans to establish a rival to the CTAL. In pursuance of this objective an Interamerican labor congress met in Lima, Peru in January 1948. At that meeting, Francisco Aguirre was elected a vice president of the new Confederación Interamerican de Trabajadores (CIT), and Eusebio Mujal was named secretary of organization of the CIT.[69]

On a world scale, the undivided CTC had been affiliated with the World Federation of Trade Unions (WFTU). However, after the withdrawal from the WFTU of the British Trade Union Congress, the Congress of Industrial Organizations of the United States, and numerous other national labor groups, a new world labor organization, the International Confederation of Free Trade Unions (ICFTU), was established, and as we have noted earlier, the legal

CTC had joined it, a decision that was ratified by the Sixth Congress in 1949.

With the establishment of the ICFTU, steps were immediately taken to establish an American regional organization of the new world confederation. That regional grouping would take the place of the CIT.

The Cubans took an important role in establishing this new regional labor grouping. The Second Congress of the CIT met in Havana in September 1949. It endorsed the establishment of the ICFTU American regional organization and voted to move the headquarters of the CIT from Santiago, Chile, to Havana, "so as to be closer to most of the organizations that were expected to form part of the new regional body," according to Serafino Romualdi's account. The Havana meeting also voted to create the post of general secretary as the CIT's chief executive officer and elected Francisco Aguirre to that post.[70]

The founding conference of the new Organización Regional Interamericana de Trabajadores (ORIT) was held in Mexico City in January 1951. Francisco Aguirre was one of the two secretaries of the meeting.[71] Eusebio Mujal spoke for the Cuban delegation in opposing the seating of a "fraternal delegate" from the Peronista-controlled Confederación General del Trabajo of Argentina.[72]

It was decided that the headquarters of the ORIT would be in Havana, and Francisco Aguirre was elected as regional secretary, that is, the chief administrative officer of the organization. Eusebio Mujal was elected as one of the fourteen members of the ORIT Executive Committee.[73]

The CTC strongly supported the exclusion from the ORIT of the Confederación del Trabajo of Argentina, controlled by the government of General Juan Perón. Eusebio Mujal published a pamphlet consisting of a speech of his at the ORIT Congress and recounting a trip he had made to several South American countries, including Venezuela, Peru, and Argentina, as part of the preparation for the ORIT Founding Congress. He had sought unsuccessfully to persuade military dictators of the first two to stop their persecution of their national labor movements, as a consequence of which he had supported membership in ORIT of the exiled and underground labor groups in those countries. Insofar as Argentina was concerned, he expressed opposition "because of the present political regime in Argentina . . . to the Argentine CGT's participating in the Congress."[74]

THE LEGAL CTC AND THE AUTÉNTICO PARTY
AND GOVERNMENT

Although the CTC, headed first by Angel Cofiño and then by Eusebio Mujal, was largely dominated by elements of the Comisión Obrera Nacional of the Partido Auténtico, the CON had a quite autonomous position within the party. As a consequence, the CTC's support of the Auténtico administrations of Presidents Grau San Martín and Prío Socarrás was by no means without reservations.

On the one hand, President Prío was invited to speak at the opening sessions of both the Sixth and Seventh Congresses of the CTC. For his part, Prío had done a number of things that met with the approval of the CTC leadership and membership, such as setting up the central bank, the Banco Nacional, and the Agricultural and Industrial Development Bank, as well as issuing several decrees favorable to all or parts of the labor movement, such as nationalizing the foreign-owned Omnibus Aliados bus and trolley car system of Havana.

However, the CTC leaders were quite willing to bring pressure to bear on Prío and his administration. For one thing, they continued the tradition of presenting a long series of demands to the president on the occasion of the annual May Day parade in front of the presidential mansion. For instance, the 1951 list of demands included goals of the CTC's national industrial federations, such as general wage increases, varying from 30 percent to 40 percent; for the government protection of Cuban industries; nationalization of substantial parts of the economy; and establishment of social security systems for various sectors of the economy.[75]

Also, the CTC did not hesitate to pressure the Auténtico regime. In October 1950, it went so far as to call a half-day general strike to protest a supreme court decision declaring a considerable body of labor legislation unconstitutional. In his subsequent report on this movement to the National Council of the CTC, Secretary General Mujal was very critical of the attitude of both his own party and the Ortodoxo Party (which had broken away from the Auténticos a couple of years before) toward the strike. He said, "The Ortodoxos and the Auténticos, who should have made declarations agreeing with the CTC . . . said nothing." The council decided to send a delegation to talk with Auténtico and Ortodoxo members of Congress who had not backed the walkout.[76]

On another occasion, when the Sugar Workers Federation was making a series of demands—including that workers have greater participation in the income generated by the industry, that union dues be paid by the employers and not be deducted from the workers' wages, and that there be a large-scale program to build decent housing for sugar workers—the FNTA threatened a general strike if these demands were not met. When President Prío promised at a meeting of the FNTA to meet these demands, the CTC secretary general, Mujal, commented that in view of the president's promise, there would be no sugar strike until Holy Week, but he added: "Then Holy Week will come, if what has been promised is fulfilled, we shall applaud, without it mattering to us that he is Auténtico and some of you are Ortodoxo, Liberal or Batistianos. . . . If, to the contrary, his word is not fulfilled, we remain willing to take our own decisions. We shall go on a general sugar strike in Holy Week or in a 'non holy' week."[77]

NATURE OF CUBAN UNIONISM BEFORE 1952

Efrén Córdova has well summarized the nature and functioning of the Cuban labor movement after 1947:

The trade unionism of the years after the exit of the Communists diminished a great deal its ideological orientation while at the same time strengthening its negotiating efforts and multiplying the forums in which it was present in representation of workers. Gradually it was thus being converted into a "trade unionism of results." In 1951 the number of registered collective contracts had increased to 4,152, which was an increase of 60 percent compared to the figure for 1943. The great majority of these contracts had enlarged their scope with the inclusion of new benefits and protections. It is important to add that in addition to the collective contracts registered in the Ministry there were countless "pacts of agreement" which were signed each year to end a conflict which also contained small gains of interpretation favorable to the workers.[78]

The Ministry of Labor not infrequently intervened where a deadlock in collective bargaining developed. Thus, for instance, in January 1952 the ministry issued a resolution in a dispute between the union representing truck drivers and their employers' organization, in which the negotiators had reached agreement on a number of points but had failed to do so on certain others. The ministry itself decided the questions at issue, apparently to the satisfaction of the union, which gave publicity to the decision.[79]

Córdova noted that although strikes still were a weapon used by the unions, there were relatively few of them in this period: "With the exception of the sugar industry in which strikes were feared, given the need for continuous work during the harvest, in the majority of industries, strikes were expressions of protest that could not last long because of lack of strike funds."[80]

Some of the unions established auxiliary organizations for their members. For example, the Telephone Workers Federation organized in 1951 a cooperative to which all members of the federation, including those who were retired, as well as its employees, could belong. It was in fact a credit union, which had among its objectives the encouraging of saving by federation union members, as well as "the creation of a vast plan of construction of houses for the members."[81]

As to the quality of trade union leadership, Córdova noted that during the whole "constitutional period" (1940–1952) the leaders "were showing their efficacy, whether in direct dealings with employers, or in the dealings they carried on in the Ministry of Labor and the provincial offices."

However, Córdova also noted corruption in the labor union hierarchy:

A great shame that some allowed themselves to be carried away by avarice and accepted bribes or lent themselves to dirty negotiations. One must say, however, that the majority maintained their integrity and never gave way to pressures or temptations. It is also good to make clear that even the impure ones never compromised the basic rights of the workers, preferring to carry out transactions with respect to pending demands.[82]

The leaders of the legal CTC were very much aware of the charges of corruption that were being made against some of them and against their confederation. Eusebio Mujal, the CTC secretary general, in a speech before the Sugar Workers Federation, recognized the existence of corruption but argued that it should be dealt with by the CTC itself, and not by groups outside the organization:

Who does not know that in our ranks there are workers who have sold out, traitors who receive money from employers to calumniate and discredit? We all know it. But those comrades guilty of unworthy actions, those traitors, must be accused and judged by us in our disciplinary organisms, never before public opinion. Insofar as I am concerned, any accusations made against me, I swear by all I hold most dear that it will be dealt with in the Executive Board of the CTC.[83]

Also, Samuel Powell, a leader of the Sugar Workers Federation in charge of its regular radio program, wrote a public letter to José Pardo Llada, a leader of the Orthodox Party who had attacked CTC corruption on his program. Powell challenged: "To be a leader of the working class is to have personal and public honesty, and insofar as I am concerned, you can investigate my person, fortune and the properties I have, to see if in any of your broadcasts you can point out to me how I have violated the interests of my class." He also challenged Pardo Llada's claim that the old Communist leaders had been honest, in contrast to their successors. He said that when the Communist leader of the Omnibus Aliados Union had been ousted, he had left the union's treasury empty, whereas his Auténtico successor had accumulated $100,000 in the organization's treasury, "which demonstrates that the people of our political affiliation not only say that they are honest but prove it by their activities."[84]

CONCLUSION

Between 1937 and 1952 Cuban organized labor became more powerful than it had ever been before or was ever to be again. It included in its ranks most of the country's industrial, port and maritime, tobacco, and land transport workers; a majority of those employed in the sugar industry; and substantial numbers of commercial and other white-collar employers. Collective bargaining became more or less the rule in labor-management relations, supplemented by a Ministry of Labor that not only frequently acted as a mediator and conciliator, but also often complemented the unions themselves in obtaining gains for their members. Overall, the labor movement was able to assure the workers of a degree of participation in the economic prosperity that marked much of this period.

The organized labor movement was also extensively politicized. It first arose from the shambles left by the failure of the March 1935 revolutionary strike through the alliance between Fulgencio Batista and the Communist Party, which was a key to securing Communist predominance in the labor movement until 1947. When political power shifted from Batista to the Auténtico Party in 1944, the way was opened for a challenge, encouraged by the Auténtico regime, to Communist control of the Confederación de Trabajadores de Cuba and most of its constituent parts. This struggle led in 1947 to a split within the CTC, and to victory within a few months of the Auténtico faction and elements allied with it. In spite of considerable violence during the transition, this shift of political control within organized labor did not fundamentally change the nature of the trade union movement, and the collective bargaining cum Ministry of Labor pressure that had existed for more than a decade.

However, the very success of the labor movement in the economic field helped to depoliticize to a large degree its rank and file membership. The trade unionists' loyalty in their organizations increasingly was based on the unions' ability to win continuing, if marginal, gains for their members in terms of wages, hours, and working conditions, rather than on any political considerations. Consequently, Cuban organized labor was ill prepared to confront the crisis it began to face on March 10, 1952.

NOTES

1. *Historia del Movimiento Obrero Cubano 1865–1958, Tomo II, 1935–1958*, Instituto de Historia del Movimiento Comunista y de la Revolución Socialista de Cuba anexo al Comité Central del Partido Comunista de Cuba, Editoria Politica La Habana, 1985, page 147; see also Efrén Córdova, *Clase Trabajadora y Movimiento Sindical en Cuba, Volumen I (1819–1959)*, Ediciones Universal, Miami, 1995, pages 294–295.

2. *Historia del Movimiento Obrero Cubano etc., Tomo II*, op. cit., page 148.

3. Córdova, op. cit., page 295.

4. Ibid., pages 295–296.

5. Ibid., page 296.

6. *Historia del Movimiento Obrero Cubano etc., Tomo II*, op. cit., pages 135–138.

7. Interview with Earl Browder, former secretary general of Communist Party of the United States, in Yonkers, NY, March 23, 1953.

8. *Historia del Movimiento Obrero Cubano etc., Tomo II*, op. cit., page 137.

9. Ibid., page 139.

10. Interview with Earl Browder, op. cit., March 23, 1953.

11. Interview with Luis Serrano Tamayo, secretary general, Federación Nacional de Trabajadores Tabacaleros, in Havana, March 19, 1952.

12. See Phillip J. Jaffe, *The Rise and Fall of American Communism*, Hergon Press, New York, 1975.

13. *Historia del Movimiento Obrero Cubano etc., Tomo II*, op. cit., page 138.

14. Interview with Luis B. Serrano Tamayo, op. cit., March 19, 1952.

15. Córdova, op. cit., page 298.

16. Interview with Angel Cofiño, secretary general of Confederación de Trabajadores de Cuba; secretary general of Federación de Trabajadores de Plantas Eléctricas, in Havana, August 12, 1947.

17. Córdova, op. cit., 298.

18. *Historia del Movimiento Obrero Cubano etc., Tomo II*, op. cit., page 175.

19. Interview with Fausto A. Waterman, a leader of Comisión Obrera Nacional of Partido Auténtico, subsequently secretary of youth and sports affairs of Confederación de Trabajadores de Cuba, in Havana, August 9, 1947.

20. Córdova, op. cit., page 299.

21. Ibid., page 200.

22. Interview with Carlos Fernández R., sub-delegado before Official and Employers' Organizations of Confederación de Trabajadores de Cuba headed by Lázaro Peña, in Havana, August 11, 1947.

23. Interview with Emilio Surí Castillo, secretario de asistencia social, Federación Nacional de Trabajadores Azucareros, secretary general of Comisión Obrera Nacional of Partido Auténtico; subsequently secretary general of Federación Nacional de Trabajadores Azucareros, in Havana, August 4, 1947.

24. Córdova, op. cit., pages 301–302.

25. Interview with Modesto Barbeito, secretario sindical of Asociación Libertaria de Cuba, subsequently official of Federación de Trabajadores de Plantas Eléctricas, in Havana, August 4, 1947.

26. Interview with Carlos Fernández R., op. cit., August 11, 1947.

27. Interview with Fausto A. Waterman, op. cit., August 9, 1947.

28. Interview with Angel Cofiño, op. cit., August 9, 1947.

29. Interview with Vicente Rubiera, secretary general, Federación de Trabajadores Telefónicos, in Havana, August 4, 1947.

30. Interview with Alfredo González Freitas, secretary general of Federación Nacional de Vendedores y Auxiliares, secretary of correspondence of CTC of Angel Cofiño, in Havana, August 8, 1947.

31. Interview with Jesús Coca Mutis, secretary general, Federación Nacional de los Trabajadores del Comercio, member of Executive Committee of CTC of Cofiño, in Havana, August 3, 1947.

32. Interview with Jesús Artigas, secretary general of Federación Nacional de Trabajadores de la Medicina, subsequently treasurer of Confederación de Trabajadores de Cuba, in Havana, August 4, 1947.

33. Interview with Pablo Balbuena, member of Executive Committee of Confederación de Trabajadores de Cuba of Cofiño, in Havana, August 4, 1947.

34. Interview with Emilio Surí Castillo, op. cit., August 4, 1947.

35. Interview with Fausto A. Waterman , op. cit., August 9, 1947.

36. Harold Dana Sims, The Cuban Sugar Workers' Progress Under the Leadership of a Black Communist, Jesús Menéndez Larrondo (1941–1948)," *MACLAS Latin American Essays*, Volume VI, 1993, page 14.

37. Interview with Gilberto Goliat, member of Executive Committee of Confederación de Trabajadores of Angel Cofiño, in Havana, August 4, 1947.

38. Interview with Carlos Fernández R., op. cit., August 4, 1947.

39. Interview with José Enseñat Polit, secretary general of Sindicato de Marineros, Fogoneros y Similares, and secretario de relaciones of Federación Obrera Marítima Nacional, in Havana, August 8, 1947.

40. Dana Sims, op. cit., page 15.

41. *Historia del Movimiento Obrero Cubano etc.*, *Tomo II*, op. cit., page 209.

42. Interview with Eusebio Mujal, secretary general of Confederación de Trabajadores de Cuba, in Havana, September 4, 1949.

43. Interview with Eusebio Mujal, op. cit., September 10, 1949.

44. Interview with José Luis Martínez, secretary general of Federación Nacional de Trabajadores de la Industria Azucarera, in Havana, March 17, 1952.

45. *Historia del Movimiento Obrero Cubano etc.*, *Tomo II*, op. cit., page 229.

46. Ibid., page 231.

47. Ibid., page 232.

48. Córdova, op. cit., page 309.

49. Ibid., pages 303–304.

50. *Historia del Movimiento Obrero Cubano etc.*, *Tomo II*, op. cit., pages 229–230.

51. Ibid., pages 220–225.

52. Ibid., page 223.

53. Ibid., page 218.

54. *Superación*, Cuban labor newspaper, Havana, May 27, 1949, page 1; for more on the two Sixth Congresses of the CTC see Evelio Tellería, *Los Congresos Obreros en Cuba*, Editorial de Ciencias Sociales, Havana, 1984, pages 266–283.

55. Córdova, op. cit., 314–315; see also Tellería, op. cit., pages 384–391.

56. Interview with Vicente Rubiera, secretary general, Federación de Trabajadores Telefónicos, in Havana, March 20, 1952.

57. Interview with Modesto Barbeito, op. cit., August 6, 1947.

58. Interview with Modesto Barbeito, Havana, March 18, 1952.

59. Interview with Antonio B. Bayer, secretario de propaganda, Acción Revolucionaria Guiteras, in Havana, August 8, 1947.

60. Córdova, op. cit., pages 309–310.

61. Ibid., page 310.

62. *Historia del Movimiento Obrero Cubano etc.*, *Tomo II*, op. cit., pages 218–219.

63. Letter to "Estimado Compañero" signed by Angel Cofiño García and Vicente Rubiera F. for Comité Obrero Nacional Independiente and Helio Nardo and Modesto Barbeito for Asociación Libertaria de Cuba, March 25, 1949 (mimeographed).

64. Córdova, op. cit., page 310.

65. "Al Pueblo de Cuba en General y a Los Trabajadores en Particular Unidad Obrera," signed by Vicente Rubiera Feito, Angel Cofiño García and Eusebio Mujal Barniol, undated, but 1949 (throwaway).

66. Confederación de Trabajadores de Cuba, *Respueta a la Asociación de Industriales*, Havana, April 1951, page 6.

67. See *El Mundo*, Havana, May 2, 1951, page 1.

68. Serafino Romualdi, *Presidents and Peons: Recollections of a Labor Ambassador in Latin America*, Funk and Wagnalls, New York, 1967, pages 65, 75.

69. Ibid., page 79.

70. Ibid., page 94.

71. Ibid., page 113.

72. Ibid., page 117.

73. Ibid., page 119.

74. Eusebio Mujal, *Contesta a la C.G.T. de la Argentina*, Editorial CTC, Havana, n.d. (circa 1951), page 3.

75. "Confederación de Trabajadores de Cuba 1 de Mayo de 1951."

76. Confederación de Trabajadores de Cuba. "Acta de la Reunión de XVIII Consejo Nacional de Trabajadores de Cuba, Celebrado en el Segundo Piso del Pacio de los Trabajadores, Sito en Carlos y Peñalver en La Ciudad de La Habana el Dia 25 Noviembre de 1950" (mimeographed).

77. "Hacía el Triunfo de las Demandas Azucareras," page 5.

78. Córdova, op. cit., page 312.

79. "Sindicato de Trabajadores de Camiones de Carga Por Carretera y Sus Anexos: Lider Nacional," Havana, January 1952 (throwaway).

80. Córdova, op. cit., page 312.

81. Federación Sindical de Trabajadores Telefónicos, *Cooperativa de Trabajadores Telefónicos de Cuba: Reglamento 1951*, Havana, 1951.

82. Córdova, op. cit., pages 312–313.

83. "Hacía del Triunfo de las Demandas Azucareras," op. cit., page 7.

84. Letter to José Pardo Llada from H. Samuel Powel, March 5, 1952 (mimeographed).

5

Labor Under the
Second Batista Dictatorship

On March 10, 1952, General Fulgencio Batista broke the Cuban "constitutional rhythm" that he himself had established in 1940, by overthrowing the elected government of President Carlos Prío Socarrás less than three months before an election scheduled to choose Prío's successor.

There were three candidates running for president until March 10, Carlos Hevía, nominee of the Auténtico Party; Roberto Agramonte of the dissident Auténtico Party, the Ortodoxos; and General Batista, supported by his own Partido Acción Unitaria. Polls indicated that it was a very close race between Hevía and Agramonte but were unanimous in showing Fulgencio Batista at third.[1]

The new dictatorship established by Batista doomed Cuban political democracy for more than a generation. Its hallmarks were tyranny, violence, and vast corruption. It proved disastrous to the Cuban labor movement.

BATISTA'S COUP

The coup of March 10, 1952, began in the early hours of the morning, when General (and Senator) Batista arrived at the country's largest military base, Camp Columbia, on the outskirts of Havana and, in connivance with some of the officers there, seized control of the base. Troops under his orders then moved quickly to take over important centers in the Havana area, including the principal broadcasting stations of radio and television and the headquarters of the Confederación de Trabajadores de Cuba, the Palacio de los Trabajadores.

Prío and his government did very little to defend themselves against this onslaught. The president refused the request of students to use arms that had been stored in the Presidential Palace to defend the regime against the rebellious soldiers—the exact purpose for which the arms had been accumulated there. One of the student leaders who met with Prío told me several years later that the president claimed that he "did not want the shedding of blood," and that was why he refused to make available the arms.[2]

Prío failed to notify the labor movement about the coup until it was too late for the CTC to launch an effective general strike in support of Cuba's democracy. Prío was said to have given little or no encouragement to military officers, in Havana or in the provinces, who wanted to confront the Batista forces. By the late afternoon of March 10, President Prío had taken refuge in the Mexican Embassy, and soon afterward he flew off to the Aztec Republic—thus, constitutionally, ceasing to be president, since he had left the country without the permission of Congress.[3]

There were conflicting opinions about why Batista pulled his coup. Some found enough explanation in Batista's desire to return to power and to continue to enrich himself, as he had during his first period in office. Others felt that he hoped that in a Perón fashion he might from a position of power be able to win enough popular support to be honestly elected to the presidency.

Whatever Batista's motivations in seizing power, his actions were very clear. The official history of Cuban organized labor issued by the Castro epoch Communist Party sketched these measures:

The government dissolved the Congress of the Republic, and in its place established a so-called Consultative Council, a reactionary organism made up fundamentally of bankers, landlords, large merchants, rich proprietors and politicians. . . . It dissolved the political parties, postponed the general elections, and drew up a code which assured the electoral confirmation of the coup d'etat, deposed and named arbitrarily, mayors and councilmen, concentrating the functions of a political character; prohibited meetings, assemblies and public demonstrations of any kind, breaking up with blows and shots the pacific meetings convoked by the workers; initiated a new epoch of detentions, kidnappings and jailing of men and women of the people; . . . provoked the breaking of relations between Cuba and the Soviet Union, while at the same time establishing even closer ties with the tyrannical governments of America.[4]

THE ABORTED GENERAL STRIKE

The Confederación de Trabajadores de Cuba did attempt to organize a general strike against Batista's seizure of power. However, they moved slowly in doing so. Although I do not know how typical his experience was, one leader of the hotel and restaurant workers told me that he had first heard about the coup at 3:30 in the morning of March 10 but for several hours did not know what to do about it. Only at 9:30 did he meet with Francisco Aguirre and several other members of the Executive Committee of the CTC, who waited some time for the CTC secretary general, Eusebio Mujal, to appear. The members of the CTC Executive who were present then decided to call a general strike.[5] The meeting at which this decision was taken was held outside the Palacio de los Trabajadores, which was already occupied by Batista's soldiers.[6]

Since representatives of most of the CTC's affiliated federations were not present at the meeting that called the general strike, it was necessary to notify them of the walkout, with the decision to join it in effect being left up to the individual federations.[7] Some, including the telephone workers, deliberately decided not to walk out.[8]

A leader of the Electrical Workers Federation informed me that the group never received an official notification of the call for a general strike. However, the Executive of the federation met several times on the morning of March 10, to decide whether they should walk out in protest against the coup. They also met with leaders of the telephone workers about the problem. They sent a delegation to the Presidential Palace to see Carlos Prío, as well as to the Morro Castle garrison, to determine whether or not there was going to be organized military opposition to Batista. Convinced that there would not, the electrical workers' leaders decided not to call a strike.[9]

As a result, the general strike was a failure. Efrén Córdova wrote: "There was, it is true, a paralyzation of urban transport in Havana, there were also strikes in two petroleum refineries, various railroad delegations and one or another labor center. There was partial abstention in the Ariguanabo Textile Firm and some other enterprises, but the rest of the workers in other economic activities either did not hear about or ignored the calls of the CTC."[10] Troops were used to run the Havana buses.[11]

Perhaps the situation and actions of the port workers of Havana were typical of those of a number of other unions. They had a hard time making up their minds what to do. They finally started to wander off their jobs late in the morning but did not leave the docks, fearful that strikebreakers might be sent to take away their jobs. Finally, the employers got in touch with Batista's soldiers, who arrived and drove the workers back to work.[12]

Outside the capital, the strike was as scantily supported as in Havana. An official of the Federación de Trabajadores of Camaguey Province reported to me a couple of years later that the

March 10, 1952, strike "did not have much affect" there.[13] However, José Luis Martínez, the secretary general of the Sugar Workers Federation, said that insofar as that industry was concerned, the response of the sugar workers in Camaguey was more widespread than that anywhere else, as workers in all but one of the province's *centrales* responded to the strike call. Martínez suggested that the troop commanders in the province did not decide to support Batista until well into the afternoon of March 10.[14] Finally, however, troops seized headquarters of at least seven *centrales* in Camaguey, as well as two in Oriente.[15]

Certainly one of the reasons that there was so little response to the CTC's general strike call was that the workers did not hear about it. Almost all of the union leaders I talked to within the following week stressed the difficulty they had had in communicating with their followers as a result of the military's seizure of most of the means of communication. By the time the strike call was issued, the television and radio stations were in the hands of Batista's troops.

Clearly the case of Angel Bravo was not unique. He was a Venezuelan unionist who was working at the headquarters of the Organización Regional Interamericana de Trabajadores (ORIT), which was located in the Palacio de los Trabajadores. He knew nothing about the Batista coup, even less of a call for a general strike, until he attempted to go to work in the Palacio, only to be told by a soldier that the building was closed by the troops.[16]

However, Efrén Córdova offered what he called "a more profound" reason for the failure of the general strike:

The emphasis that the CTC had given to economic demands, its gradual transformation into a trade unionism of results, was imposing on the leaders and the masses a kind of economistic and materialist culture that made them indifferent to political developments. The workers saw in the CTC and its affiliated unions an organization of services from which they could demand increases and benefits; they were not, on the contrary, in any way habituated to listen to ideas of a political type or to respond with mass action to extra-labor calls. The unions . . . had been converted into cells of an economic animal; events outside of that range lacked interest for them.[17]

THE AGREEMENT WITH BATISTA

Dr. Jesús Portocarrero, a leader of Batista's party and author (as member of Congress) of some of the country's social legislation, whom Batista had named as minister of labor, had contact with the CTC general secretary, Eusebio Mujal, at seven o'clock in the evening of March 10, seeking an agreement with the CTC to call off the general strike.[18] Within four hours an accord had been reached, and at 11:00 p.m. the CTC leadership officially broadcast a suspension of the general walkout.[19]

According to a leader of the Hotel and Restaurant Federation, the basis of the agreement to call off the general strike was that there would be no dismissal by the government of trade union leaders; there would be no interference with gains the unions had made; there would be no impediments to the unions' legitimate economic activities. At least in the period immediately after the agreement, the Batista regime seemed to be conforming to this accord, when the minister of labor actually reversed several oustings of union officials by elements of the Batista party, the Partido Acción Unitaria.[20]

The decision to call off the general strike was taken by the Executive Committee of the CTC after long discussion and had the support of all the factions in the leadership of the Confederación de Trabajadores de Cuba.[21] The so-called Independents as well as the Auténtico Party members of the CTC Executive supported the move, arguing that Batista had agreed to "protection" of the unions and of the gains the labor movement had made.[22] Even Francisco Aguirre, who had at first urged violent resistance to the coup, went along with the agreement.[23]

This "deal" with Batista must have been particularly embarrassing for Eusebio Mujal, the CTC secretary general. A couple of weeks before the coup, the CTC had held a demonstration to celebrate the anniversary of the martyrs of the March 1935 general strike. All of the speakers except Mujal had made apolitical speeches, but Mujal had made a particularly violently partisan one, attacking both the Ortodoxos and General Batista, whom he accused of a wide variety of crimes.[24]

Minister of Labor Portocarrero, in explaining to me the circumstances of the settlement with the CTC leaders, claimed that "the first item on the Batista government's program for the trade unions is absolute freedom for the workers to carry on their own affairs." He said that the new regime was opposed to any intervention by the government in the internal affairs of the labor movement and that the ministry would be open to the leaders of any "democratically controlled" unions, adding that this did not include the Communists.[25]

The U.S. labor attaché said that he thought that the labor leaders in calling off the general strike sought "to save what they could of their organizations," adding that if there had not been an agreement, Batista would have been "ruthless" in his treatment of the labor movement. However, he added that the organized workers could have caused Batista "a great deal of trouble" before he could have overcome them, and that the general strike was canceled almost before it had really begun.[26]

Angel Miolán, an exile from the Dominican Republic who worked for the Transport Workers Federation, agreed with the U.S. labor attaché's explanation of the causes of the CTC leaders' agreement to call off the strike.[27]

The agreement between the CTC leadership and Batista was confirmed on March 14, when he turned control of the Palacio de los Trabajadores, the CTC headquarters, to the Confederación de Trabajadores de Cuba.[28]

ORGANIZED LABOR'S PROSPECTS AFTER MARCH 10

The agreement with Batista to end the March 10 general strike left at best an uneasy peace between the dictator and the organized labor movement. The leaders of the CTC and its constituent unions had no clear picture of what attitude Batista intended to take toward the workers and their unions once the immediate crisis of his seizure of power had passed. There were several widely prevalent notions about what policies he would follow in long run.

One possibility that was widely discussed among the CTC leaders was that Batista might try to emulate Juan Perón, launching from power a program of concessions to the workers and their organization such as to win him enough support to be elected president in a more or less real election.[29] One leader of the Electrical Workers Federation, himself an anarchosyndicalist, suggested to me that if Batista should decide on that line of approach, there were important groups of workers to whom he could appeal. He noted that the unions had not paid as much attention as they should have to the most poorly paid workers in the industries in which they were organized—citing the situation in the tobacco industry, in which although some workers received as much as $100.00 a week, others earned only about $0.50 a day. He also noted that only a week after the coup Batista had promised to complete and turn over to the workers a housing project on the outskirts of Havana, which had been five years in the building under the Auténtico governments.[30]

Another union leader, of the Petroleum Workers Federation, noted that Batista had been talking of carrying out an agrarian reform, of extending the social security system to include all workers, and of stimulating the establishment of new industries to expand employment. This unionist felt that if Batista did these things, he might have the possibility of gaining the popular support he lacked in March 1952.[31]

The Peronistas had been active in Cuba for some time before the March 10, 1952, coup and had organized a Comité Nacional Cubana, ATLAS (the acronym of Perón's continental labor group). Although they made exaggerated claims of their influence in the Cuban labor movement, it was really very small. One of the local admirers of Perón, who had attended the founding congress of ATLAS, was told by the CTC leadership on his return from Mexico that he would have to decide between keeping his trade union post and maintaining his affiliation with ATLAS. He decided to keep his position in his union.[32]

Those who thought that Batista might try to impose a Peronista mold on Cuba presumed that in doing so, he would try to press his own Partido Acción Unitaria (PAU) on the leadership of the labor movement. However, they emphasized the weakness of the PAU in organized labor as of March 1952. A leader of the Hotel and Restaurant Workers Federation suggested that there were not more than twenty "Paupistas" active in his organization.[33] A leader of the Telephone Workers Federation noted that there were no members of Batista's party active in the leadership of that organization and punned that they ought to be called "pap-pistas," that is, people interested in getting posts in the government, rather than "Paupistas."[34] Finally, an official of the Cattle Workers Federation noted that although the PAU had had the secretary generalship of one of his federation's unions, it had lost that post in elections in December 1951.[35]

Some of the CTC leaders feared that Batista might renew his old alliance with the Communists in the labor movement. When the Executive of the CTC met with Batista on March 14, shortly before the Palacio de los Trabajadores was returned to the Confederación's control, the labor leaders pressed the dictator on whether or not he intended to return to his old alliance with the Communists. He assured them that he would not do so.[36]

However, several CTC leaders insisted to me that the Communists had heavily infiltrated Batista's own party, the Partido Acción Unitaria, particularly its small labor wing, and feared that to the degree that Batista insisted on incorporation of Paupistas into the CTC leadership, this would in fact mean the return of Communists to top positions in the Confederación de Trabajadores de Cuba.[37]

In the immediate aftermath of the coup, there was considerable reason to believe that in fact Batista might renew his old alliance with the Communists. In Oriente Province, in particular, there were a number of cases in which members of Batista's party, the PAU, and Communists seized union headquarters, and the military had taken over the provincial headquarters of the

CTC. Eusebio Mujal dispatched Pedro Domenech, a native of Oriente and secretary general of the Cinemategráfico Federation, to the province to urge the return of the various headquarters to their elected officials. Within a few days, he had succeeded in this effort.[38]

EARLY GOVERNMENT INTERVENTION IN UNIONS

During the first months of the second Batista dictatorship, the government openly intervened in several important unions. These included the Havana construction workers union, the Sindicato McFarland Electro-química (of the Chemical Workers Federation), and the union of workers of Autobuses Modernos.[39]

The most important of these interventions was that in the Autobuses Modernos union. Early on the morning of June 28, when the night shift of bus personnel were going off duty, soldiers suddenly appeared at all of the posts where shifts were being changed; they first took away the licenses of all the workers and shortly afterward returned those of selected drivers whom the government would allow to continue in their jobs. At almost the same time, Marco Hirigoyen, the head of the union, was arrested.

Soon after this, "elections" were called in the union, resulting in victory for a slate composed of Communists and members of the Partido Acción Unitaria. However, when Eusebio Mujal objected strenuously to this procedure, the Ministry of Labor declared the elections illegal and named a government "interventor" to run the union.[40] Subsequently, some 500 bus drivers were fired."[41]

The intervention in the Autobuses Modernos was particularly significant. That union had participated more fully in the March 10 general strike against Batista's seizure of power than virtually any other labor group and was regarded as one of the country's most militant unions. Also, the Autobuses Modernos union was controlled by Acción Revolucionaria Guiteras (ARG), the only so-called terrorist group that had any influence in organized labor. The firm itself was government-owned; ran at a deficit, which the government subsidized; and was also largely controlled by the ARG.[42]

Marco Hirigoyen had strongly criticized the deal made by the CTC leadership and Batista. He had also bitterly and publicly attacked not only Batista but Eusebio Mujal. As a consequence, the CTC leadership's defense of Hirigoyen and the Autobuses Modernos Union was something less than enthusiastic.[43]

By mid–1953 there was considerable tension between the government and the CTC. The U.S. labor attaché commented that there was a "tug of war" between Batista and the CTC leadership.

He cited strikes of the port workers (over the issue of allowing train ferries to enter Havana) and a strike of the workers of Omnibuses Aliados over economic issues that were broken by the government. He also noted a statement by the acting minister of labor that no more strikes would be allowed because they were all political—a stand from which he backed down when Mujal and others protested to Batista.[44]

THE ROLE OF EUSEBIO MUJAL

Eusebio Mujal, the secretary general of the Confederación de Trabajadores de Cuba, played a pivotal role in the Cuban labor movement during the second Batista dictatorship. Whether or not he had originally intended to, he established a de facto alliance with Batista that was to have crucial importance in the labor movement during the Batista dictatorship and helped prepare the ground for the direction organized labor would take after the overthrow of Batista.

The growing alignment of Mujal (and his supporters within the CTC leadership) with Batista was perhaps first indicated on March 14, 1952, at the time of a meeting of the Executive Council of the CTC with Batista and Minister of Labor Portocarrero, after which the minister formally returned control of the Palacio de los Trabajadores to the CTC. After the formal transfer, Mujal not only shook hands with the minister and gave him an *abrazo*, but also said that the workers were solidly behind General Batista in his struggle for a better Cuba. A number of the other leaders of the CTC very much disapproved of this endorsement of the dictator.[45]

One immediate "practical" reason for Mujal and his supporters in the CTC leadership to strike a deal with Batista was that with the overthrow of the democratic regime, the CTC ceased to receive the $300,000 a year subsidy that the Auténtico governments had paid the Confederación. Dues payments by union members were not sufficient to cover the costs of the organization, and Mujal and other leaders were certainly anxious to have the government subsidy reestablished.[46]

By 1953, the government was again subsidizing the CTC, principally by giving the Confederación the proceeds from several drawings of the national lottery.[47]

Clearly, if Mujal was to succeed in realigning the CTC with Batista, he had to sever his and most key CTC figures' association with the Auténtico Party, which Batista had overthrown. In pursuance of this objective, a few weeks after the coup, Mujal announced that the Comisión Obrera Nacional of the Partido Au-

téntico had decided to withdraw from that party and to form a
Labor Party.[48]

One of Mujal's important supporters in the CTC leadership
explained to me the supposed rationale for this move. He said
that in Cuba the trade union movement needed a strong political
party behind it in order to prosper, adding that that was why the
Communists were so successful in organized labor. He said that
since the Auténtico Party could no longer provide the kind of
backing the labor movement needed, the CTC had to establish its
own party.[49]

Eusebio Mujal's apostasy was the more striking because of
the important role that he had played in the Auténtico Party and
his close relationship with the Auténtico governments of Ramón
Grau San Martín and Carlos Prío. Together with the martyred
Sandalio Junco, he had organized the Comisión Obrera Nacional
of the party and he had succeeded Junco as its chief. In that capacity, he had been a key figure in the capture of control of the
CTC from the Communists. He had been elected senator by the
Auténtico Party, and had been a candidate for reelection in the
1952 election that was never held. We have already noted his very
partisan attack on General Batista only a few days before the
March 10 coup.

During the Prío regime, Mujal was the recipient of some
$70,000 a month from the government, of which he passed on
$30,000 to the CTC. He was also reported to have had as many as
3,000 government jobs at his disposal.[50]

By no means all of the Auténticos in the CTC leadership went
along with this idea. Among those opposing it were Pablo Balbuena, head of the Printing Trades Federation; César Lancis of
the Federación de Medicina; Antonio Collada of the Construction
Workers Federation; as well as important figures in the transport,
wheat workers, and sugar workers federations.[51]

By July 1952, the Auténticos in the leadership of the CTC
were reportedly divided into at least four different groups. One of
these consisted of those giving unquestioning support to Eusebio
Mujal. A second group went along with the idea of establishing a
Labor Party but insisted that that party take a position of strong
opposition to the Batista regime; these included, Calixto Sánchez
of the Airline Workers and Pascasio Lineras of the Textile Workers. A third group was working with Batista's Minister of
Information Ernesto de la Fe, who was fighting within the regime
against the alliance that then existed, particularly in the labor
movement, between the Communists and leaders of Batista's
party. Finally, there was a group led by Pablo Balbuena, Lancis,

Collada, and others who had remained loyal to the Auténtico Party and had reestablished the Comisión Obrera Nacional.[52]

A few of the Auténtico labor leaders who were opposed to the deal with Batista resigned their posts in protest against this policy. This was the case with Antonio Collada, a leader of the Construction Workers Federation and member of the CTC Executive. He resigned from these two posts, although continuing for some time to be head of the Marble Workers Union. He also was a member of the Comisión Obrera Nacional of the Auténtico Party, which was reestablished by those Auténtico labor leaders opposed to the policies of Eusebio Mujal and his colleagues.[53]

Another such case was that of Pedro Martínez, who was an official of the Rubber Workers Union. A little over a month after the coup, he resigned from his position in the union, and soon afterward he entered into underground work against the dictatorship.[54]

The proposed Labor Party was never established. However, in effect, Mujal's announcement of his withdrawal from the Auténtico Party and dissolution of the CON, of which he (together with Sandalio Junco) had been a founder, in effect signaled his and his supporters' alliance with Batista and his regime.

Efrén Córdova sketched the nature of the quagmire into which Mujal and his supporters in the CTC leadership were dragged by their alliance with Batista. The demands imposed on them by this alliance were at first relatively light:

In the beginning, Batista sought from the CTC recognition of his military power and to obscure the illegitimate character of his government. The CTC could provide the masses who would attend public meetings, thus offering the regime an appearance of support by the working class. The regime promised, for its part, a policy of sympathy toward labor demands and to provide benefits.

However, as the Batista regime was unable to establish any degree of legitimacy, and opposition to it widened and became more dangerous, the nature of the regime's demands on its collaborators in the CTC changed. As Córdova wrote:

It was thus that the confederation was transformed into an instrument of the regime to assure the failure of political strikes and of demonstrations of protest that had a labor origin. The CTC assumed the responsibility of controlling or keeping within acceptable limits worker and citizen protests. When these intensified in the last years of the dictatorship, the CTC leadership even provided armed groups that patrolled the streets of Havana in moments of crisis and the sugar zones during the harvest of 1957–1958.[55]

The alliance between the Mujal group and Batista became so close that in the final reorganization of his cabinet before his overthrow the dictator appointed Raúl Valdivia, the head of the Sugar Workers Federation, as a minister without portfolio. After the fall of Batista, Valdivia's wife (he himself was in hiding) told me that her husband had not wanted to take that position, but Eusebio Mujal insisted that he do so, arguing that the labor leadership "could not afford" to have any "problem" with the government at that point, and that Valdivia's membership in the Batista administration would assure that there would be none.[56]

At the same time, protest against the policy of Mujal and his collaborators intensified. It became particularly acute in the Sugar Workers Federation, as that organization's secretary general, José Luis Martínez, "sought to strengthen its autonomy from the CTC." Mujal reacted to this, "interviewing first with the police in the offices of the FNTA, then deposing the disloyal, convoking in April 1956 a Workers Congress which ratified all his measures (including the designation of Raúl Valdivia as secretary general of the FNTA) and expelling . . . the disaffected."

Subsequently, several other federations were purged by the CTC leadership. These included the organization of cattle workers and the telephone and electrical workers federations.[57]

Efrén Córdova commented that those CTC leaders who sooner or later opposed Eusebio Mujal

were subdivided into those who assumed positions of active struggle and those who adopted a more discrete position. Leaders of recognized militancy against Batista like Pascasio Lineras of the Textile Federation, Antonio Collada of Construction and Marco A. Hirigoyen of transport, lost their positions in the CTC and were later jailed or went into exile. In the electric sector, there was a radical group that made itself responsible for sabotage of the Calle Suárez plant in 1958, while a part of the leadership headed by Oscar Samalea produced a break of his old relationship with Cofiño, who in 1957 had to leave the island. Together with Cofiño in opposing Batista were Amado Maestri, Guillermo Mestre and others. In 1957–1958 many unionists of that sector, including Amaury Fraginals, were joining the nascent 26th of July Movement which led the struggle against Batista.[58]

That struggle was particularly intense in the sugar sector. Among the leaders of that federation who were purged were not only José Luis Martínez, the FNTA secretary general, but provincial leaders, including Conrado Bécquer, Gerardo Rodríguez, Rodrigo Lominchar, and Humberto Mursuli, as well as officials of a number of local sugar unions.[59]

Some significant CTC leaders became involved in plotting against the Batista regime. One of these was Calixto Sánchez, head of the Federación Aerea Nacional, which included all airline employees except pilots. Sánchez had been an Auténtico, having joined the party during the Prío administration. However, at first he supported both the original CTC leaders' deal with Batista and Mujal's move to withdraw from the Auténtico Party and establish a Labor Party.[60]

However, by 1957 Sánchez was involved in plotting against the dictatorship. He was arrested but on the intervention of Eusebio Mujal was allowed to go into exile. Subsequently, he led a small invasion by exile forces, which was easily defeated, and died in the process of the struggle.[61]

CTC CONGRESSES DURING THE BATISTA DICTATORSHIP

Two congresses of the Confederación de Trabajadores de Cuba were held during the second Batista dictatorship. The first of these, the Eighth Congress, met in Havana in May 1953. It was officially announced that there were present some 2,365 delegates, representing 1,553 unions.

The Communists, by that time working within the legally recognized CTC, claimed to have delegates representing some 600 unions. However, the Credentials Committee, controlled by Mujal's group, rejected the credentials of most of these—claiming that the unions involved were not affiliated with the CTC, were delinquent in paying their dues to the confederation, or were "paper" unions, with no actual membership. In the end, the number of delegates in the anti-Mujal camp was reduced to a mere forty.

Efrén Córdova noted: among the resolutions approved by the Eight Congress, the most notable demanded measures for the economic protection of the workers, such as the struggle against wage reductions, rejection of any attempt to increase working hours, respect for collective contracts and promotion procedures, price control, and a subsidy of 60 pesos a month for unemployed workers in the textile industry." It also passed resolutions calling for new impetus for industrialization of Cuba.

However, one resolution sponsored by elements opposed to Mujal and his associates was also passed. This "covered entry into the CTC of whatever *bona fide* unions sought admission, and an end to the Credentials Committee's intervention in the workers' organizations." Córdova commented:

It is probable that this last resolution . . . was the reason that a bit later, on June 7, 1954, the Executive Committee met in an emergency session in which it was decided that no Communist could attend any future congress of the CTC or its affiliated organizations. The latter must also relieve from their posts any known Communists who occupied them; refusal of any union to do so would lead to the canceling of its affiliation to the relevant federation, and hence from the CTC. . . . This tended, mistakenly, to convert the Communists into victims and push them toward an opposition to Batista that they had not until then manifested.[62]

A new Executive Committee of the CTC was chosen at this congress. Its membership represented all of the blocs then existing in the leadership. The onetime Auténticos were represented, as were the Independents, including representatives of the Electrical Workers. Finally, José Pérez González, the principal figure of the Labor Bloc of Batista's Partido Acción Unitaria, was also admitted to the new Executive.[63]

José Pérez González had been a very secondary leader of the Cuban labor movement before March 10, 1952, as a member of the Executive of the railroaders union, the Hermandad Ferroviaria. However, he had a close relationship with Batista, and on hearing of the coup, he hastened to Camp Columbia, where Batista then was. He was soon dispatched to Havana to establish contact with the CTC leaders, to try to get them to call off the general strike. Thereafter, he emerged as the most significant PAU member in the labor movement.[64]

The Ninth Congress of the CTC was held in the Palacio de los Trabajadores late in April 1956. Córdova noted:

Purged by then of oppositions from the ranks of the trade union confederation, the meeting was apparently peaceful, since there was no need to reject credentials or to have disturbing internal debates. Although the PSP claimed that in that year they still had the support of 83 unions, either those did not dare to send delegates to the Congress, or thought that to do so was useless or contrary to the interests of the party.[65]

The official labor history of the Castro period Communist Party explained how the "peaceful" nature of the Ninth Congress was assured by Mujal and his supporters:

The delegates were submitted to a minute search upon entering the building where the congress was meeting, and Gestapo-like control inside the building reaching the extreme that the delegates were not permitted to converse with one another or circulate freely. Not a single delegate was given the floor to oppose the reports and propositions of the officials, or to criticize them, and the few who insisted on the right to speak were coerced, attacked or expelled from the building by the police.

Before and during the congress, the Palacio de los Trabajadores was occupied by the police and by the so-called Commission of Internal Order of the CTC, reinforced by a sizable contingent of agents from the Servicio de Inteligencia Militar (SIM) and other repressive groups.[66]

At the Ninth Congress emphasis was placed on the reduction of the workday in several industries, and on the problems of economic development. Among the measures proposed were diversification of the sugar industry through development of by-products, expansion of the merchant marine and stimulation of electrification, reforestation, and irrigation.

Córdova noted an anomaly in the resolutions passed in these two congresses. Without explicitly mentioning the dictatorship of Batista negatively, they went on record denouncing the dictatorships of Trujillo in the Dominican Republic and Pérez Jiménez in Venezuela. Also, at the Sixth Conference of American State Members of the International Labor Organization in 1957, the Cuban labor delegation proposed the expulsion of the Dominican Republic from the ILO.[67]

INTERNATIONAL ACTIVITIES OF THE CTC

During the second Batista dictatorship, the CTC continued to be very active in the anti-Communist segment of the international labor movement on both a regional and a worldwide level, as it had been from the time that the Auténticos and their allies joined in forming the Confederación Interamericana de Trabajadores (CIT) in 1948. Then, in 1951, when the Organización Regional Interamericana de Trabajadores (ORIT) was established to take the place of the CIT and to be the American regional organization of the International Confederation of Free Trade Unions (ICFTU), Havana had been chosen as the seat of the ORIT headquarters and Francisco Aguirree of the Cuban Hotel and Restaurant Workers Federation was chosen as ORIT secretary general.

Aguirre continued to be ORIT secretary general after the fall of the democratic Cuban regime. Cuba also became the center of a number of other important international labor groups. Thus, in 1955 Havana was the scene of the First World Congress of Sugar Workers, and the International Transport Workers Federation established its regional headquarters in the Cuban capital.[68]

A U.S. Department of Labor source noted:

Being well off financially, the CTC and the federations uniformly pay full dues to these international centers and send full strength delegations to represent them at international labor congresses. The CTC sends out and finances numerous representatives to do ORIT organizational work in

Latin America. Within ICFTU, it proposed and financed the major share of the newly established ICFTU Plantations offices.

This source also noted that "in the international field, the CTC is militantly anti-Communist. The great activity in the field is accounted for largely by ideological and prestige considerations."[69]

CTC figures also continued to play significant roles in a United Nations organization, the International Labor Organization (ILO). The Plantations Committee of the ILO met in Havana in 1955 and the American regional congress of the ILO was held there in 1956. Several Cubans sat on the Administrative Council of the ILO.[70]

The association of the CTC leadership with the Batista dictatorship created an increasingly embarrassing problem for labor leaders of other countries who were associated with the Cubans in international organizations. Luis Alberto Monge, the Costa Rican unionist who had been secretary general of the ORIT, tried to persuade that organization to denounce the Batista regime (as it was denouncing other Latin American military dictatorships of the time) but to no avail.[71]

The same issue was raised at an ORIT congress in Bogotá in December 1958. There was present an unofficial delegation from Fidel Castro's 26th of July Movement's Labor Section, which sought to induce the congress to denounce strongly the Batista dictatorship and to repudiate the incumbent CTC leaders. The U.S., Mexican, and Cuban delegations to the meeting strongly opposed such action.

One member of the unofficial Cuban group talked with Serafino Romualdi, member of the U.S. delegation and an assistant secretary of the ORIT, and told him that within a matter of weeks Batista was going to fall. But Romualdi replied that he knew Latin America very well and was sure that such was not the case; he refused to alter his, or his delegation's, attitude toward the Cuban problem.

Only a few of the delegations of smaller labor movements represented at the Bogotá conference supported the position of the 26th of July people. In the end, only the delegates from Peru voted not to recognize the official CTC delegation.[72]

CTC IN THE LAST YEARS OF THE DICTATORSHIP

A U.S. Labor Department source noted in May 1957 that over half of the Cuban wage and salary earners belonged to unions affiliated with the CTC. It noted:

The organized sectors of the economy include the extremely important sugar industry where virtually all the agricultural workers as well as the mill and office workers are unionized; practically all of the manufacturing industries; transportation (railroads, port operations, buses, etc.); communications; electric power; hotel and restaurant operations; banking; and some of the smaller commercial enterprises which together comprise an important segment of the Cuban economy; in cattle raising; in coffee growing; and on small farms other than those attached to the sugar industry.

The same source noted that the lowest level of organization was the local union of workers in a particular enterprise. These were joined in national industrial federations, some of which had subsidiary provincial federations. All of the federations were affiliated to the CTC. This source added that the confederación "also has provincial federations to which its local affiliates belong. The provincial federations function almost as branch offices of the CTC."[73]

In 1957, the CTC had thirty-two national federations, which had 1,641 affiliated unions, with 1.2 million members. The U.S. Labor Department source noted:

In practice, the CTC has considerable control over most of its affiliates. Not infrequently, the CTC, at the request of the Ministry of Labor, "intervenes" various CTC affiliates after they have disregarded CTC policy and directives. In June 1956 at the time of the last CTC Congress, for instance, 40 unions, mostly very small ones, were "intervened" by the CTC.

However, this report added: "Nevertheless, the federations and some local unions have considerable influence within the CTC. Most of the influential CTC leaders are also important officers of the federations."

The same U.S. source noted that government employees were not legally allowed to establish unions, a prohibition dating from 1934. However, in many branches of government the workers had organizations that often had "the outlook and functions of trade unions." But these organizations could not and did not belong to the CTC. [74]

COMMUNIST LABOR ACTIVITIES DURING THE BATISTA DICTATORSHIP

Communist opposition to the new Batista dictatorship was somewhat slow in developing, particularly in the labor field. There were a number of instances in the first days of the new regime in which Communists—sometimes in conjunction with members of

Batista's own party—took advantage of the collapse of the democratic government to seize control of local unions. More generally, as Efrén Córdova noted, "Although the PSP condemned the coup d'etat, the protest action directed by Lázaro Peña was practically nonexistent. For various years he had insisted that the mass of workers and peasants remained loyal to him, in the critical hours of March 10, the leader and his comrades were conspicuously absent."[75]

Although subsequently the Communists claimed to have been severely persecuted from the beginning of the second Batista regime, my personal experience indicates that this was something less than the whole truth. Some considerable time after the coup of March 10, 1952, I visited the headquarters of the Partido Socialista Popular, where I talked with the party's president, Juan Marinello, and was introduced to Lázaro Peña (although I did not get a chance to talk to him at any length).

Although subsequently the Communists sought representation at the two congresses of the CTC held during the second Batista dictatorship, they principally concentrated their efforts on labor groups outside the structure of the confederación. They organized what they called Comités de Defensa de las Demandas (Committees for Defense of the Demands) (CDD).

The official labor history of the Castro-era Communist Party described the nature of these committees:

The CDD was not a parallel union or an element of division in the trade union movement, but an organism which would contribute to labor unity; assuring that the union was really a class struggle organization and not a passive entity or an appendix to the interests of the boss as Mujal and his followers wanted. The CDD did not arise to substitute for the union, but to make it function, go give it impulse, to force its leaders to work in defense of the demands and rights of the workers.

This account went on, "These Comités, which were constituted directly by the workers in assemblies and meetings, assured a continuing function and adopted very simple and operative forms of organization that permitted them to act under all circumstances and maintain the closest and most direct contact with the masses."[76]

In some cities and provinces the local Comités de Defensa were brought together in larger scale organizations. Then, at a conference in February 1956, more than 180 delegates met to establish a national organization, the Comité Nacional de la Defensa de las Demandas Obreras y por la Democratización de la CTC. This committee consisted of twenty-five members; the official labor history of the Castro period Communist Party claimed that "in it were represented all industries and work sectors, as well as all the provinces and most important regions of the country." Its function was "to act as a center of direction and coordination of the movement which was developing in all the island."[77]

Efrén Córdova noted one significant way in which the Comités de Defensa were of significance for the post-Batista development of the labor movement: "The action of the Committees fostered the training of a new host of future trade union leaders, among them David Salvador, trade union leader of Central Stewart in the province of Camaguey quickly began to stand out."[78]

By the beginning of 1956, a report of the Communist Party (Partido Socialista Popular) claimed that there existed 219 Comités de Defensa at particular workplaces, although this enumeration was incomplete. The same report said that there were eighty unions "directed by Communists," as well as "approximately 200 which . . . responded fundamentally to its orientation." The unions led by Communists included ten in the tobacco sector, four sugar unions, four of port workers, five in transport, one metallurgical union; "and the rest were in shoe, construction, graphic arts and other sectors."[79]

After the overthrow of the Batista government, non-Communist elements within the new labor leadership claimed that the Communists, although publicly expressing strong opposition to the Batista regime, in fact were not as severely persecuted by that regime as were its non-Communist opponents. One leader of the Juventud Obrera Católica pointed out to me that all of the Communists' periodicals except the newspaper *Hoy* continued to be published, and although technically illegal, they circulated freely through the mails, as did foreign Communist periodicals.[80]

There were also charges that the Communists had heavily infiltrated the labor section of Batista's own party. It was even claimed that José Pérez González, the most notable Batistiano labor figure, who admittedly had been a Communist, had not given up that affiliation when he became the leading Batistiano labor figure. Arsenio González, who for a while was Batista's minister of labor, was alleged also never to have foresworn his Communist affiliation.[81]

Efrén Córdova also commented that it was not until the entry of the Communist labor underground into the Frente Obrero Nacional Unido in October 1958 that the Communists

effectively demonstrated the determination of the party to participate in the movements directed toward overthrowing the regime of Batista. The Communists had been active in the presentation of economic demands, particularly in the sugar industry, but their political posture had been rather ambiguous. Their principal leaders had sought refuge abroad and its other known militants had been absent from the large confrontation of the opposition with the regime; nor did they play an important role in the two general strikes. . . . It was clear that the party had rejected the armed struggle as the most appropriate method for opposing Batista.[82]

COLLECTIVE BARGAINING AND LABOR LEGISLATION IN SECOND BATISTA REGIME

Efrén Córdova noted:

In the first five years of the dictatorship of Batista . . . the government permitted and fomented collective bargaining. Even in 1957, the negotiations that the CTC and FNTA carried out with regard to the sugar industry resulted in wage increases amounting to 40 million dollars and the extension of the grinding season by sixteen days. In that same year, an intense campaign by the workers in medicine . . . resulted in a general increase of 20 percent.[83]

In 1958, there were in effect more than 5,000 collective agreements.[84]

The second Batista regime also enacted some important legislation dealing with issues of particular importance to organized labor. It prohibited mechanization of the cigar industry, limited the shipping of sugar *en masse* without bags, and established a considerable number of social security systems for particular groups of workers.[85]

However, as Córdova pointed out:

Toward the end of this period, the protective measures had political objectives and many times were designed to avoid popular insurrection. The general minimum wage increase decreed in April 1958 had for its objective dissuading workers from participating in the general strike announced for this same month. The monthly wage of urban workers of Havana and Mariano was raised to 85 pesos (when the peso and the dollar were at parity), that of he workers of other cities to 80 and for workers outside the perimeter of the cities to 75.[86]

In 1953 there was an unusual number of strikes and labor protests. More than a dozen such major events took place. Sugar workers protested layoffs and cuts in benefits, textile workers protested the setting of minimum output rules, and bakers fought against wage reductions, as did Omnibus Aliados employees. Workers in pharmacies struck to protest failure to pay a 48-hour wage for a 40-hour week, which had been agreed to by employers. Other important walkouts on economic issues took place among railroaders, seamen, and port workers.

Córdova noted that "it was not normal that so suddenly there were so many conflicts. It seemed that the absence of a rule of law and the failure of the political parties to effectively oppose the regime of Batista had generated a state of labor discontent which caused disorder and required, on many occasions, the use of the police."[87]

GOVERNMENT STRENGTHENING OF POSITION OF MUJAL

As the commitment to the Batista dictatorship of Eusebio Mujal and his CTC associates became more intense at the same time that working-class opposition to the regime became increasingly great, the dictatorship took several important steps to try to maintain Mujal's control over the Confederación de Trabajadores de Cuba. With each such step, the control over the confederation by its rank and file members became more illusory. Two such moves of the Batista government were of particular importance and at the same time aroused opposition to the regime, as well as to the Mujalista leadership of the CTC.

The first of these measures was the imposition of compulsory payment of dues by all workers to their respective unions—and to the CTC. Efrén Córdova noted the spread of this system, which

appeared first in 1951 in the sugar industry, then officialized in Decree Law 1364 of April 1954, and later extended, by successive decree—laws to almost all labor sectors of the nation. This kind of trade union tax meant the collection of various millions of pesos each year. However, the compulsory form of its deduction and the distribution of those funds (30 percent went to the CTC), provoked unhappiness and resentment among the workers.[88]

The second government measure to fortify the Mujalistas' control over the CTC and its affiliates was a decree providing for the continuance in office of trade union officials until further notice. Efrén Córdova commented that this measure was "imposed by Batista as a consequence of the abnormal situation which existed and which provoked many protests."[89]

The Mujal leadership itself sought to strengthen its grips on power within the CTC. For instance, the constitution of the CTC itself was modified to give the top officials of the Confederación the right to intervene in and take over control of any of its affiliates; in 1957, this power was used to remove Angel Cofiño from control of the Electrical Workers Federation.[90]

THE RISING OPPOSITION TO THE BATISTA DICTATORSHIP

The need the Batista regime felt to help its allies keep control of the labor movement underscored the basic failure of that regime. The dictator did not develop the basis of popular support that he undoubtedly hoped to achieve when he seized power.

For a year or so after March 10, 1952, the shock of the sudden demolition of the democratic regime had been developing in the previous dozen years left the opposition to the Batista dictatorship largely demoralized. However, in time four different types of opposition developed, each committed to a different strategy for getting rid of the dictatorship.

The first group was headed by the former President Ramón Grau San Martín, who continued to lead a part of the Auténticos, apparently in the hope of inducing Batista to repeat his "voluntary" retirement from power of 1944. Grau sought to keep his opposition legal and was the only oppositionist to participate in the rigged presidential and congressional elections that the government organized late in 1954. However, in the end even Grau had to recognize the failure of that strategy; a few days before the election, he withdrew his candidacy for president, saying that the results of the election had been determined even before the votes were cast.

The former President Carlos Prío adopted another strategy that had historical roots, that of military conspiracy. There were still numerous officers who had entered the armed forces or had advanced their careers during the Auténtico period, not a few of whom were opposed to the Batista regime. Prío returned from exile in 1955 and conspired with those officers. However, a well-organized plan for a military coup was thwarted when its secrets were disclosed to the regime shortly before the coup was scheduled to take place. Prío returned to exile, in Miami.

A third strategy that also is a long-standing tradition in Cuba, dating from independence in the late nineteenth century and the struggle against the Machado regime in the 1920s and early 1930s, was put into practice by the University Students Federation and its offshoot, the Directorio Revolucionario (DR). This was the use of individual terror against the leaders of the dictatorial regime. It reached its climax in March 1957, when a DR group penetrated the Presidential Palace and only barely missed carrying out their objective of murdering President Batista. Subsequently there was widespread physical extermination of anyone involved in this attack who fell into the hands of the police or the Service of Military Intelligence (SMI).

The fourth strategy used by oppositionists had no historical antecedents in Cuba and, at the beginning at least, seemed to be quixotic. This was the organization of a guerrilla war struggle, commencing in the hinterlands of Oriente Province, against the relatively well-armed and trained Cuban Army of some 25,000 soldiers. The leader of the use of this strategy, of course, was Fidel Castro, a young lawyer who had been a candidate for Congress of the Ortodoxo Party in the 1952 elections that were never held.

Castro and his followers had broken with the Ortodoxo Party and established their own group, the 26th of July Movement. Particularly after a tiny band of guerrillas succeeded in establishing a base in the Sierra Maestra mountains in eastern Cuba, the 26th of July Movement had a rapidly expanding underground organization, which had increasingly large numbers of followers in the trade union movement.

The Batista dictatorship became increasingly brutal after the landing of the Castro-led guerrilla force in November 1956. Arrest, tortures, and murders by the coercive forces of the dictatorship, and particularly the Servicio de Inteligencia Militar, became commonplace. When I was in Cuba about a week after the fall of Batista, the number of people murdered by the SIM and other police forces that was most commonly mentioned was 20,000.

With the intensification of terror by the dictatorship, the opposition grew in numbers and militancy. The Castro forces more or less established bases in the mountains of eastern Cuba and grew from a baker's dozen to several hundred guerrillas, whom the army, in spite of superior numbers and firing power, was unable to defeat.

Other armed opposition groups appeared. The Directorio Revolucionario established their own "front" in the Escambray mountains east of Havana, a splinter of the Auténtico Party, calling itself the Triple A and headed by Aureliano Sánchez Arango, set up their own small guerrilla operation in the westernmost province, Pinar del Río. In 1957 there was an unsuccessful naval insurrection in the port city of Cienfuegos.

By 1958, the vast majority of the people of Cuba were against the Batista dictatorship; its fall was only a matter of time. However, it was by no means clear just what kind of regime would follow it. Nor was it clear what the impact of the change would be on organized labor.

POLITICAL STRIKES

As the disintegration of the Batista regime developed, the number of strikes increased, and it became increasingly difficult to differentiate between purely economic walkouts and those with antiregime political objective. Sometimes strikes that began for economic reasons developed into—or came to be regarded by the government as—political ones.

Two walkouts that began as economic strikes but quickly took on political overtones were those of the sugar workers of Las Villas in December 1955 and of the bank employees of Havana of August 1956. The first began as a result of the failure of the sugar firms of the province to pay the so-called differential, an increase in pay related to the profitability of the harvest. At first, the CTC and the Sugar Workers Federation supported this strike, but it soon escaped from their control. The Communists became active in the struggle, but much more important was the support of the University Students Federation, which dispatched many of its members to the area to encourage the workers to walk out. The strike had wide support from other workers in the area, and there were a number of local general strikes in solidarity with it. Elements of the Auténtico and Ortodoxo Parties also were active in working up support for the walkout. Two local leaders of the sugar workers union, Conrado Bécquer and Conrado Rodríguez, played a particularly important role in organizing and leading the strike, as a result of which they were subsequently purged by the CTC and FNTA leadership. Finally, the Las Villas sugar strike was broken by the army and the police.[91]

The Havana bank workers' walkout arose as the result of a dispute between the Bank Workers Federation and the employers' organization, the Banks Association, over the renewal of their collective agreement. The workers demanded a 20 percent increase in salaries and the suppression of a clause in the contract forbidding the unionization of "confidential" employees.

The issue of confidential employees who were not allowed to join the union was particularly bitter at the time. A very large part of the work force was designated by the employers as confidential, obviously in the hope that this designation would give the people involved a feeling of superiority to their fellow employees and make them unlikely to join any movement for higher salaries or other improvements. Reportedly, many of those declared to be confidential employees were so named against their will.[92]

The strike of Havana bank workers lasted for a month and a half and had the support of neither the national Bank Workers Federation nor the CTC. However, it aroused wide support in the

Havana area, where there were many short sympathetic walkouts by different groups of workers. The employers fired most of the workers active in organizing the strike. The walkout was finally ended through the intervention of Cardinal Manuel Arteaga. The employers ultimately granted a 10 percent wage increase but refused to reemploy any of the strikers who had been dismissed.[93]

Two other major strikes were clearly politically motivated from their inception. These took place in August 1957 and April 1958.

The August 1957 walkout started as a result of the murder by government agents of Frank País, the national leader of the 26th of July Movement underground organization. It first spread more or less spontaneously through the Eastern part of the island, but was less well organized in Havana. However, underground opposition elements there—including the 26th of July, the Organización Auténtica, Resistencia Cívica and Juventud Obrera Católica—met and launched a call for a general strike in the city on August 5, Neither official trade union elements nor the Communists were represented at this meeting.

The August 5 general strike call had only limited effectiveness. There were some acts of sabotage, and some limited strikes, and temporary seizure of radio stations, but no real general strike movement.

However, Efrén Córdova suggested that this August 1957 movement had had much greater political potential than it finally fulfilled: "It is very probable, however, that if the CTC had joined the movement and had brought to it its experience and its labor network, the strike of '57 would have put an end to the Batista dictatorship. Proof of the magnitude and potential possibilities of the citizen strike is shown by the fact that in Pinar del Río and other cities it continued for a week."[94]

The April 1958 general strike was called on the direct initiative of Fidel Castro and the 26th of July Movement. It was the result of a meeting early in March of guerrilla and underground elements associated with the 26th of July Movement in rebel held territory, which launched a call for a general strike on April 9, 1958. In Havana, the planning for the strike was carried on in the headquarters of the Juventud Obrera Católica, the Catholic group working within the labor movement, particularly in the anti-Batista labor underground. There was a certain protection afforded by the association of the JOC with the Roman Catholic Church.[95]

The direction of this proposed movement was divided among three groups. One was the recently established Frente Obrero Nacional (FON), charged with getting workers out on strike; the second was the Movimiento de Resistencia Cívica, a largely middle-class group, which was to undertake sabotage and limited armed action against the government in the cities; the third was the Frente Estudiantil Nacional, which was to mobilize the students in support of the movement.

Of course, the announcement of such an event so long before it was supposed to take place gave Batista and his government wide opportunities to prepare for it and to round up as many as possible of those the authorities considered likely to be involved in the movement. In addition, the FON, which was charged with actually organizing the workers to walk out on April 9, was too new and its influence was still too weak to confront the government, the employers, and the trade union apparatus of the Mujal-controlled CTC.

As a matter of fact, the leadership of the CTC made its opposition to the walkout very clear: It called on the workers to reject the "political and adventurous general strike."

The April 1958 general strike was a failure in Havana. Although there were sporadic stoppages in some factories and other enterprises, and a few more in some of the cities of the interior, most workers stayed on the job and ignored the call to walk out. The elements of the Movimiento de Resistencia Cívica who sought to seize arms, sabotage government and public utility installations, and otherwise confront the regime with force, had limited success, and many of the participants in the movement were killed, not a few after they had been captured by the police or the army. Over all, the attempted revolutionary general strike was inadequately organized and failed to arouse the support that Castro apparently hoped for, in spite of the general disapproval of the Batista regime by the citizenry, particularly the workers.[96]

However, it was much more successful in Santiago than elsewhere. Maurice Zeitlin noted that there "the strike completely paralyzed industry and commerce . . . workers stayed out despite the regime's threat of arrest and its offer of immunity from prosecution to anyone killing an advocate of the strike."[97]

Some of those who had participated in the activities of the April 1958 strike subsequently joined the guerrilla military groups, particularly in the western province of Pinar del Río, where the strike had lasted considerably longer than in most other parts of the republic.[98]

THE UNDERGROUND LABOR OPPOSITION

In the last year of the Batista dictatorship there developed a substantial underground opposition to the regime within the labor movement. The most extensive element in this underground was that of Fidel Castro's 26th of July Movement. However, other groups were also active. In the closing phases of the fight against Batista, most of these underground forces were associated on a national level, first in the Frente Obrero Nacional (FON), then in the Frente Obrero Nacional Unido (FONU).

When Castro was still in Mexico, he asked for the formation of a labor section of the 26th of July Movement. After Castro and his small group of guerrillas had established themselves in the Sierra Maestra, Frank País, the head of the general 26th of July underground, and Antonio Torres and other trade unionists took a plan for the organization of a labor underground to Castro, who gave it his approval. They worked in Oriente Province, then moved to Camaguey, Santa Clara (where Conrado Bécquer joined the movement), then on to Matanzas, Havana, and Pinar del Río. In each place, they made contact with leaders who undertook the job of organizing there. Some of these were dead by the time the struggle was over, others survived to help rebuild the labor movement after Batista's downfall.

There were many casualties among members of the 26th of July underground, as they were imprisoned, tortured, or killed. It became necessary to replace those who had fallen, as the result of which quite a few of those who survived by January 1, 1959, had relatively little trade union experience.[99] However, many others were experienced trade unionists, who had held positions in the labor movement. Octavio Lloit, for instance, who emerged as the number two person in the Sección Obrera, had been on the executive of Hermandad Ferroviaria in Camaguey Province.[100]

Some of the members of the Sección Obrera had a long trajectory in the underground opposition to the Batista regime. For instance, Javier González, who became the principal leader of the Sección Obrera in the Liquor Workers Federation, told me that he had been active in the underground opposition even before the 26th July Movement was established.[101]

After the revolution, David Salvador, the head of the Labor Section of the 26th July, claimed that by the time Batista fell, the section was organized throughout the island and had groups within virtually every union in the country. He estimated that there were some 15,000 workers in the Sección Obrera.[102]

The port and maritime workers were among the best organized underground groups. Antonio Gil Brito, whose only previous labor leadership experience had been as secretary general of a union of fifty members, had established eighteen organized groups in the Port of Havana alone. Gil Britto served as secretary of organization of the 26th of July in the port. At one point, in September 1958, he was jailed, was beaten, and lost the joint of one finger. He was finally freed after twenty days, because the police did not know who he actually was and because his father was a friend of an important Batista politician.[103]

There were organized 26th of July groups in all twenty-five sections of the railroad workers union, Hermandad Ferroviaria. Generally, a section had a four-man committee: secretaries of organization, finances, propaganda, and press. The secretary of organization coordinated all underground work in the section; that of finance raided money for the revolutions in the Sierra Maestra and other revolutionary work. The secretary of propaganda distributed various kinds of underground literature; the secretary of press gathered information of interest to the railroaders and circulated it. In some cases, there was a fifth secretary, of supply, in charge of getting food, clothing, medicine and other things and channeling it to the Rebel Army.[104]

All of the leaders of local labor sections of the 26th July were not men. In the case of the Continental Can workers union, the leader was a woman, who headed the local section made up of half a dozen workers. Until the end of the Batista regime, much of the work of that group was taken up with selling "bonds," sold by the 26th of July Movement to finance its activities, to their fellow workers.[105]

There were a number of other political groups that also were active in the labor underground. We have already noted the Comité Nacional de Defensa de las Demandas Obreras, organized and directed by the Communists. Of less importance were elements of the Auténtico and Ortodoxo Parties and of the University Students Federation. A new element in the picture were the activists of the Juventud Obrera Católica (Catholic Labor Youth), a subsidiary group of Catholic Action.

During the closing months of the Batista regime, two organizations were established to unite the various elements involved in the labor underground: FON and FONU.

The FON was formed, according to Efrén Córdova, by "Auténtico, Ortodoxo, Catholic and independent revolutionaries, united in the proposition to restore democracy and the Constitution of 1940." Although many of its people did not have much trade union experience, "they had the enthusiasm and cleanliness of objectives necessary to recruit adherents and become the trade union wing of M-26-7," that is, of the 26th of July Movement.

As we have seen, the FON was charged with persuading the workers to leave their jobs in the general strike–rebellion of April 1958. With the strike's failure, pressure mounted—some of it apparently from Fidel Castro—to include the Communists in its ranks. As a consequence, the Frente Obrero Nacional Unido was formed in October 1958 by a merger of the FON with the Communists' Comité Nacional de Defensa de las Demandas Obreras. Elements of the Directorio Revolucionario and of the Auténtico and Ortodoxo Parties that had not belonged to the FON were also included in the FONU.[106]

The FONU put forth a twelve-point "minimum program" for the labor underground. This program included demands for a general 20 percent wage increase, price controls, protection of workers from the negative effects of mechanization, unemployment insurance, stimulation of economic development, "a real agrarian reform," opposition to discrimination against black workers, special protection for women and children, and reestablishment of the Constitution of 1940. It also demanded "the reestablishment of union democracy in all worker organizations; against the corruption and class collaboration introduced in the labor movement; against the obligatory deduction of trade union dues, and for the constitutional right of the workers to meet, parade and organize strikes and boycotts."[107]

There was at least one attempt of the CTC leadership to negotiate with Castro, and at least by implication with the pro-Castro labor underground. Huber Matos, one of Castro's principal "comandantes," and Celia Sánchez, one of the most important women in the 26th of July Movement, were intermediaries in these discussions. According to the U.S. labor leader Serafino Romualdi, these contacts were totally unsuccessful—the 26th of July negotiators demanded the resignation of the CTC leadership, which (understandably) they turned down.[108]

LABOR MEETINGS IN REBEL TERRITORY

As the approaching collapse of the Batista's regime became more evident, several important "congresses" were held in territories under the control of the Rebel Army. These included regional meetings in areas of the Second Front, in the vicinity of Guantánamo and under the command of Fidel Castro's brother, Raúl, as well as sessions held in parts of the province of Las Villas conquered by the columns commanded by Camilo Cienfuegos and Ernesto Ché Guevara.

Raúl Castro had established a Labor Buro of the 26th of July Movement in the region under his control. That body summoned, in the name of the Frente Obrero Nacional Unido, a congress that met on December 8–9, 1958. It paid particular attention to the problems of the sugar workers but also dealt with more general issues. Some 110 delegates attended the meeting. According to the official labor history of the Castro period Communist Party:

The delegates represented practically all sectors of production. There were sugar workers (from 16 centrales), railroaders, port workers, miners, agricultural workers, telephone workers, those of construction, electricity, commerce, medicine, graphic arts, bakeries, musicians, carpenters, pharmaceutical workers, liquor workers, and those of the Naval Base of Guantánamo; in expression of the worker-peasant alliance, there was representation of the Asociación Campesina "Frank País."

This congress repudiated the Mujalista leaders of the CTC, the Sugar Workers Federation, and the local unions. It called for meetings of workers in each work center to officially depose those leaders and to elect a new leadership democratically. It also repudiated the compulsory dues collection established by the CTC and the Batista government and made a number of economic demands of particular relevance to the sugar workers.[109]

In the areas of Las Villas conquered by the column of Camilo Cienfuegos, a labor commission was established. A number of groups made up of five workers of the Cienfuegos column were organized

to put in practice in the liberated zones the following directives given by Camilo: a) celebration of free elections in each union to elect their leaders; b) destitution of the mujalista leadership imposed on the workers; c) elaboration of a list of demands, particularly of the sugar workers, in view of the harvest; d) creation and constitution of the basis for a strong labor movement, energetic and combative, which would be converted into a determining factor in the struggle against the Batista tyranny.

As a result of these decisions, there were numerous meetings, on sugar *centrales* in particular, where new leaders were chosen for the local unions. A number of peasant organizations were also established.

In the areas taken over by Ché Guevara's column there was held at the beginning of December 1958 a provincial congress of the Labor Section of the 26th of July Movement. Ché Guevara himself attended some sessions of this congress.[110]

In the area controlled by Guevara's column there was also held on December 20–21, 1958, the First National Conference of Sugar Workers in Liberated Territory. It was officially sponsored by the FONU and was attended by eighty delegates from forty centrales in various parts of the country, except Oriente, where fierce battles were then under way. This meeting adopted resolutions dealing specifically with the sugar workers, including demands for wage increases, stability of employment, and reduction of working hours for clerical personnel in the industry. It also declared deposed the then-current leaders of the Sugar Workers

Federation and decreed that all unions within areas controlled by the Rebel Army should hold meetings to depose their local officers. It demanded democratization of the CTC, as well as full freedom to strike, and dissolution of the repressive organisms of the Batista regime.

The meeting also resolved to "to give knowledge of each of the demands contained in this document to all the Military chiefs of our Glorious Rebel Army, and in particular to Comandante Jefe Dr. Fidel Castro, as well as the provisional president of the Revolutionary government, Dr. Manuel Urrutia Lleo, from whom we expect cooperation and support."[111]

Efrén Córdova saw in the labor meetings held in rebel territory before the final overthrow of Batista seeds of conflicts within the labor movement once the revolution was victorious:

These decisions help in understanding the differences that existed between the directors of the M-26-7 and those who descended from the mountains. The program of the FONU appeared to correspond to the objectives of a trade union movement designed to operate in a democratic regime and a market economy. The references to reestablishment of the Constitution of 1940 and respect for all democratic freedoms of the people are unequivocal. The agreements and proposals of the congresses and meetings held under the auspices of the Rebel Army indicated a different situation and had within them already the ferment of the changes of structure which were going to be produced in Cuba.[112]

NOTES

1. Efrén Córdova, *Clase Trabajadora y Movimiento Sindical en Cuba, Volumen I (1819–1959)*, Ediciones Universal, Miami, 1995, page 317.

2. Interview with Roberto Ferrer Guzmán, responsable of 26 de Julio, Federación de Trabajadores de la Provincia de La Habana, in Havana, January 11, 1959.

3. Interview with Modesto Barbeito, secretario sindical of Asociación Libertaria de Cuba, official of Federación de Trabajadores de Plantas Electricas, in Havana, March 18, 1952.

4. *Historia del Movimiento Obrero Cubano 1865–1958, Tomo II, 1935–1958*, Instituto de Historia del Movimiento Comunista y de la Revolución Socialista de Cuba anexo al Comité Central del Partido Comunista de Cuba, Editoria Política, La Habana, 1985, page 258.

5. Interview with Juan Beguer, secretary general of Caja de Retiro de Trabajadores Gastronómicos, in Havana, July 16, 1952.

6. Interview with Gilberto Goliat, secretary general of Federación Obrera Marítima, in Havana, March 18, 1952.

7. Interview with Pablo Balbuena, Secretary of Organization of Confederación de Trabajadores de Cuba, secretary general of Federación Sindical de Trabajadores Gráficos, in Havana, March 17, 1952.

8. Interview with Manuel Martínez Ezcurra, secretary of culture of Federación Sindical de Trabajadores Telefónicos, in Havana, March 20, 1952.

9. Interviews with Modesto Barbeito, op. cit., March 12, 1952, and Manuel Martínez Ezcurra, op. cit., March 20, 1952.

10. Córdova, op. cit., page 318.

11. Interview with Marco Hirigoyen, secretary general of Federación de Transporte, member of Buro of Confederación de Trabajadores de Cuba, in Havana, March 15, 1952.

12. Interview with Irving Lippe, labor attaché, U.S. Embassy, in Havana, March 17, 1952

13. Interview with Armando Baudet, building manager of Federación de Trabajadores de la Provincia de Camaguey, in Camaguey, June 18, 1954.

14. Interview with José Luis Martínez, secretary general of Federación Nacional de Trabajadores de la Industria Azucarera, in Havana, March 17, 1952.

15. Interview with Herbert Samuel Powell, member of Executive of Federación Nacional de Trabajadores de la Industria Azucarera, in Havana, March 17, 1952.

16. Interview with Angel Bravo, Venezuelan trade union leader, official of Organización Regional Interamericana Trabajadores, in Havana, Cuba, March 17, 1952.

17. Córdova, op. cit., page 319.

18. Interview with Jesús Portocarrero, minister of labor of Batista second dictatorship, in Havana, March 19, 1952.

19. Interview with Gilberto Goliat, op. cit., March 18, 1952.

20. Interview with Castro Moscú, secretary of interior of Federación de Trabajadores Gastronómicos, in Havana, March 16, 1952.

21. Interview with Pablo Balbuena, op. cit., March 17, 1972.

22. Interview with Vicente Rubiera, secretary general of Federación de Trabajadores Telefónicos, in Havana, March 20, 1952.

23. Interview with Irving Lippe, op. cit., March 17, 1952.

24. Ibid.; see also interviews with Castro Moscú, op. cit., March 16, 1952, and Angel Bravo, op. cit., March 17, 1952.

25. Interview with Jesús Portocarrero, op. cit., March 19, 1952.

26. Interview with Irving Lippe, op. cit., March 17, 1952.

27. Interview with Angel Bravo, op. cit., March 17, 1952.

28. Interview with Ramón León Renterría, leader of Federación Obrera Maritima, in Havana, March 15, 1952.

29. Interview with Pablo Balbuena, op. cit., March 17, 1952.

30. Interview with Modesto Barbeito, op. cit., March 18, 1952.

31. Interview with Roberto Hoyos, organization secretary of Federación de Petroleo y Minas, in Havana, March 17, 1952.

32. Interview with Octavio Díaz Benítez, secretary general of Sindicato de Trabajadores de Camiones por Carretera, in Havana, July 25, 1953; see also interviews with Angel Guina, secretary of press, Comité Nacional ATLAS, in Havana, July 25, 1953.

33. Interview with Castro Moscú, op. cit., March 15, 1952.

34. Interview with Manuel Martínez Ezcurra, op. cit., March 20, 1952.

35. Interview with Francisco González del Cristo, delegado ante Organismos Oficiales y Patronales of Federación Nacional de Trabajadores Ganaderos, in Havana, March 17, 1952.

36. Interview with José Luis Martínez, op. cit., March 17, 1952.

37. Interviews with Modesto Barbeito, op. cit., March 18, 1952, Pablo Balbuena, op. cit., July 13, 1952, and Pablo Mena, secretario de Juventud y Deportes of Confederación de Trabajadores de Cuba, in Havana, March 17, 1952.

38. Interview with Pedro Domenech, secretary general of Cinematográficas Federation, in Havana, March 17, 1952.

39. Interview with Pablo Balbuena, op. cit., July 15, 1952.

40. Interview with Irving Lippe, op. cit., July 15, 1952.

41. Interview with Pablo Balbuena, op. cit., July 15, 1952.

42. Interview with Modesto Barbeito, op. cit., July 16, 1952.

43. Interview with Angel Miolán, refugee from Dominican Republic, employee of Transport Workers Federation of Cuba, in Havana, July 15, 1952.

44. Interview with Bruce Crooks, labor attaché in U.S. Embassy, in Havana, July 24, 1953.

45. Interview with Angel Bravo, op. cit., March 17, 1952.

46. Interview with Buenaventura López, secretary of organization of Confederación de Trabajadores de Cuba, in Havana, July 16, 1952.

47. Interview with Bruce Crooks, op. cit., July 24, 1953.

48. Interview with Pablo Balbuena, op. cit., July 15, 1952.

49. Interview with Herbert Samuel Powell, op. cit., July 15, 1952.

50. Interview with Modesto Barbeito, op. cit., July 16, 1952.

51. Interview with Pablo Balbuena, op. cit., July 15, 1952.

52. Interview with Modesto Barbeito, op. cit., July 15, 1952.

53. Interview with Antonio Collada, secretary of organization of Federación Nacional de Trabajadores del Ramo de la Construcción, in Havana, September 13, 1959.

54. Interview with Pedro Martínez, head of labor affairs for Directorio Revolucionario, in Havana, January 13, 1959.

55. Córdova, op. cit., pages 328–329

56. Interview with Sra. de Valdivia, wife of Raúl Valdivia, former president of Sugar Workers Federation, in Havana, January 13, 1959.

57. Córdova, op. cit., pages 329–330.

58. Ibid., page 322; see also Robert Kenneth Brown, "The Impact of Revolutionary Politics on the Autonomy of Organized Labor in Cuba, 1959–1960," University of Colorado M.A. Thesis, 1965, page 16.

59. Córdova, op. cit., page 322.

60. Interview with Calixto Sánchez, head of Federación Aerea Nacional, in Havana, July 15, 1952.

61. Interview with Modesto Barbeito, op. cit., January 13,

62. Córdova, op. cit., pages 334–335; see also *Historia del Movimiento Obrero Cubano etc.*, *Tomo II*, op. cit., pages 318–319.

63. Interview with Ignacio González Tellechea, a leader of Maritime Workers Federation of Cuba, in New York City, December 10, 1955.

64. Interview with José Pérez Gonzalez, member of Buro de Dirección of Confederación de Trabajadores de Cuba, labor leader of Partido Acción Unitaria, in Havana, July 25, 1953.

65. Córdova, op. cit., pages 336–337.

66. *Historia del Movimiento Obrero Cubano etc.*, Tomo II, 1985, op. cit., page 318.

67. Córdova, op. cit., pages 336–337.

68. Ibid., pages 350–351.

69. *Foreign Labor Information: Labor in Cuba*, U.S. Department of Labor, Bureau of Labor Statistics, Washington DC, May 1957, pages 7, 9.

70. Córdova, op. cit., pages 350–351.

71. Interview with Luis Alberto Monge, Costa Rican labor leader, former secretary general of ORIT, in Havana, January 12, 1959.

72. Interviews with Reino González, in charge of international affairs for CTC, former secretary general, Juventus Obrera Católica, secretary general of Unión de Trabajadores Cristanos, in Havana, June 12, 1959; Jose Plana, member of Executive of Confederación de Trabajadores de Cuba, member of Executive of Unión de Trabajadores Cristianos, in Havana, June 5, 1959; Robert Gladnick, head of International Ladies Garment Workers Union in Puerto Rico, in Santurce, PR, June 25, 1959.

73. *Foreign Labor Information: Labor in Cuba*, op. cit., page 3.

74. Ibid., page 6.

75. Córdova, op. cit., page 320.

76. *Historia del Movimiento Obrero Cubano etc.*, Tomo II, op. cit., pages 284–285.

77. Ibid., page 286.

78. Córdova, op. cit., page 338.

79. *Historia del Movimiento Obrero Cubano etc.*, Tomo II, op. cit., page 319.

80. Interview with Gilberto García, secretary general of Juventud Obrera Católica, in Havana, January 12, 1959; see also interview with José Plana, op. cit., June 5, 1959.

81. Interview with Rodolfo Riesgo, editor of Juventud Obrera Católica Publications, in Havana, January 12, 1959.

82. Córdova, op. cit., page 339.

83. Ibid., page 325.

84. Ibid., page 348.

85. Ibid., page 325.

86. Ibid., pages 325–326.

87. Ibid., page 326.

88. Ibid., page 325.

89. Ibid., page 338.

90. Interview with Serafino Romualdi, Latin American representative of American Federation of Labor, assistant secretary of ORIT, in New York City, October 8, 1962.

91. Córdova, op. cit., page 327; see also *Historia del Movimiento Obrero Cubano etc.*, Tomo II, pages 290–294.

92. Interview with Raúl Muñoz Robledo, secretary of organization of Sindicato Bancario de La Habana, in Havana, June 6, 1959.

93. Córdova, op. cit., pages 330–338; see also *Historia del Movimiento Obrero Cubano etc., Tomo II*, op. cit., pages 288–290.

94. Córdova, op. cit., pages 327–328; see also Maurice Zeitlin, *Revolutionary Politics and the Cuban Working Class*, Harper Torchbooks, New York, 1970, page 226.

95. Interview with Gilberto García, op. cit., January 12, 1959.

96. Córdova, op. cit., pages 331–334; see also *Historia del Movimiento Obrero Cubano etc., Tomo II*, op. cit., pages 343–350.

97. Zeitlin, op. cit., pages 226–227.

98. Interview with Neill Macaulay, history professor in University of Florida, former lieutenant in Rebel Army of Fidel Castro, in Rio de Janeiro, Brazil, August 27, 1965.

99. Interview with Antonio Torres, member of Provisional Executive of Confederación de Trabajadores de Cuba, in Havana, January 11, 1959.

100. Interview with Octavio Lloit, director of propaganda of Confederación de Trabajadores de Cuba, in Havana, January 15, 1959.

101. Interview with Javier González, leader of Sección Obrera of 26th of July in Liquor Federation, in Havana, June 2, 1959.

102. Interview with David Salvador, delegate of 26th of July Movement in charge of Confederación de Trabajadores de Cuba, in Havana, January 10, 1959, January 11, 1959.

103. Interview with Antonio Gil Britto, secretary general of Federación Obrera Marítima, in Havana, September 14, 1959.

104. Interview with José Miguel Juan Aizpurua, responsable of 26 de Julio of Hermandad Ferroviaria on Ferrocarriles Occidentales, in Havana, January 11, 1959.

105. Interview with Maria Luisa Fernández, leader of 26 de Julio of Sindicato Metalúrgico Continental Can, in Havana, January 11, 1959.

106. Córdova, op. cit., page 338.

107. Ibid., page 339; see also *Historia del Movimiento Obrero Cubano etc., Tomo II*, op. cit., pages 357–359.

108. Interview with Serafino Romualdi, op. cit., October 8, 1962.

109. *Historia del Movimiento Obrero Cubano etc., Tomo II*, op. cit., pages 361–362.

110. Ibid., pages 362–363.

111. Ibid., pages 363–366; see also Robert Kenneth Brown, 1965, op. cit., pages 21–22.

112. Córdova, op. cit., page 341.

6
Organized Labor in Castro's Cuba: Seizure of the CTC

About midnight December 31, 1958–January 1, 1959, President Fulgencio Batista fled Cuba, together with some of his leading associates. His flight not only ended Batista's personal dictatorship, but set in train a process that was to convert Cuba into the Western Hemisphere's first—and so far, only—Marxist-Leninist dictatorship. The new regime's treatment of organized labor played a major part in this transformation.

EARLY EVOLUTION OF CASTRO REGIME

With the fall of Batista's rule, Fidel Castro emerged immediately as the virtually unchallenged leader of the regime that took its place. Castro had organized the "Rebel Army," the guerrilla group that started with a baker's dozen of combatants in the Sierra Maestra mountains of eastern Cuba and developed into an army that after two years defeated the 25,000 man, supposedly "modern" army of Batista. However, the Castro victory also owed a great deal to the underground organization of the 26th of July Movement and several other clandestine groups, which had mobilized much of the nearly universal opposition to Batista that developed in the final phase of his regime. Dissident trade unionists, fighting against the alliance of he CTC leadership of Eusebio Mujal and his associates with Batista, played a major role in this clandestine struggle against the general-president's tyranny.

Writing a couple of weeks after Castro made his triumphal entry into Havana, I commented:

At the present moment, the 26 de Julio Movement of Castro has carried all before it. It was the 26 de Julio which selected the President, the cabinet, which is running the government at the moment. It is the 26 de Julio which is organizing the new army. . . . It seems to me that the whole situation, both political and trade union, depends a great deal on what Castro does. He is at the moment the absolute master of the situation. He is the popular hero, and everyone is waiting for him to make some of the fundamental decisions.[1]

The collapse of the Batista regime undoubtedly was more sudden than its opponents had expected. The 26th of July Movement, which quickly emerged as the dominant element in the revolutionary government after January 1, 1959, had not yet clearly decided what kind of a "New Cuba" it wanted to build on the ruins of the fallen regime.

The 26th of July Movement was in fact a very heterogeneous group. However, in the first few months of the revolutionary regime, it was broadly divided into two factions or tendencies. One of these may be dubbed "national revolutionary." It wanted, after an appropriate interval, the full reestablishment and enforcement of the Constitution of 1940, with full civil liberties and elections. It advocated a mixed economy, in which the state would have a major role in its direction and development, but most sectors would remain in the hands of private firms and individuals, operating principally through the market.

The national revolutionaries also favored broad agrarian reform, which would limit the size of rural landholdings and give many family farms to tenants and agricultural laborers. It also advocated a major effort to industrialize the economy, the reorganization and strengthening of the social security system, and other major social programs such as low-cost housing, massive educational efforts and extension of medical services to those whom poverty had deprived of such facilities. In terms of foreign policy, hey urged that Cuba establish a more or less dependent stance, not fully aligned with either party in the Cold War.

The other tendency within the 26th of July during these early months of the revolution was Marxist-Leninist. It sought the indefinite extension of the provisional de facto regime established after January 1, 1959, and its conversion as rapidly as possible into a "dictatorship of the proletariat" exercised by an unchallengeable "vanguard" party. That regime would bring about the establishment of a "socialist" economy in which virtually all means of production and distribution would be in the hands of the state. They wanted an agrarian reform that would establish a Soviet-style rural economy. The 26th of July Marxist-Leninists supported close collaboration with the traditional Communist

Party (Partido Socialista Popular [PSP]), in spite of the PSP's failure to support the revolution until it was convinced that the Castro-led forces were going to win. They also advocated full alignment with the Soviet Union in the Cold War.

During the early months of the revolution there is little doubt that the strong majority of the 26th of July leadership and rank and file supported the national revolutionary position. Those in that camp included most of the members of the cabinet, important leaders of the Rebel Armed Forces (the new army based on the guerrilla forces), and the overwhelming majority of the new leadership that emerged in the labor movement. Elements outside the 26th of July, including the remnants of the Auténtico Party and the Revolutionary Directorate, also favored the national revolutionary position.

The two most prominent figures in the Marxist-Leninist camp were Fidel Castro's brother, Raúl, who quickly became head of the Rebel Army as Fidel assumed the political leadership of the regime, and Ernesto "Che" Guevara, the Argentine doctor who had emerged as one of the principal leaders of the Rebel Army. During this early period, the support of the Marxist-Leninists was certainly most significant within the Rebel Army, particularly those segments of it that had been commanded by Raúl Castro and "Che" Guevara during the civil war. It also had the backing of a minority within organized labor, as well as of the Partido Socialista Popular outside the 26th of July.

During the first nine months of the revolution Fidel Castro did not take a clear position in favor of either faction. At times he took steps that seemed to align himself with the national revolutionaries. These included his advocating a vaguely defined "humanism" which would avoid the evils of both capitalism and communism, while denying strongly that he was or ever had been a Communist, and of stating that in elections within the labor movement the 26th of July would go it alone and not make any alliance with the Communists—or anyone else. On the other hand, other moves by Fidel, such as his ouster and humiliation of the first man he had made president, Manuel Urrutia, when Urrutia became too vocally anti-Communist, seemed to put Fidel on the side of the Marxist-Leninists.

During this early period of the Cuban Revolution, Fidel Castro received a degree of support, and even adulation, from a large part of the Cuban people that one who had not observed it would find hard to believe. Efrén Córdova has noted:

The bearded and audacious guerrilla who had defeated the army of a hated dictatorship was respected and venerated in what was from any

viewpoint an exaggerated form by a large part of the people. . . . It was
the period of the glorification and almost the deification of the figure of
the leader of the revolution. It was the time when periodicals published
images of Castro that looked like Jesus Christ.[2]

However, by September 1959, it appeared to me that the
situation was basically evolving toward the apparent emergence of
a government party and establishment of a representative democratic regime. I reported to Jay Lovestone (the "foreign minister"
of the AFL-CIO):

The 26th of July Movement is now in the process of reorganization and
solidification. I don't know just what their time table is, but they are beginning a process of electing local authorities, which in time will be
capped by a national congress of the movement. When that is accomplished, the 26th of July will be a political party, instead of the kind of
loosely-organized "movement" which it has been since January 1st.

I continued:

The principal opposition at the present time is the Partido Revolucionario
Cubano (Auténtico), the old Auténtico Party. Its reconstruction is now
well advanced. Its revolutionary arm, the Organización Auténtica, has
been merged into the party organization. The party has now reconstituted its provincial committees in all provinces, and the town-by-town
and ward-by-ward organizational structure is rapidly being reestablished. The party now has a weekly newspaper, which is very well edited.[3]

Early in September there were still articles in the 26th of July
newspaper *Revolución* strongly attacking the Communists, including one signed by Euclides Vázquez Candela, "Balance of a
Polemic":

Our truths must have struck very deeply; the political sins must be very
great and the errors of the oligarchy which commands in the PSP and
which must torment them since a brief accusation of mine that the organization could not head the revolutionary opposition to Batista, due to
their former complicity with the tyrant and certain lack of confidence
which their compromised past had to inspire, to achieve what very few
have obtained from this party, that its high leadership publicly engaged
in self criticism in two kilometer long editorials and admit false past positions which over and over and during many years they refused to
recognize.[4]

It has long been my conviction that Fidel Castro made his decision to support definitively the Marxist-Leninists within the
26th of July, and the PSP outside it, at the time of the Huber Ma-

tos incident late in September 1959. Matos, one of the major leaders of the Rebel Army and at the time its commander in Camaguey Province, submitted his resignation and asked to resume his old job as a schoolteacher, giving as his reason his objection to Communist Party infiltration in the 26th of July Movement and the government, which he had drawn to Fidel's attention without Fidel's taking any action on the matter. Instead of accepting Matos's resignation, Castro; his brother, Raúl; and Camilo Cienfuegos went to Camaguey, arrested Matos, and had him taken back to Havana for a trial that resulted in a twenty-year jail sentence. It is perhaps also significant that in the process of this incident, Camilo Cienfuegos mysteriously disappeared; he was the second- or third-ranking officer in the Rebel Army, was the only figure whose popularity somewhat approached that of Fidel, and had shown his hostility to the Communists by banning circulation of their literature in Camp Columbia, the military installation outside Havana of which he was commander.

Perhaps even Fidel Castro himself does not know for sure why he finally decided to support the Marxist-Leninists within the 26th of July and so establish the direction of the Cuban Revolution toward the installation of a Marxist-Leninist-Stalinist society. However, at least two elements seem likely to have been of great importance in this decision. One was that the two principal advocates of such a decision—Raúl Castro and Ernesto "Che" Guevara—were much closer personally to Fidel at that time than any of the leaders of the opposite faction. The second was that Castro had come to love governing the country as he was then doing, as whatever idea he wanted to put into practice became the law. Also, it would have taken a man of particularly strong democratic convictions to resist the almost unlimited adulation to which Fidel was subject during the first phase of the revolution, convictions that he did not have.

TRANSITION TO A MARXIST-LENINIST REGIME

With Fidel's decision to adhere to Marxism-Leninism there began the transition of the regime in that direction. The freedom of press, organization, and discussion that had characterized the regime in its earliest months quickly disappeared. All promises of early elections ceased, and raising the issue became "subversive." The independence of the labor movement was destroyed in the months after the Tenth Congress of the Confederación de Trabajadores de Cuba in November, and the function of organized labor was converted from that of pushing for the improvement of the lot of the worker, and defending their interests, to that of stimulating production and supporting whatever the Castro government want to do in the economy.

By the autumn of 1959, also, there began to be arrests of leaders of the Revolution who did not agree with the regime's turn toward Marxism-Leninism, while others, including members of the revolutionary government, were forced into exile. One trade union leader who went into exile told me that in some ways the situation of oppositionists became worse under Castro than it had been under Batista. For one thing, what he called *amigismo* had disappeared. Under Batista, one who was jailed who had some kind of relationship with someone in authority usually was able to persuade that person to use influence to obtain his or her release. However, there was no such possibility under Castro.[5]

In 1960, various steps that were taken put under the control of the state most elements of the economy. Seizure of land under the 1959 agrarian reform law, taking over all U.S. firms in the country, and then confiscation of all large- and medium-scale Cuban-owned private enterprises were part of this process. This was followed by establishment of a Central Planning Group (JUCEPLAN) and a Ministry of Industries (headed by Ernesto "Che" Guevara) to control and plan the economy.

Once the government had taken over the largest part of the economy, it began a process of consolidating small industries and workshops that had been confiscated and merging them into larger enterprises.[6] In 1968 there was a so-called revolutionary offensive in which virtually all small handicraft firms (electricians, barbers, etc.) as well as "mom and pop" commercial enterprises were seized by the government.

To some degree, the Castro regime "went beyond" the Soviet Union and East European Communist regimes in establishing "socialism." Thus, for example, although in the beginning the larger part of agriculture—particularly the sugar industry—was converted into Soviet-style collective farms, by 1962 a policy of transforming most of those into (equally Soviet-modeled) "state farms" (People's Farms), in which the workers were purely wage earners instead of members of supposed cooperatives, was announced.[7]

Meanwhile, the Cuban economic situation became increasingly difficult. The increased demand for consumer goods resulting from 1959 income redistribution measures; inefficiency and errors in state-controlled sectors; and growing balance of payments problems, intensified by increasing difficulties with the United States that culminated in an almost complete embargo of Cuban-U.S. trade in 1961, which deprived Cuba of both U.S. consumer goods and replacement parts for industrial and other equipment were among the causes for these economic problems.[8] As a consequence of them, "In March 1962, Fidel Castro had no choice but to decree rationing for a broad variety of staples: rice, beans, eggs, milk, fish, chicken, beef, oil, toothpaste, and detergent."[9] Subsequently, the list of rationed items was extended to virtually everything consumers bought, and to a greater or lesser degree rationing continued for the next three decades and beyond.

In 1961, the "vanguard" party was established to lead the revolution and monopolize power. The remains of the 26th of July Movement, the Partido Socialista Popular, and the Directorio Revolucionario were merged into the Organizaciones Revolucionarias Integradas (ORI). In the following year, after a showdown between Fidel Castro and the old-line Communists, who had dominated the process of establishing the new vanguard party, ORI was reorganized as the Partido Unico de la Revolución Socialista (PURS), of which Fidel Castro was secretary general, Raúl Castro was assistant secretary general, and a hand-picked Central Committee of twenty-five was named, fifteen from the old 26th of July, five from the PSP, and five from the Directorio Revolucionario. Finally, a further reorganization in 1965 brought into being the Partido Comunista de Cuba (PCC), with the same secretary general and assistant secretary general and a new Central Committee.

With the formal establishment of a new Communist Party, an effort was made to recruit members. Maurice Zeitlin described how this was done:

The workers in the plant nominate those who they believe merit Party membership, because of their outstanding qualities as workers and because of their "advanced" consciousness, "Marxist-Leninist" ideology, study and self-education, and devotion to the revolution. When the Party nucleus has investigated them thoroughly, an explanation and justification of the reasons why some are accepted and others are rejected for membership is given to the workers at large, and the decisions may be "ratified" or questioned by the workers, requiring the Party to investigate further those who the workers claim should not have been rejected. The Party may then admit them to membership in the plant—but final decisions remain the Party's.[10]

Although it was promised in 1965 that the PCC's First Congress would meet in the following year, that event was in fact "postponed" and did not take place until a decade later. Maurice Zeitlin, writing in 1969, noted that "there was no public debate about this decision, and there has been none about the fundamental questions concerning the revolution for several years." He also commented: "There is little question that in practice the Party is responsible to itself—and above all, to Fidel—and not to the citizenry at large. . . . The Central Committee was not chosen by the rank and file of the Party throughout the country, and there seems to be no inclination to carry out such elections within the party itself."[11]

During the period of transformation of the Castro regime, the international situation of Cuba was completely changed. Instead of the island's economy's being closely tied to that of the United States, its principal markets and sources of financing came to be the Soviet Union and the Soviet-controlled nations of Eastern Europe.

CASTRO'S BID FOR WORLD MARXIST-LENINIST LEADERSHIP

By the mid–1960s, the Marxist-Leninist reorganization of Cuban political life, society, and economy had been completed. Then, beginning in 1966 and extending for a bit more than two and a half years, there began one of the most interesting phases of the Cuban Revolution. During that period, Fidel Castro sought to make Havana the third center of world revolution, together with Moscow and Peking, and to make Cuba become the leader of the so-called Third World, the "developing" countries.

During that period, relations between Cuba and both the Soviet Union and China were very much strained. Castro and other Cuban leaders were voluble in their criticisms of both of the leading Communist-controlled countries.

In bidding for world leadership, the Castro regime presented its own "theoretical" position concerning both the Communist road to power and what a Communist regime should do with power once it possessed it. In the first instance, Castro and other Cuban leaders put forth the supposed model of their own road to power, arguing that the *foco* method of guerrilla warfare that Castro had used was the only feasible way for Communists to get control of a country. It argued that a revolution could be successful without an existing Communist Party that would prepare the political ground for the revolution, and that such a party would be established only after the revolution was successful.

In terms of the internal policies of Communist regimes that had gained power, Castroite theoretical doctrine in this period preached that "material" incentives should be supplanted by "moral" incentives. That is, workers should not be paid more for doing more work—a "capitalist remnant"—but should instead receive honors—medals, titles, pendants and so on—and should be appealed to in the name of patriotism and loyalty to the revolution (and if those appeals failed, should be coerced) to work harder, longer, and more intensively, rather than being compensated in economic terms for such efforts. This was an old controversy in the Soviet Union and China, one that Stalin had largely resolved in terms of material incentives, and on which the Chinese Communist regime had taken a mixed position, using both of moral and material incentives.

Maurice Zeitlin, before it was entirely clear that the Cuban leadership had abandoned their bid to establish Havana as the third center of the world revolution, wrote: "The revolutionary leaders have conspicuously rejected the Soviet model of 'how to construct Communism.' Cuba is 'the black sheep of the family,' as Fidel put it, 'because it does not follow the beaten path even if that path leads nowhere!' "[12]

The late Professor Sergio Roca summed up this particular period of the Cuban Revolution:

In 1965–66, Castro was vying for leadership of the worldwide revolutionary movement. The Cuban premier attempted to establish Havana as the political and ideological center of the Third World nations. During this time, Castro openly attacked Soviet and Chinese diplomatic efforts and economic policies, vigorously supported the creation of the Organization for Solidarity with African, Asian and Latin American Peoples, strongly backed African and Latin American guerrilla movements, and widely publicized Regis Debray's work on the *foco* theory of revolution. The ideological thrust of this movement scorned Soviet techniques of economic management (such as material incentives and profit as performance index), and rejected Soviet preferences for peaceful coexistence in the struggle for liberation in developing countries.[13]

The bid for world Communist leadership collapsed in 1968. At that time, Fidel Castro indicated his surrender to Soviet leadership by endorsing the Soviet and Eastern Bloc invasion of Czechoslovakia, although he did so in a speech conceding all of the charges made against the USSR in the Czechoslovakia situation were true but arguing that the invasion was justified anyway.

This surrender of Fidel was undoubtedly prompted by the growing economic difficulties of Cuba. Rationing had been introduced as early as 1962, and shortages intensified thereafter. Furthermore, the regime was faced with its promise to reach the goal of producing 10 million tons of sugar in 1970, which seemed in 1968 to be an all but unobtainable goal.

The 10-million-ton campaign was the result of another surrender to the Soviet leadership, in 1963. At that point, the Castro regime gave up its efforts—largely led by "Che" Guevara as minister of industry—to carry out the kind of rapid industrialization of Cuba that the Stalin regime had carried out a generation earlier in the USSR. Castro agreed instead to a "socialist division of labor," in the process of which Cuba would return to doing what it knew how to do, that is, growing sugar, which it would supply to the rest of the Soviet bloc—with, ideally, some extra to sell where it could earn hard currency.

In the eyes of the Castro regime, the 10-million-ton campaign was a failure. Although in 1970 the harvest in Cuba produced more sugar than ever before or since, some 8.5 million tons, Castro had made such a fetish of achieving the 10-million-ton goal as the supreme test of the Cuban Revolution that falling short by 1.5 million tons was a clear failure.

THE INSTITUTIONALIZATION OF THE REVOLUTION

There then followed what came to be known as the "institutionalization" of the Cuban Revolution. There were at least two aspects to this process. One was the calling of congresses of all the "mass organizations" that functioned under the Marxist-Leninist regime—the labor movement, the "independent" peasants' organization, the Cuban Federation of Women, the Committees for the Defense of the Revolution (city block organizations established in the early 1960s to spy on and discipline their neighbors), and finally the Communist Party of Cuba.

A new constitution was also adopted in 1976. It was patterned after the new constitution introduced by the Brezhenev regime in the Soviet Union, which made the president of the republic, rather than the prime minister, the principal governmental functionary and established a species of "supreme soviet," as the parliamentary body of the regime.

The other aspect of the institutionalization period were the increasing control by and economic dependence of Cuba on the Soviet Union. In 1972, after a trip to the USSR, Castro announced the establishment of a system of Cuban-Soviet binational committees, ostensibly to supervise the use of Soviet aid to Cuba. In fact, these committees for some period provided overall supervision of most sectors of the Cuban economy and society—including education.

During this period of institutionalization the Cuban economy became even more dependent on the Soviet bloc. One important innovation in the structure of this dependence was a process by which the USSR provided Cuba not only the petroleum necessary for its own economy, but a large surplus, which Cuba was then free to sell in the world market for hard currency. By the late

1980s, Soviet oil surpassed sugar as a source of foreign exchange.

In this period, too, the "international revolutionary solidarity" of Cuba with the Soviet Union was predominant in the country's foreign policy. From the early years of the revolution, international solidarity had been an important part of the Castro government's policies. The Cuban regime supported revolutionary attempts in a variety of Latin American countries, most notably "Che" Guevara's efforts in Bolivia in 1966–1967. Those efforts involved the Soviet Union very little or not at all.

However, in the 1970s this situation changed. Cuban troops were dispatched in large numbers, particularly to African countries in which the Soviet Union was trying to develop or maintain influence. Most notable were such incursions in Angola and Ethiopia; as over a period of years hundreds of thousands of Cuban troops were engaged in Angola.

In the later 1970s and early 1980s, Cuba also followed the Soviet lead in terms of internal economic policy. The government allowed establishment of peasant markets, where supply and demand rather than government fiat largely set prices. There was also a limited relaxation of control over individual artisans, electricians, plumbers, and the like, allowing them to ply their trades with relatively little government supervision or control.

Marifeli Pérez Stable noted that in this period the "struggle for the peso" superseded the "struggle for the Revolution." There was considerable corruption, labor discipline relaxed, and many workers worked for themselves, leaving their official jobs early to fix plumbing or to do some other private work that was then permitted. She also noted that there was considerable improvement in labor conditions, and that this was the only period since 1959 in which there was marked economic growth.[14]

However, in 1986 Fidel Castro reversed these policies. He decreed an end to peasant markets and other petty private enterprise, at the same time largely dismantling the Soviet-type central planning apparatus that had been characteristic of the regime in the institutionalization period. Castro seemed to be reverting to utter reliance on "moral incentives" once again.

THE "SPECIAL PERIOD"

The advent of Mikhail Gorbachev to the leadership of the Soviet Union presaged grave difficulties for the Cuban Marxist-
Leninist regime. Even in the early years of his regime, Gorbachev
gave evidence of a desire to cut back on Soviet obligations to the
Castro regime, most notably by beginning to limit the amount of
oil the Cubans could sell for hard currency in the world market.
Of course, with the fall of Gorbachev and the end of the Soviet
Union in 1991, all aid and most preferential terms of trade with
the USSR and what had been the Soviet Bloc in Eastern Europe
came to an end.

This catastrophe gave rise to what Castro labeled the "Special
Period in Times of Peace." There was a catastrophic fall in the
output of the Cuban economy: not only were there the customary
shortages of consumers' goods, but electricity (largely produced
by petroleum) and all kinds of raw materials, replacement parts
for Soviet-bloc produced machinery, and a wide variety of other
things were in exceedingly short supply.

Although the full impact on Cuba of the collapse of the Soviet-
East European Communist regimes was felt after the period that
is the focus of the present volume (after 1990), the beginning of
the crisis was evident considerably before that date, and the Castro regime's answer to it—a limited recourse to the market system
and encouragement of private foreign investment in the Cuban
economy, without forgoing the domination of the Communist
Party—had begun to become apparent.

The history of the Cuban labor movement from January 1,
1959, onward can only be understood against the background of
the implantation in Cuba, starting later in that year, of Marxist-
Leninist-Stalinist (and Fidelista) economy, society, and polity.

REVOLUTIONARY SEIZURE OF THE UNIONS

The labor movement felt immediately the impact of the fall of
the Batista dictatorship. At least nominally, the future of organized labor became the responsibility of the Frente Obrero Nacional
Unido (FONU), the underground group that had been established
a few weeks before the triumph of the Revolution.

At the same time as the flight of Batista the FONU consisted of seven representatives of the 26th of July Movement, five from the Communist Party (Partido Socialista Popular), four from the Ortodoxo Party's Labor Section, and three each from the Directorio Revolucionario and Auténticos. The 26th of July members of the FONU were David Salvador, Conrad Bécquer, José María de la Aguilera, Octavio Lloit, Jesús Soto, Antonio Torres, and José Pellón. The Communists were Ursinio Rojas, Vicente Valdéz, Benito Sánchez Diego, José Miguel Expino, and Octavio Fernández Roig. Isidoro Figueroa, Blas Castillo, Ramón Guirola, and Cecilio Guirola represented the Ortodoxos; Orlando Blanco, Pedro Martínez, and Leandro Borrera, the Directorio Revolucionario; and Rodrigo Lominchar, Oscar Martínez, and Pablo Balbuena, the Auténticos.[15]

In the days after the flight of General Batista, virtually all of the country's unions were physically seized by elements of what had before January 1, 1959, been the underground. In the great majority of cases, it was members of the 26th of July Movement who took over the base unions, federations, and CTC, although in some cases people in the Directorio Revolucionario, the Auténticos, and other groups, including the Communists, did so.

As the fall of Batista seemed imminent, the Sección Obrera of the 26th of July Movement had worked out an emergency plan, fearing that Batista might give way to some kind of military junta that essentially would continue his regime. It was decided that four people of the 26 de Julio in each workplace would take the initiative the moment Batista fell to go to their workplaces and proclaim the general revolutionary strike and seize control of the union involved. To a considerable degree, this is what happened on January 1, 1959.[16]

A week and a half after the flight of Batista, David Salvador, the new provisional head of the Confederación de Trabajadores de Cuba, told me that the headquarters of every union in the country, from the humblest local to the CTC itself, had been seized by the Labor Section of the 26th of July Movement, and representatives of that section had been put in charge of every union on a provisional basis.[17]

The process of seizure varied somewhat from case to case. In the Tobacco Workers Federation, the 26th of July people named a five-man committee, members of the 26 de Julio, provisionally to run the organization.[18] In the teachers' organization. the Colegio Nacional de Pedagogos, it was the leaders of the colegio's municipal organization in Havana who belonged to the 26 de Julio who ousted the national leadership; they then soon called an assembly of the Colegio Nacional, which confirmed the new group in office.[19] Among the metal workers, the 26 de Julio seized control of the Federación Metalúrgica, and members of the 26 de Julio were named as *responsables*, to head each of the federation's constituent unions.[20]

The 26th of July was particularly well organized among the dock workers. The secretary of organization of the movement in the port of Havana took control of the Maritime Workers Federation.[21]

This revolutionary seizure of the unions was soon legalized by the new government. Efrén Córdova noted: "A presidential decree provided for the constitution of all trade union officials and recognized the validity of the de facto executive organs which had been formed by the representatives of the various tendencies. These executives would remain in office until trade union elections were held."[22]

It was not always elements of the 26th of July who first seized control of individual unions. The leader of the Directorio Revolucionario underground group among the electrical workers recounted to me what he and others did on January 1. When it was announced that Batista had fled, people were not sure whether this was in fact true or was a trick being played by the Batista regime. For a while, no one dared leave home. However, he had arms and uniforms in his house, so at eight o'clock in the morning, he sallied forth with his uniform and weapon, got together at the Electrical Workers Federation headquarters with others of his group, and from there went to capture the city's principal electric plant, where they met no resistance. He then took fifteen others and seized radio-television station CMQ. Then they took the headquarters of the Investigations Bureau and the telephone building, as well as several other places. He added that they gave up each of these to the 26th of July people when those arrived.[23]

In the case of the Textile Federation, the headquarters were first seized by Communists. However, when 26 de Julio people arrived, the Communists turned over those headquarters to them. In this case (which was unusual), the 26th of July people agreed to share federation leadership with the Communists.[24]

The revolutionary seizure of the unions took place in the provinces as well as in Havana. For instance, in Matanzas, the first union to be taken over by the revolutionaries was that of the bank clerks. Elements of the 26th of July Movement underground seized that organization and established a temporary executive committee; they then on January 17 had a general assembly of the union that ratified the revolutionary committee as the provisional executive committee of the union.[25]

The underground labor leaders on the railroads had particularly grave problems. On both the Ferrocarriles Occidentales in the western part of the island and the Ferrocarriles Orientales in the east, the administrators of the railroads abandoned their jobs when they heard of the fall of Batista. As a consequence, the 26th of July unionists who took over control of the railroads had multiple jobs to accomplish. In addition to seizing union leadership, seeing to it that the railroaders adhered to the general strike call issued by Fidel Castro, they had to take over the task of restoring the railway operation once the strike was over. To run each of these railroads, they named Workers Administrative Councils, who remained in charge for several weeks.[26]

The process of seizure and temporary reorganization of the leadership of the Cuban labor movement of course involved the Confederación de Trabajadores of Cuba itself. After some confusion, a nine-man provisional national directorate for the CTC was named, presumably by the Labor Sector of the 26th of July Movement. It consisted of David Salvador as secretary general and Conrado Bécquer, José María de la Aguilera, Octavio Llouit, José Pellón, Reinol González, José de Jesús Plana, Jesús Soto, and Antonio Torres.

Although all members of this provisional executive group were from the 26th of July Movement, they represented varied points of view. David Salvador was an ex-Communist who by 1959 was quite opposed to the Communists; Conrado Bécquer was an ex-Auténtico, who had joined the 26 de Julio while fighting with Castro's guerrilla army and was also outspokenly opposed to the Communists. Reinol González and José de Jesús Plana were of Christian Democratic origin. The only two who were to a greater or lesser degree sympathetic to the Communists were José M. de la Aguilera and Jesús Soto.[27]

Aside from the 26th of July Movement and the Communists, some other political groups were also active in the labor movement during the first months of the Revolution. One of these was the Auténticos. The Comisión Obrera Nacional (CON) had been reestablished in 1953 by Auténtico labor people who opposed Eusebio Mujal's attempt to establish a "Labor Party" and had been very active in the labor underground in subsequent years, although quite a few who had been Auténticos joined the 26th of July Movement. A number of Auténtico labor leaders were jailed by the Batista regime, including Pablo Balbuena, the head of the revived CON, and Rodrigo Lominchar, the principal Auténtico figure among the sugar workers. Balbuena died a short time after the overthrow of the Batista regime as a result of torture he had received while in one of the dictator's poisons.

After the revolution, the CON came out into the open. It began reorganizing its followers in Havana and the provinces. The Auténticos had a policy of not serving in any of the provisional directorates of the CTC and its affiliates. When union elections were held, the Auténticos had some, but limited, successes in them.[28]

Early in January, I attended the first postrevolutionary open meeting of the CON. Different people reported on the political situation of the Auténticos in various union groups and the need for those who had joined the 26th of July Movement but still considered themselves Auténticos to reaffiliate with CON. There was some discussion of the process of reestablishing the Partido Auténtico itself as a legal party, and there were several expressions of optimism about the future of the party and of the CON in particular.[29]

THE RENEWAL OF COLLECTIVE BARGAINING

The provisional leadership of the unions and federations that took over after January 1, 1959, almost immediately began the process of collective bargaining with the employers. This continued after elections had put in office what were supposedly more permanent executives in the local unions and the federations, and by September 1959 most labor organizations had worked out new collective agreements with employers.

In this early phase of the Cuban Revolution, collective bargaining and the general administration of the labor movement were undertaken with a different orientation from that which had prevailed since the late 1930s. David Salvador, the interim general secretary of the Confederación de Trabajadores, spoke for most of his colleagues when he told me in January 1959 that they wanted to build a labor movement on the basis of "complete independence of the government." He added that organized labor should not be "a dependency of the Ministry of Labor," as it had in the past.[30]

However, the conciliation and arbitration units of the Ministry of Labor were exceedingly active during the first months of the Revolution. Efrén Córdova estimated that as many as 10,000 meetings of this kind were held in the ministry and its provincial offices during the first half of 1959.[31]

Understandably, one of the most persistent demands by the new union leaders was that for wage increases. At first, the new CTC leadership decided to seek a general over-the-board wage increase for all workers. However, they soon abandoned this idea and left the issue to the various unions to negotiate individually with their respective employers' groups.[32]

Agreements on wages varied considerably. In the tobacco industry, upward wage adjustments varied between 13 percent and

45 percent, depending on the particular union involved. These unions also gained enforcement of the legal provision for nine days of sick leave per year, payable at the end of the year if it had not been used during that period.[33] Food industry workers obtained increases varying from 20 percent to 40 percent.[34]

In the case of the hotel and restaurant workers, emphasis in bargaining was on negotiating equalization of wages rather than general increases. However, a number of fringe benefits were also obtained.[35]

The reorganized Miners Federation helped its unions get substantial wage increases, which ran as high as 35 percent. That federation and its unions put major stress, however, on ensuring that provisions of collective contracts that were already in place were in fact enforced, as the new leaders claimed that they had not been in the Batista-Mujal period.[36]

In the construction industry, too, the unions succeeded in getting some wage increases. However, they regarded the establishment of a minimum wage, which no previous union leadership had accomplished, their most important gain. They also obtained agreement to the 1934 legal provision for nine-day paid sick leave.[37]

In the drug and pharmacy industry, the unions put emphasis in their bargaining on issues other than wage increases. Several of these unions obtained group insurance policies, paid for by the employers, covering life, medical attention and hospitalization, and accidents outside the workplace. These benefits applied only to the workers themselves, but the union leaders were hoping to extend them subsequently to members of the workers' families.[38]

Among the shoe workers unions, collective bargaining was directed toward trying to standardize wages. This was designed to overcome the kind of cut-throat competition among workers that resulted from the piecework wages that predominated in that industry.[39]

In the case of the Grazing and Slaughterhouse Workers Federation, its unions were able to obtain wage increases totaling about $1,500,000 a year; and one big milk pasteurizing plant agreed to pay an additional $170,000 to its workers. But that federation put special emphasis on trying to assure that the legal minimum wage in agriculture and grazing of $75 a month was actually paid by the employers.[40]

Some union groups had particular problems in their industries that they sought to deal with in collective bargaining. Thus, the bank workers unions had considerable success in securing a reduction of the number of bank workers who were officially classified as "confidential employees" and thus ineligible for membership in the union. Insofar as wages were concerned, the bank workers union adapted their demands to the capacity of the various banks to pay more. They made a close study of the situation of each bank, to see how much it could afford to give, and then fit their demands to the capacity of the bank.[41]

In the case of the sugar workers, the unions at first demanded substitution of four six-hour shifts for the three eight-hour shifts that were customary. They also wanted reestablishment of the system whereby the workers got a share of the income from the sugar harvest if the price of sugar exceeded a fixed amount—a provision that had largely been abrogated during the Batista dictatorship.[42]

The overthrow of Batista occurred virtually at the beginning of the 1959 sugar harvest. As a result, the sugar workers gave up their demand for the four-shift system, when Fidel Castro generally appealed to the union leaders to do so, arguing that such a sudden shift in work would interfere with the harvest. However, the sugar unions did receive wage raises ranging from 12 percent to 30 percent, through the mediation procedure of the Ministry of Labor.[43]

In a few instances, the new collective agreements called for checkoff of union dues by the employers. Although the compulsory checkoff (and payment of dues directly to the CTC) was one of the most hated aspects of the labor policy of the Batista dictatorship, some unionists favored it on a voluntary basis. It was part of the collective agreements signed by the unions of the Bank Workers Federation and some of the local units of the Sugar Workers Federation, among others. However, there was provision in such agreements that the employer could not deduct union dues from worker's wages or salaries without written permission of the individual worker.[44]

Efrén Córdova noted that "the position of the Cuban worker achieved in reality its highest level of well being in 1959."[45]

In the early months of the new regime, the government more or less openly supported the workers' demands in the collective bargaining process. However, in September, Fidel Castro, in a three-hour speech to a meeting of the National Council of the Confederación de Trabajadores, urged the assembled union leaders to moderate their demands, arguing that the workers' increased purchasing power was increasing the demand for imports, which had to be paid for in foreign currency, which was in increasingly short supply. He also argued that both the private sector and the government needed increased resources for investment, so that the Cuban economy could produce more of the goods that the workers wanted to purchase with their wages and salaries. This speech presaged the kind of line that Castro would begin to take a few months later in a more extensive and peremptory form. At this meeting, his appeal met what might be best called a mixed reception.[46]

Collective bargaining proceeded during these early months of 1959 with few strikes. There were probably several reasons for this. Given the revolutionary situation, employers were hesitant to be recalcitrant in negotiating with their workers. Perhaps the desire of much of the new union leadership to establish for the labor movement a degree of independence that it had not had in the past led them to try to prevent situations that might provoke government intervention in labor disputes.

It is also the case that top government officials, particularly Fidel Castro, used their influence generally to avoid strikes. Fidel made personal appeals to both the oil workers and the sugar workers not to strike.[47]

ISSUES IN LOCAL UNION ELECTIONS AND
FEDERATION CONGRESSES

At the time the unions were seized by the anti-Batista underground in the first days of January 1959, the 26th of July Movement Labor Section announced its intention to hold union elections within thirty to ninety days. This had been promised by the 26th of July at meetings in rebel held territory before the victory of the revolution. In fact, the electoral process in virtually all of the country's base unions went on during the first months of the regime, followed by congresses of each of the thirty-three labor federations to choose the definitive leadership of those organizations.

In the run-up to union elections at least two important issues arose. One was whether people who had held union offices during the Batista period would be able to run for office in the reorganized unions. The other was whether the 26th of July Movement, which dominated most of the provisional union officialdom established right after the overthrow of Batista, should run its own slates in the elections or should have joint lists of candidates, and particularly whether such joint slates should include Communists.

In the discussions of who could run for union office in the first few months of the Cuban Revolution, the people who held those posts at the time of the fall of the Batista dictatorship were not a consideration. As we have noted, they had been removed from their positions by decree of the new government, and there was virtually unanimous agreement that they should under no circumstances be allowed to return to office in the foreseeable future.

In any case, most of the important Mujalista trade union leaders disappeared from the scene. Efrén Córdova noted, "No prominent leader of the Mujalista CTC was executed, but a large number of them sought asylum, others were jailed and not a few escaped from the country in a more peremptory fashion."[48]

Although those who had been supporters of Eusebio Mujal throughout the Batista period were clearly banned from taking part in the union elections of early 1959, there was considerable debate over whether those who had continued for some time in the union leadership during the second Batista period but had broken with Mujal and consequently had been ousted from their leadership positions should be able to do so. The most important figure of this kind was Angel Cofiño, founder and long head of the Electrical Workers Federation, who had been removed from that position by Mujal and spent the last two years of the Batista regime in exile.

Opinions were divided, in his federation and more generally, concerning whether Cofiño should have the right to seek reelection to his old position. He admittedly still had considerable support among the electrical workers.[49] The issue was finally decided by an assembly of Cofiño's base union, that of the electrical workers of Havana. That body voted to ban him from holding office in the union for ten years, citing as a justification the fact that he had signed his name to a declaration denouncing the March 13, 1957, attack by the Directorio Revolucionario on the presidential palace. Cofiño did not appeal the decision and for the time being returned to his job with the electric company in Havana.[50] César Lancis, long a leader of the Federation of Traveling Medical Salesmen, an Auténtico and an opponent of Mujal in the second Batista period, was similarly banned from holding office by an assembly of his organization.[51]

There were obviously exceptions to the banning of those who had for some time held important positions in the union leadership during the second Batista period. One of the most important of these was Conrado Bécquer, who in 1959 emerged as secretary general of the Sugar Workers Federation (FNT). He had been an Auténtico, had remained a member of the national executive of the FNTA until 1955, had participated in the Batista regime's 1954 election, and had been elected to Congress on the ticket of Grau San Martín's faction of the Auténtico Party. However, in 1957 he went to the mountains to join Castro's forces and joined the 26th of July Movement.[52]

More widely debated than the possible role in 1959 union elections of those who had held union office during the second Batista dictatorship was the issue of the types of political alliances, if any, that should be formed during these elections. This issue was particularly important in the 26th of July Movement.

In the early months of the revolution, the great majority of the unionists supported the 26 de Julio, and it dominated the provisional leadership of the CTC and its affiliates established immediately after the flight of Batista. However, the 26th of July labor leaders were by no means a homogenous group; there was particular division of opinion concerning the attitude that should be adopted toward the Communists within the labor movement, and in general.

One 26 de Julio member of the Provisional Executive of the CTC, who was also a leader of the Unión de Trabajadores Cristianos, explained to me in June 1959 that there were divisions among the 26th of July of labor people insofar as relations with the Communists were concerned. A few, he said, were overtly pro-Communist. Most of the new union leaders were "non-Communists" in the beginning. But he claimed that the rank and file were generally anti-Communist, and they put pressure on these people to form no alliance with the Communists.[53]

There also undoubtedly existed a number a number of 26th of July labor leaders who might be labeled Communist fellow travelers, asserting their independence from the Communists but working more or less closely with them. In Cuban parlance of the period they were *melones*, that is, green (the color of the 26th of July) on the outside, but red (the color of the Communist Party) on the inside.

Most of the top 26th of July labor leaders argued from the beginning that their group should run their own candidates and make no deals with other political groups. Early in January, David Salvador, speaking to a meeting of the 26th of July union leaders, said that although the 26 de Julio would not try to bar any political group from running candidates, they would not make any deals, as previous union leaders had, to parcel out positions among various political groups. They would not back anyone who did not belong to their own ranks and insist that the workers vote for these people because of a deal they had made.[54] In that same period, Octavio Lloit, then the second most important 26th of July labor leader, was more explicit in conversation with me, saying that the 26J would not under any circumstances run any joint slates with the Communists.[55]

The Communists were very eager for a deal with the 26th of July for the union elections. It was reported at the time that they had first proposed an arrangement with the 26th of July to divide all union posts one to one between the two groups, which the 26 de Julio quickly turned down. The Communists then suggested a broader arrangement whereby, by previous agreement, union posts would be divided among the 26 de Julio, Partido Socialista Popular (Communist Party), Directorio Revolucionario, and other groups, which the 26J also rejected. As a consequence, in most cases, the Communists were forced to go it alone in the elections that took place in the base unions, and then in the congresses of the various federations of the CTC.[56]

The 26th of July trade unionists received support in their decision not to make any deal with the Communists from Fidel Castro. He issued a statement to the effect that the 26th of July Movement would not make pacts with any other political group in the trade union elections, which heartened many of the 26J leaders who did not want to have any agreements with the Communists but were afraid that refusal to do so might run against the 26th of July Movement's policy.[57] At about the same time, Fidel Castro accused the Communists of "perturbing" the progress of the revolution.[58]

RESULTS OF UNION ELECTIONS AND FEDERATION CONGRESS

The 26th of July Movement was overwhelmingly victorious in the local union elections held during the first months of the new regime. A few examples will indicate the extent of these triumphs.

In the key Federación Nacional Trabajadores Azucareros (sugar workers), the Communists won control of only 17 of the 140 unions in the federation; the 26th of July swept most of the others.[59] In the congress of the federation that was held in May to complete its reorganization, about 90 percent of the delegates were members of the 26th of July.[60] The delegates to that congress had been the four top officials of each local union. Of the more than 900 delegates present, only 13 were Communists.[61]

In the Tobacco Workers Federation, like that of the sugar workers a onetime bulwark of Communist support in the labor movement, the 26th of July was also generally victorious. It won control of all of the unions in Havana, although the Communists were victorious in a few unions in the interior—in Oriente, for instance, they captured four of the eighteen unions in the province; the rest went to 26J.[62]

The Maritime Workers Federation, also a onetime stronghold of the Communists, also saw a wide victory of the 26th of July in the local union elections. Of the 218 unions, only 6 were captured

by the Communists; the rest were won by the 26th of July. All of
the unions won by the Communists were in Havana, and only one
of these, the stevedores, was considered of strategic importance.
When, after the elections, the Federación Obrera Maritima Nacional
held its congress, it chose an exclusively 26th of July executive
committee.[63]

In the Electrical Workers Federation there were two lists of
candidates, one backed by the 26th of July, the other by the ex-
leader of the federation, Angel Cofiño. The 26J ticket won by
about 2,000 votes. There were no Communists elected; one of the
new leaders claimed that there were only 12 Communists among
the 5,000 members of the federation. The 26th of July list included a member of the Directorio Revolucionario, who became
secretary of organization of the Havana electrical workers union.[64]

In a few other unions, the 26th of July included members of
other groups on its list of candidates. For instance, in the construction workers union, the Sindicato de Albaniles, Carpinteros
y Anexos of Havana, there were members of the Directorio
Revolucionario and the Triple A, a dissident Auténtico group,
among the candidates supported by the 26J.[65]

In a handful of unions, the 26th of July ran joint lists of candidates with the Communists. However, in one such case, the
Liquor Workers Union of Havana, many union voters crossed out
the names of the four Communists and wrote in the names of
four 26th of July members, who were elected in place of the
Communists.[66]

In the Metal Workers Federation, the 26th of July Movement
won the elections in all of the local unions in the interior. However, the Communists won in several of the unions in Havana. At
the subsequent congress of the federation, there were sixty-eight
delegates of the July 26th Movement and twenty-three Communists.[67]

The 26th of July Movement swept the union elections in the
interior of the republic as well as in Havana. For instance, in Matanzas, of the 125 unions in the province, only 10 did not elect
26J administrations. The Communists won control of 2—the
printers union and one sugar union—and the Auténticos and Directorio Revolucionario both were victorious in a few unions.[68]

One of the few clear victories of the Communists was in the
Shoemakers Union of Havana. There, after the election had been
postponed twice as a result of 26 de Julio pressure, the Communists' ticket defeated that of the 26th of July by 1,400 to 800
voters; a third group received 400 votes.[69]

Efrén Córdova summed up the results of the union elections:
"The M-26-7 [26th of July Movement] won the elections over-

whelmingly. . . . Only in the hotel and restaurant, textile and aviation sectors could the candidates of the PSP prevail. In total, it was calculated that the M-26-7 triumphed in more than 1,800 unions. The Communists thus paid the price for their ambiguous attitude during the dictatorship of Batista."

Córdova went on, "After the elections in the base unions came the national assemblies to elect the leaders of the federations. There were no surprises here either, since the results indicated that of the 33 industrial federations, 26 elected anticommunist leaderships, three were on the side of the PSP and the other four chose to elect mixed or neutral directing bodies." In the case of the FNTA, it not only elected no Communists but rejected the credentials of Ursinio Rojas, the ranking Communist leader in the organization.

Finally, Córdova noted: "Other national Congresses, including those of the construction workers, commercial employees and workers in medicine adopted resolutions opposing any form of collaboration with the PSP. In some of the others, the Communist minority felt so frustrated that it abstained from voting and left the scene of the congress."[70]

One important exception to the general triumph of non-Communist 26 de Julio people was the Federación Gastronómica, the organization of hotel and restaurant workers, which had long been the base of Francisco Aguirre. The *responsable* originally put in charge of that federation in January was a Communist or fellow traveler. He insisted on a "unity" slate of 26th of July and the Communists, the latter of whom largely dominated that federation later.[71]

The weak position of the Communists in the labor movement after the base unions' elections and the congresses of the federations was shown at the time of the meeting in September 1959 of the National Council of the Confederación de Trabajadores de Cuba. Only 3 of the 163 delegates to that meeting were Communists.[72]

The Communists attacked many of the local union elections and the federation congresses as "dishonest and antidemocratic." However, an official statement of the National Labor Section of the 26th of July Movement, made in answer to an attack by Joaquín Ordoqui, one of the PSP's principal leaders, commented:

However, we have observed that the socialists virtually attack the congresses and union elections, alleging dishonest and antidemocratic procedures only where the result has been adverse to them. However, they have defended and continue defending frankly antidemocratic elections where they have won representation. There is Mujalism or democracy, depending on what is convenient.[73]

DISSIDENCE WITHIN CTC TOP LEADERSHIP

As we have noted, the Labor Section of the 26th of July Movement was by no means homogeneous. In part, the differences within the group resulted from personal ambition, but they also reflected different ideological tendencies within the 26 de Julio.

One controversy arose over a Statement of Humanism, which put forward the position which Fidel Castro was presumably then supporting, that the Cuban Revolution was "humanist" in inspiration, rejecting the evils of both Communism and capitalism. It was endorsed by a majority of the newly elected 26th of July leaders of the various federations of the CTC. However, it was opposed and strongly denounced by Jesús Soto, of the Textile Workers Federation, who claimed that it did not reflect the position of the CTC.[74] In this controversy, Soto gave evidence, which was to be confirmed a few month later, that he was one of the "melons," green on the outside and red on the inside.

Another controversy that brought up the Communist issue centered on Antonio Collada, newly elected secretary of organization of the Construction Workers Federation. He had a long record—both as an Auténtico and subsequently as a member of the 26 de Julio—of opposition to the Communists, and in the early months of the revolution he came under severe attack from them, who alleged that he had been a "Mujalista." This issue was raised in the XXIV National Council meeting in September 1959, when he gave a passionate defense of his role during the second Batista dictatorship. He said that he remained an Auténtico. He had resigned from a leadership post in the Construction Federation right after the March 1952 coup but had continued to head the Marble Workers Union, which he had led out on a successful strike in December 1956 against the wishes of the Mujal leadership of the CTC. Soon afterward, he had gone into the underground, where he had worked with, among others, David Salvador and Jesús Soto.[75] Although many of the 26 de Julio labor leaders felt that the attacks launched against Collada at the National Council meeting were principally motivated by the Communists,[76] that meeting decided to establish an investigating committee to look into the charges that had been made against him.[77]

The most publicized dissidence within the 26th of July leadership in the labor movement was that raised by José María de Aguilera and the Bank Workers Federation, of which he was the secretary general. He told me in June that the National Council of his federation had formally nominated him for the post of CTC secretary general in preparation for the confederation's first postrevolutionary congress.[78]

The campaign of Aguilera and his federation against Salvador and other top 26th of July figures in the CTC and its federations intensified as time went on. Early in September, the Bank Workers Federation issued a Declaration of Principles, which, together with reiterated pledges of loyalty to Fidel Castro, attacked the CTC leadership. It alleged "Erroneous practices used in some industry congresses and in certain trade union elections and the presence of well known Mujalista elements in the leadership of unions and federations." It also claimed that it was "inexplicable that in the provisional leadership of the Revolutionary CTC rightist attitudes and erroneous concepts prevail which place the labor movement not in the vanguard of the Revolution but in contradiction with developments, provoking dissent and unhappiness among the workers."

The tenth and final point in this Declaration of Principles proclaimed:

Finally we issue a call to all the trade union leaders and all the workers to unite their actions and efforts to make of the Revolutionary CTC an organization which supports the wishes of the workers, trade union democracy, classist principles, and which marches in accord with the postulates of the Revolution and of its leader Fidel Castro, whom we support with all our forces and our greatest enthusiasm.[79]

In conversation with me, Aguilera asserted that the CTC Executive had "not paid enough attention to the quality of personnel in the executives of the various unions and federations," adding that "a number of bad people" had thus obtained important positions. He did note, however, that by then all of the union officials were elected. Aguilera said that his position had the support not only of his own federation but of the hotel and restaurant, chemical, textile, and airline workers' federations.[80]

Some of Aguilera's colleagues went even further in criticizing the CTC leadership. One of the Bank Workers Federation officials claimed to me that there was a crisis in the CTC because "the leaders of the various organizations have been imposed from the top" and were people who were not prepared for the jobs that they had assumed.[81]

Those under attack claimed that Aguilera was motivated by a desire to be CTC secretary general. Conrad Bécquer noted that Aguilera had never presented his complaints to the CTC Provisional Executive, adding that there was no truth in his claim that elections in the unions and federations had not been honest and correct. Bécquer added that Aguilera was playing into the hands of the Communists, in their campaign against the 26 de Julio leadership of the CTC.[82] The U.S. labor attaché agreed with Bécquer's claim that Aguilera's attacks on other CTC leaders were motivated by the desire to be CTC secretary general, adding that Aguilera "did not have a chance" of getting that post.[83]

For his part, Aguilera said that his criticisms of the CTC leadership were motivated by his fear that if the evils he criticized continued, the Communists would be able to gain ground in the labor movement. But he added that he had no hesitation to join the Communists in their criticisms of the CTC leadership at times.[84] One case in which he clearly did so was in the campaign against Antonio Collada in the XXIV Council of the CTC.[85]

THE QUESTION OF EXTERNAL AFFILIATION

One of the issues that was extensively debated within the labor movement during the months before the Tenth Congress of the CTC in November 1959 was whether the Confederación de Trabajadores de Cuba should continue to be a member of the International Confederation of Free Trade Unions (ICFTU) and its Inter American affiliate, the ORIT. The CTC, of course, had been a founding member of the ICFTU, as well as of the ORIT and its predecessor, the Interamerican Confederation of Workers (CIT).

There was general unhappiness among the leaders of the Cuban labor movement about the way ORIT (and to a lesser degree, ICFTU) had dealt with "Cuban problem" (the Mujal group's relations with Batista) during the years of the second Batista dictatorship. However, there was at first a feeling among many of the new leaders of Cuban labor that the CTC should continue in the ORIT and ICFTU and seek to "reform" the former. Those opposed to that position proposed the idea of the Cubans' taking the lead in establishing a new Latin American labor confederation.

In one of the early meetings of the Provisional CTC Executive Committee there was a long discussion of the international affiliation of the confederación. A notion to have the CTC withdraw from the ORIT, and denouncing the behavior of the U.S. and Mexican delegations to the December 1958 Bogotá Conference of the ORIT, had substantial support but was finally tabled.[86]

In January, Octavio Lloit, the second most important figure in the new provisional leadership of the CTC, told me that the intention of the new labor leadership was that the CTC stay in the ORIT and ICFTU. He added that although there was a great deal of resentment about the way these organizations had dealt with the Cuban situation, they thought that the ORIT could be changed and wanted to stay in it and help make the changes.[87]

As late as September 1959, Conrado Bécquer, the secretary general of the Sugar Workers Federation, told me the same thing. He added that the FNTA belonged to the Plantation Workers International Federation, associated with the ICFTU; that the president of that group was a Cuban, Samuel Powell, who, said Bécquer, although a friend of Eusebio Mujal, had not been a "Batistiano," but had always remained a supporter of Carlos Prío's faction of the Auténtico Party. The new FNTA leadership intended to stay in that organization and was willing to accept Powell's remaining in his post until the next congress of the Plantation International.[88]

Similarly, one of the new leaders of the Maritime Workers Federation (FOMN) told me that they supported letting the CTC remain in the ICFTU and ORIT and intended not only to let the FOMN remain in the ICFTU-connected International Transport Workers Federation, but to become more active in that organization.[89]

Reinol González, the secretary of international affairs of the Provisional CTC Executive Committee, an ex-secretary general of the Juventud Obrera Católica (Catholic Labor Youth), also favored keeping the CTC in ICFTU and ORIT. He took this position in January 1959, even though a few weeks before the fall of Batista, he had had an unhappy personal experience, as representative of the 26 de Julio Labor Section, in trying unsuccessfully to get the Bogotá Conference of the ORIT to condemn strongly the Batista regime and the then leaders of the CTC's collaboration with that regime. His conviction that continued affiliation was the correct policy was reinforced by the fact that by midyear he had been named the Cuban member of the Executive Committee of the ORIT, confirming his belief that the ORIT could be reformed and the Cubans should remain in it to create such transformation.[90]

During this period, the dominant elements in the CTC leadership made it clear that they wanted to maintain friendly relations with the U.S. labor movement. One example of this was a cable sent by David Salvador to David McDonald, head of the United Steelworkers of America, which was then on strike. It read: "A million and a half affiliates of the Revolutionary CTC offer total moral support to the 500,000 metallurgical workers' strikes. STOP We hope quick triumph in demands made. STOP We offer our solidarity as a principle of social justice and trade union rights. STOP."[91]

The Auténticos strongly supported continued affiliation with the ORIT and ICFTU.[92]

One major opponent of continued CTC affiliation with the ORIT was José María de Aguilera of the Bank Workers Federation. He told me in September that he felt that the ORIT "had not fulfilled its purposes," as was shown by its continuing to work with the Mujal leadership of the CTC until the overthrow of the Batista regime. He professed to believe that it was impossible to reform the ORIT, so he opposed the CTC's remaining in it.[93]

By September 1959, it seemed most likely that the CTC would stay in the ORIT and ICFTU. I reported to Jay Lovestone of the AFL-CIO:

During the 24th Council of the CTC a motion was introduced, urging that the CTC withdraw from the ORIT and ICFTU pending the November congress of the Confederación de Trabajadores de Cuba. This motion was voted down almost unanimously, with only three votes being cast in its favor. The only speech given on the occasion was one supporting the motion, but Octavio Lloit, who was presiding the at the time, treated it with virtual contempt, and there were numerous representatives of various Latin American labor groups in Havana, and Venezuelan and Chilean representatives urged the CTC to take the lead in establishing a new Latin American confederation, the Cubans refused to do so.[94]

PREPARATIONS FOR THE TENTH CONGRESS OF THE CTC

By the time the first postrevolutionary congress of the Confederación de Trabajadores de Cuba (Tenth Congress) began its sessions on November 18, 1959, it is clear (at least in retrospect) that Fidel Castro had made his decision to side with the faction of the 26th of July Movement that wanted to convert the Cuban Revolution into a Marxist-Leninist revolution. This decision was amply reflected during the labor congress.

At least two kinds of preparations were made for the Tenth Congress of the CTC. One of these was made by Fidel Castro, who dismissed the man who had served as minister of labor since the beginning of the year, Manuel Fernández García, and replaced him with Augusto Martínez Sánchez. Fernández García had a political background in Acción Revolucionaria Guiterista and was described as having "little administrative experience and irreproachable intentions." He had connections with the Catholic labor element in the 26 de Julio and had "tried to foster the creation of labor tribunals and to favor other measures designed to improve the climate of worker-management relations."

Martínez Sánchez, on the other hand, had been a comandante in the part of the Rebel Army headed by Raúl Castro, had been minister of defense before being transferred to labor. He took with him several pro-Communists to man key parts of his new ministry.[95] The task of the new minister of labor, as soon became clear, was to help change the nature of the labor movement.

With the replacement of Fernández by Martínez Sánchez, there was a massive turnover in the personnel of the Ministry of Labor. Robert Kenneth Warren noted, "Other non-Communist Labor Ministry personnel were smeared and harassed to the extent that practically all left their jobs en masse and were quickly replaced by personnel that the Communist had already trained."[96]

The second form of preparation for the CTC Tenth Congress was the election of delegates to that meeting. As had been true in the local sindicato elections and those for the various federation congresses, various political groups competed in the elections for CTC Congress delegates. The two most important contestants were the 26th of July Movement and the Communists, although there were also candidates presented by the Directorio Revolucionario, the Organización Auténtica and the dissident Auténtico group Triple A, headed by the onetime Minister of Education Aureliano Sánchez Arango.

As in the earlier union elections, the 26th of July won overwhelmingly, getting 2,784 of the 3,200 delegates, some 87 percent, whereas the Communists won only 224 delegates, or 7 percent, and other groups together elected 193 delegates, about 6 percent. However, as indicated by Efrén Córdova, the 26th of July delegates were by no means a homogeneous group.[97]

LEADERSHIP STRUGGLE IN THE CTC TENTH CONGRESS

The Tenth Congress of the Confederación de Trabajadores de Cuba opened on November 18, 1959. In addition to the 2,948 regular delegates seated by the credentials committee, there were present at this session a number of foreign invitees. These include Vicente Lombardo, head of the Communist Latin American group the CTAL, representatives of the Soviet and Yugoslav trade unions, as well as people from three world trade union groups (the Communists' World Federation of Trade Unions, the International Confederation of Free Trade Unions, and International Federation of Christian Trade Unions), as well as from the ORIT.[98]

Although a variety of different resolutions were passed during the nearly six days that the congress met, the great majority of the time spent and the preponderant issue debated related to the election of new leadership for the confederation. This issue arose at the opening session and continued to be the principal order of business until shortly before the meeting came to an end.

At the opening session of the CTC Congress there were four speakers: David Salvador, Minister of Labor Martínez Sánchez, and Raúl and Fidel Castro. Salvador argued that the congress should dedicate itself to support of the revolution and to this end urged that the workers donate 4 percent of their wages to a fund for the industrialization of the country and the CTC should forgo the compulsory checkoff of union dues.

The labor minister and the two Castro brothers called for "unity" in the labor movement; the clear indication was that the Communists should share in the leadership of the CTC. Particularly during Fidel Castro's speech there were conflicting chants for "Unity" and "Twenty-six" from the Communist and 26 de Julio delegates. Fidel concluded that the labor movement should be characterized by "discipline, brotherhood and unity."[99]

The suggestion of the Castro brothers and Martínez Sánchez that the Communists' small minority should have equal weight with the overwhelming 26th of July majority in the future direction of the labor movement became the major subject of debate in the congress. Delegates of twenty-five of the thirty-three federations announced their categorical opposition to inclusion of the Communists in the future leadership of the CTC. Only five— airline, hotel and restaurant, textile workers, salesmen, and insurance and finance workers—supported an "arrangement" with the Communists; the remaining three took no clear position.

A Uruguayan trade unionist who attended the conference, Juan Acuña, recorded what was taking place:

While the federations deliberated and transmitted to Fidel Castro their decisions, in the hall of the congress and in the nearby streets there was an extraordinary and exemplary spectacle. Thousands of workers and delegates argued with vehemence, provoking not a few incidents and fist-fights which brought intervention of the police, arrests, etc., denouncing or insulting communism for its betrayals, for its connivance and collaboration with the dictatorship of Batista. . . . The multitude demanded as fundamental and essential the exclusion of Communist elements from the Executive Council of the CTC.[100]

Efrén Córdova summarized what was happening in the congress.

During more than ten hours the room in which the congress was under way was practically taken over by the delegates of M-26-7 who showed and waved signs, sang the hymn of the revolution and accused and repudiated communism. . . . A feverish atmosphere charged with passion had invaded the Congress. Two bands faced one another, one of the majority but lacking official support and the other in the minority but patronized from above. The session of the Congress could hardly proceed with its debates, so many were the meetings and consultations.[101]

Córdova added that

one thing was certain: the X Congress had seen the most pronounced explosion of anticommunism that had even been seen in Cuban trade unionism. So conspicuous, for example, was the hissing of the Soviet observer P. T. Pimenov, that the President of the Congress, Conrad Bécquer, had to intervene so that he could continue his speech. Shouts of protest were heard any time alliance with the Communists was mentioned. Things got so extreme that the executives of the 25 industrial federations opposed to this alliance let it be known that they would withdraw from the CTC-R if the proposal of Castro was accepted.[102]

In the face of this clear rejection by the 26th of July trade unionists of Castro's demand that they share leadership with the Communists, Fidel decided to intervene personally in the situation. He appeared late in the night of November 22, at what should have been the closing session of the Congress "and the delegates were exhausted." He entered in a military uniform, with a pistol at his side, with its holster open, and accompanied by bodyguards.

As Castro began his speech, he was greeted by shouts of "Twenty-six, twenty-six." At that point, he shouted that the only people who had the right to use the slogan were those who had participated in the attempt to seize the Moncada barracks on July 26, 1953.

Then Castro "continuing with an aggressive tone . . . accused those who attacked the government of being counterrevolutionaries." Then he commented, "I cannot but feel myself defied when I see that the working class denies itself the opportunity of defending and guiding the revolution." He added, "That class must convert itself into an army to defend the revolution and within an army there was no room for factions." At one point, he accused those opposed to the Communists' inclusion in the CTC leadership of being "counterrevolutionaries" and "criminals."

As an apparent concession to the anti-Communist attitude of most of his audience, Castro then said that he had sought to achieve "harmony" in the labor movement and had not suggested any particular pact. He added, "The important thing is that there be elected true revolutionaries and to put aside evil."

Fidel then made a move to "solve" the situation. He suggested that "a wide vote of confidence be given to a qualified person 'who would be responsible to the workers and the government,' to choose the new leadership." There were then shouts that that person should be David Salvador, and finally it was voted that he should draw up the list of members of the new Executive Committee of the CTC and submit that list for approval by the Congress.[103]

Shortly afterward, David Salvador met in the office of the director of the government newspaper *Revolución* with the director, Fidel Castro, and Minister of Labor Martínez Sánchez. It was that group that chose the new leadership of the CTC.

Dropped from the Executive Committee that had been in office since January were two Christian Democratic members, Reinol González and José de Jesús Plana, who had been vociferously anti-Communist, as well as Antonio Torres and Conrado Bécquer, "about whose loyalty there were still reservations." Octavio Lloit, in spite of having expressed himself as opposed to conceding the Communists' positions in the leadership, was chosen for the new Executive, as were José Pellón, José María de la Aguilera, and Jesús Soto. It was decided that David Salvador would continue as secretary general. No known Communists were selected, although several of those named were among the "melons," green on the outside and red on the inside.

Efrén Córdova categorized those selected for the new Executive, which was expanded to twenty-seven members, as "a hybrid leadership, but in the majority innocuous and usable by the government." The list was then taken back to the Congress at five o'clock in the morning of November 23 and was approved by the exhausted delegates virtually without debate—although proforma a Communist representative read a statement indicating the intention of the Communists to abstain from voting for the list proposed by Salvador.[104]

In spite of the attention centering on the selection of a new leadership, a number of resolutions were passed by the Tenth Congress. One was to withdraw from the ICFTU and the ORIT and to undertake to launch a new Latin American labor confederation. (The CTC subsequently joined the Communists' World Federation of Trade Unions.) Another suggested that the holding of general elections in Cuba be postponed "until the country was well advanced on the road to honesty, economic security and welfare." There were also resolutions dealing with problems of individual worker groups.

No formal resolution calling for a further purge of the leadership of the CTC and its constituent unions was passed. However, according to Efrén Córdova, since a demand by Fidel Castro that "a broom to be used to get rid of Mujalista elements" was greeted with strong applause, this was subsequently interpreted to be an authorization for the drastic purge that went forward in the months that followed the Tenth Congress.[105]

THE POST–TENTH CONGRESS PURGE OF
THE LABOR MOVEMENT

The new Executive Committee of the Confederación de Trabajadores de Cuba lost little time in setting into operation a process of purging the leadership of the labor movement of all those who continued to support the position held by the overwhelming majority of the delegates to the Tenth Congress. In doing so, they had the clear support of the government of Fidel Castro.

Less than a week had passed since the end of the congress when the Executive Committee decided to suspend the trade union rights of Manolo Fernández, head of the actors' union, the Asociación Cubana de Artistas Teatrales (ACAT), on the charge that he had participated in social gatherings with Batista police officials. He had been one of the most vocal opponents of the Communists in the CTC during 1959. This decision had to be ratified by a general assembly of the ACAT, which met on December 15. Although the supporters of Fernández were reportedly a majority in that assembly, he decided to resign his post as head of the ACAT, and he and his supporters withdrew from the meeting. Those people remaining (including at least a few who were not even members of the union) thereupon voted to expel from the union all of those who had been elected to its executive committee a few months earlier.[106]

On January 7, 1960, the Executive Committee of the CTC, at a session attended by President Dorticós, Fidel Castro, and the minister of labor, passed a resolution providing for expulsion from their posts of any official or member of any affiliate of the CTC who "was considered a Mujalista or a counterrevolutionary." This action had been presented by Jesús Soto, head of the Textile Federation and new secretary of organization of the CTC.[107]

In the months that followed, those who were purged from the positions to which they had been elected in 1959—and in many cases, expelled even from union membership—included Auténticos, Ortodoxos, Social Christians, anarchists, and those with no particular affiliation, as well as large numbers of the 26th of July Movement.

In March, the CTC Executive announced that special assemblies would be held to choose substitutes for the general secretaries of the construction, tobacco, medicine workers, musicians, and barbers unions. By April, elected officers of twenty of the CTC's thirty-three federations and of almost two thousand unions had been expelled from the posts to which they had been elected in 1959 [by the Purge Commission of the CTC Executive Committee].[108]

In 1965, I wrote:

Within a year, the secretaries general of 1,400 of the country's 2,490 unions had been removed by the committee. The leaders of at least half of the nation's thirty-four national industrial federations were also dismissed. One of the most important victims of the purge was David Salvador himself, who was removed in May 1960. Subsequently, he was jailed, as were hundreds of other 26th of July labor leaders.[109]

Little attention was paid in the purge of labor leaders to their previous service to the revolution. For example, Mario Fontela had been with Castro in the mountains and when he returned to Havana had proposed the idea of organizing a new federation of agricultural workers and had done so with the approval of Fidel Castro. By the end of February 1959 Fontela and his associates were able formally to establish the Federación de Trabajadores Agrícolas, which held a congress that elected Fontela as secretary general. The new federation was approved by the CTC National Council meeting held in September 1959, and then by the Tenth Congress of the CTC.[110]

The CTC leadership had indicated its support for the new agricultural workers' federation, carrying a special article about it in its international bulletin. That article ended with the comment "This Federation is led and oriented by Mario Fontela, the *responsable general*, who has carried out a great job."[111]

However, Minister of Labor Martínez Sánchez refused to grant legal recognition to the new federation, because he knew that it was headed by anti-Communist union leaders. This situation was finally "resolved" when Jesús Soto, as secretary of organization, of the CTC, called a new "congress" of the federation, attended by only 70 delegates instead of the 300 who should have been present, which met in July 1960. This rump congress removed Fontela and other anti-Communist founders of the federation, shortly after which the ministry of labor legally recognized the organization. Within a short time, Fontela went into exile.[112]

Another somewhat similar case was that of Eric Garcés, head of the Musicians Federation. He served for eighteen months with Castro in the Rebel Army, rising to the rank of lieutenant. Right after the fall of Batista, Garcés was the *responsable* of the 26th of July Movement in charge of the Musicians Federation and was subsequently elected its secretary general. However, because of Garcés's open and outspoken opposition to the Communists,

Jesús Soto suddenly called a new congress of the Musicians Federation in February 1960, which, according to Garcés, was attended by only 13 of the 10,000 members of the federation. That meeting declared Garcés and the rest of the Executive of the federation deposed. He, too, soon went into exile.[113]

There were a few unions in which there was overt opposition to the purge. The most important of these was the Federation of Electrical Workers, and its Havana union. The two principal electrical workers union leaders were Amaury Fraginals and Fidel Iglesias, who with their colleagues had been elected by more than a two-to-one majority in the 1959 elections.[114]

Efrén Córdova noted that the electrical workers leaders "had resisted with success various attempts made by the Communists in 1959 and 1960 to control the federation. As much from conviction as for tactical reasons, this leadership combined a clear revolutionary militance with a decided anticommunist posture, which permitted it to survive the siege of the unconditional supporters of Castro and the PSP, supported by the Minister of Labor."[115]

In August 1960 problems for the union leaders began when the government nationalized the Cuban Electric Company, and soon thereafter, Fraginals accused the government interventor in the firm of violating conditions of the existing collective agreement and plotting against the union leadership. A general assembly of the federation supported the leadership's charges.

Then on November 20 there was sabotage of five transformers in the Havana area, and three days later a raid on the headquarters of the company resulted in the seizure of $100,000. The government-controlled press used these events to attack the federation's leadership, implying that they were connected with the sabotage raid.

Fraginals and other leaders of the federation refused to let their supporters attend a new assembly called by the government. Instead, they organized a street demonstration of more than 1,000 workers, who marched to the presidential palace. Although President Dorticós agreed to receive a delegation from the demonstrators, he rejected their demands that the company management fulfill the provisions of the collective agreement and instead charged them with being counterrevolutionaries.

Subsequently, Fraginals and Iglesias were expelled from the 26th of July Movement, and lesser leaders of the federation were called before revolutionary tribunals. Meanwhile, the government mobilized its supporters to instruct them to send telegrams and other messages demanding punishment for the electrical workers' leaders.

A meeting was also organized on December 13, of representatives of the various federations and local unions, which denounced the sabotage and robbery of the company offices; and a resolution was signed by every federation except those of the electrical workers and food workers, the leadership of which was also quickly denounced as "counterrevolutionaries."

The CTC then called a new assembly of members of the Electrical Workers Federation. However, the call for this meeting had certain peculiarities. "The CTC executive also invited to it members of the University Students Federation, students of the Schools of Arts and Crafts, sympathizers and activists of other unions and of various Communist groups." Fidel Castro and the minister of labor were also present.

Efrén Córdova noted, "There were also adopted rigorous security provisions controlling entry to the meeting place." This meeting voted to expel from the labor movement anyone involved in sabotage and also voted to depose the leaders of the Electrical Workers Federation and its Havana union. Jesús Soto, who of course did not belong to the electrical workers union, made these motions but did not submit them to a vote, merely asking whether there was anyone opposed to them. Given the situation, the motions were passed "unanimously."[116]

Major leadership in the purge of the CTC and its federations was assumed by Jesús Soto, new secretary of organization and leader of the textile workers. Efrén Córdova commented:

Soto was transformed after the congress into a kind of enthusiastic and implacable plotter and executionist, going from assembly to assembly and city to city, sometimes alone and other times accompanied by the Minister of Labor, both always seeking to give impulse to the purges. The textile leader carried to the extreme his revolutionary zeal, to the point of offering menaces and engaging in personal conflicts with the persecuted leaders.[117]

Some other Cuban labor leaders claimed that Jesús Soto was a late convert to the revolution against Batista and that he had cooperated extensively, in his capacity of treasurer of the Textile Workers Union, with Eusebio Mujal. Only near the end of 1958 did he join "Che" Guevara's guerrilla forces and finally returned to Havana with "Che's" troops.[118]

Minister of Labor Martínez Sánchez frequently intervened personally to bring about the purges. He did not cavil at using military pressure to achieve his objective. Efrén Córdova noted, "When there arose serious problems in the assembly of the Havana Construction Workers Union called to replace seven delegates, Martínez Sánchez appeared in the union, accompanied by an inspector of the Ministry, various members of the Rebel Army and eighty members of the Communist Party and proceeded to carry out the replacement."[119]

Fidel Castro himself also made clear very early on his support of the purge of the labor movement leadership. When a newspaper criticized the CTC Executive Committee's decision to carry out the purge and naming of a committee of three for that purpose, Castro attacked that paper:

What right do they have to attack the revolution when the CTC is simply fulfilling an order of its National Congress, which is itself a reflection of the desire of all the Cuban workers to eradicate the counterrevolutionaries from the labor movement at the moment when the fatherland is in danger and needs people loyal in place of those whom history has proven are unworthy of confidence.[120]

THE CASE OF DAVID SALVADOR

The fate of David Salvador was undoubtedly the most dramatic case of all. He had been one of the first trade union figures to enter the clandestine struggle against the Batista dictatorship. E. P. Whittemore sketched his participation in that struggle:

In 1952, shortly after Batista regained power through a coup Salvador went underground. For the first two years of Batista's second regime, he was a member of "Triple," the only clandestine organization then operating against the dictator. On July 26, 1958, when Castro made his armed attack on the Moncada Barracks, Salvador established contact with the *Fidelistas*, and when Fidel formed the 26th of July Movement in Mexico two years later, he was one of a small group who launched it in Cuba. By 1957 Salvador was head of the Movement's Labor Section. . . . In October 1958, while preparing for a labor congress in the Sierra Maestra, Salvador was arrested by Batista's police. He was imprisoned and tortured.[121]

As head of the Labor Section of the 26th of July Movement, David Salvador had become de facto secretary general of the CTC on the fall of Batista.

After meeting Salvador for the first time in Havana in January 1959 I wrote:

David Salvador is a young man, perhaps thirty or thereabouts, was the leader of a sugar workers local union in the Province of Camaguey, and was head of the labor underground of the 26 de Julio. He is usually referred to in deprecating terms by the old trade union leaders, as well as by our Labor Attaché, who has never met him. They say that he is "too young," "inexperienced," etc. I'm not entirely convinced this is true. He apparently has organizing ability or he would not have risen to the job he held in the Underground. He is an ex-Communist, which is sometimes a recommendation. He is a good orator, and in the speech I heard him give at a meeting of 26 de Julio trade unionists on January 11 . . . he impressed me with having an exceedingly good grasp of the problems facing the labor movement and facing the 26 de Julio in the labor movement. He has the tendency of a lot of the 26 de Julio people to play down the anti-Batista activities of every other group but his own.[122]

As an ex-Communist, Salvador was strongly opposed to Communist influence in the CTC. However, he had seemed to go along with the de facto imposition by Fidel Castro of a leadership of Fidel's own choosing at the time of the Tenth Congress, as well as the beginning of the purging process.

However, by February 1960, he had begun to object to the extent and nature of the purge. After returning from a mission to France on which he had been sent by Castro in the spring of 1960, Salvador had a violent confrontation with Jesús Soto and Minister of Labor Martínez Sánchez after learning that twenty-two of the twenty-eight elected federation secretaries general who had opposed Communist participation in the CTC leadership had been removed. After that meeting, he resigned as secretary general of the CTC and returned to the Stewart sugar plantation, where he had begun his trade union career. In June, he once more entered the underground, helping to establish what was called the 30th of November Movement, together with several other victims of the purge.

In November 1960, Salvador was arrested, whereupon the CTC Executive formally expelled him from the labor movement and called for "the severest punishment" for him. He was sentenced by a revolutionary tribunal to thirty years in jail. On his release, at the completion of his term, he traveled to the United States, where he went to live in Los Angeles.[123]

CUBAN LABOR LEGISLATION AS OF JANUARY 1, 1959

Before describing the total transformation of the Cuban labor movement after the Tenth Congress, it is appropriate to note the kind and breadth of the country's labor legislation at the time the Castro government gained power. Robert Kenneth Brown has summarized the legal framework within which organized labor and labor relations generally were supposed to function before January 1, 1959:

In 1933, the working day was limited to eight hours. In 1940, the work was limited to forty-four hours with pay for forty-eight. Legislation in 1933 also granted large numbers of Cuban employees a break of one and

a half or two hours between sessions of the work day. . . . Four days of
the year were designated as legal holidays on which the worker would
receive full pay. Approximately five other days, though not legally so designated, were granted by custom also with pay. Various legal measures
enacted after 1945 provided . . . various categories of personnel were to
receive an extra day off each week without loss of pay during June, July
and August. A variety of decrees prescribed the length of paid vacations.
All workers were granted paid sick leave up to a maximum of three days
per month but not more than nine days per year.

Brown continued: "The principle of the minimum wage was
recognized in the Constitution of 1940 and its periodical regulation was to be determined by a 'parity commission' for each
sector. Payment for overtime was set at a minimum of 25 percent
higher than normal pay. In 1938, additional decrees raised this to
one and a half the regular rate by 1959."
    Brown also noted:

The constitution of 1940 legalized collective bargaining and ruled that
labor disputes would be solved by a bipartite conciliation commission
presided over by a judicial functionary. The right to strike was recognized
in 1933 and reaffirmed in 1934 and in the constitution of 1940. Collective bargaining was defined and regulated in 1938; the constitution of
1940 stated that it was compulsory for both employers and workers to
adhere to collective agreements. The constitution of 1940 also made provision for the creation of biparty type commissions and judicial functionaries
that were to resolve labor problems and disputes.[124]

Virtually all of this legislation was ignored or done away with
de facto after the Castro government regime, and control of the
CTC and its constituent unions, was seized by the government
after the Tenth Congress.

NOTES

    1. Letter of Robert J. Alexander to Jay Lovestone, January 19, 1959.
    2. Efrén Córdova, *Clase Trabajadora y Movimiento Sindical en Cuba,
Volumen II (1959–1996)*, Ediciones Universal, Miami, 1996, page 68.
    3. Letter of Robert J. Alexander to Jay Lovestone, September 27, 1959.
    4. Euclides Vázquez Candela, "Saldo de Una Polemica," *Revolución,*
Havana, September 14, 1959.
    5. Interview with Pascasio Lineras, secretay of propaganda, Sindicato
Textil Ariguanabo, subsequently textile workers' leader of Organización
Auténtica, and member of Executive of Frente Obrero Revolucionario
Democrático Cubano, in New York City, October 14, 1960.
    6. Maurice Zeitlin, *Revolutionary Politics and the Cuban Working Class,*
Harper Torchbooks, New York, 1970, pages 164, 169.

7. *Labor Conditions in Communist Cuba*, Cuban Economic Research Project, University of Miami, 1963, pages 9–10.

8. Ibid., page 26.

9. Jorge G. Castañeda, *Compañero: The Life and Death of Ché Guevara*, Alfred A. Knopf, New York, 1997, page 216.

10. Zeitlin, op. cit., page xxxix.

11. Ibid., pages xl-xli.

12. Ibid., page 1.

13. Sergio Roca, "Moral Incentives in Socialist Cuba," *The ACES Bulletin*, Summer 1980, page 35.

14. Marifeli Pérez Stable, associate professor of sociology, SUNY Old Westbury, speaking to Columbia University Latin American Seminar, New York, February 7, 1991.

15. Interview with John Correll, U.S. Embassy labor attaché, Havana, January 12, 1959.

16. Interview with Antonio Torres, member of Provisional Executive of Confederación de Trabajadores de Cuba, in Havana, January 11, 1959; and with Juan Ramón Alvarez, former official of Sociedad de Dependientes de Restaurantes, in Havana, January 11, 1959.

17. Interview with David Salvador, provisional secretary general of Confederación de Trabajadores de Cuba, in Havana, January 10, 1959.

18. Interview with Luis Moreno, provisional secretary general, and subsequently secretary general, Federación Tabacalera, in Havana, January 14, 1959.

19. Interview with Reinaldo Cassín González, treasurer of Colegio Nacional de Pedagogos, in Havana, June 5, 1959.

20. Interview with José Antonio Hernández, secretary general, Federación Nacional de Trabajadores de la Industria Metalúrgica y Similares, in Havana, September 13, 1959.

21. Interview with Antonio Gil Brito, secretary general of Federación Obrera Marítima Nacional, in Havana, September 14, 1959.

22. Córdova, 1996, op. cit., page 30; see also Robert Kenneth Brown, "The Impact of Revolutionary Politics on the Autonomy of Organized Labor in Cuba, 1959–1960," University of Colorado M.A. Thesis, 1965, pages 32–33, 64–65.

23. Interview with Guido Muñoz Ponce de León, Directorio Revolucionario leader in Electrical Workers Federation, in Havana, January 13, 1959.

24. Interview with Fidel Benítez, secretary general of Textile Union of Mariano, in Electrical Workers Federation, in Havana, January 13, 1959.

25. Interview with Pedro M. Rodríguez Ponce, secretary general of Sindicato de Empleados Bancarios, Provincia de Matanzas, in Havana, June 6, 1959.

26. Interviews with José Miguel Juan Aizpurua, Responsable of 26 de Julio in Hermandad Ferroviaria on Ferrocarriles Occidentales, in Havana, January 15, 1959, and Humberto Aguirre, responsable of 26 de Julio Movement in Delegación #2 of Hermandad Ferroviaria, in Havana, January 11, 1959.

27. Córdova, 1996, op. cit., page 30.

28. Interviews with César Lancis, former secretary general of Federación de Viajantes, secretary general of Comisión Obrera Nacional of Auténtico Party, Havana, June 5, 1959; Sr. Cornejo, member of CON of Auténtico Party, a leader of Sindicato de Omnibus Aliados, in Havana, June 5, 1959; Emilio Rubido, secretario de propaganda, Sindicato de Licoreros y Refrequeros de La Habana, member of CON of Auténtico Party, in Havana, June 5, 1959; and Adalberto Martínez Cobiello, member of Executive of Sindicato Cinematográfico de La Havana, member of CON of Auténtico Party, in Havana, June 5, 1959.

29. Robert J. Alexander. "Notes of Meeting of Comisión Obrera Nacional of Partido Auténtico," Havana, June 5, 1959.

30. Interview with David Salvador, op. cit., June 10, 1959.

31. Córdova, 1996, op. cit., page 38.

32. Interview with José Plana, member of Provisional Executive of Confederación de Trabajadores de Cuba, member of Executive of Unión de Trabajadores Cristianos, in Havana, June 5, 1959.

33. Interview with Luis Moreno, op. cit., June 1, 1959.

34. Interview with Simeon Torres, secretary general of Federación de Obreros del Ramo de la Alimentación, in Havana, June 1, 1959.

35. Interview with Alfredo Rancano, responsable of July 26th Movement in Federación Gastronómica, in Havana, January 14, 1959.

36. Interview with Manuel Carvallo, secretary general of Federación Minera, in Havana, June 1, 1959.

37. Interview with Gerardo González López, member of Executive of Federación de Obreros del Ramo de la Construcción, in Havana, June 1, 1959.

38. Interview with Carlos Pérez Bega, responsable general of Sindicato de Trabajadores de Laboratorios, Droguerias y Farmacias, in Havana, June 1, 1959.

39. Interview with José Martínez, secretary general of Federación de Trabajadores del Calzado, in Havana, June 2, 1959.

40. Interview with Humberto Grillo, responsable of 26 de Julio in Federación Ganadera, in Havana, January 11, 1959.

41. Interview with Raúl Muñoz Robledo, secretary of organization of Sindicato Bancario de La Habana, in Havana, June 6, 1959.

42. Interview with Isidoro Salas Alvarez, member of Buro Nacional Azucarero of Federación Nacional de Trabajadores Azucareros, in Havana, January 15, 1959.

43. Interview with José Vega, secretary of propaganda of Federación Nacional de Trabajadores Azucareros, in Havana, June 2, 1959.

44. Ibid., see also interview with Alberto Baro Elías, treasurer of Federación Sindical de Trabajadores Bancarios, in Havana, September 14, 1959.

45. Efrén Córdova, El Trabajador Cubano en el Estado de Obreros y Campesinos, Ediciones Universal, Miami, 1990, page 25.

46. Robert J. Alexander, Presidents of Central America, Mexico, Cuba and Hispaniola, Conversations and Correspondence, Praeger, Westport, CT, 1995, pages 177–186.

47. Brown, op. cit., pages 54–55.

48. Córdova, 1996, op. cit., page 19.

49. Interview with Pedro Martínez, head of labor affairs for Directorio Revolucionario, in Havana, January 13, 1959.

50. Interviews with Vicente Collado, coordinador de Secciones Sindicales of Federación de Trabajadores de Plantas Eléctricas, in Havana, September 14, 1959; and Orlando Blanco, secretary of organization of Sindicato de Trabajadores de Plantas Eléctricas de La Habana, May 30, 1959.

51. Interview with César Lancis, op. cit., June 5, 1959.

52. Interview with Conrado Bécquer, secretary general of Federación Nacional de Trabajadores Azucareros, in Havana, September 14, 1959.

53. Interview with José Plana, op. cit., June 5, 1959.

54. Interview with David Salvador, op. cit., January 11, 1959.

55. Interview with Octavio Lloit, director of propaganda of Confederación de Trabajadores de Cuba, in Havana, January 15, 1959.

56. Interview with Orlando Blanco, op. cit., May 30, 1959.

57. Interview with Gilberto García, secretary general of Juventud Obrera Católica, in Havana, June 5, 1959.

58. Brown, op. cit., page 85.

59. Interview with Conrado Bécquer, op. cit., September 14, 1959.

60. Interview with José Vega, op. cit., June 2, 1959.

61. Interview with Leandro Barrera, secretario agrario of Federación Nacional de Trabajadores Azucareros, in Havana, June 2, 1959.

62. Interview with Luis Moreno, op. cit., June 1, 1959.

63. Interviews with Antonio Gil Brito, op. cit., September 14, 1959; and Luis Viña, secretario de actas, Federación Obrera Marítima Nacional, in Havana, June 1, 1959.

64. Interviews with Vicente Collado, op. cit., September 14, 1959; and Orlando Blanco, op. cit., May 30, 1959.

65. Interview with Gerado González López, member of Executive of Federación de Obreros del Ramo de la Construcción, in Havana, June 1, 1959.

66. Interview with Javier González, leader of Sección Obrera of 26 de Julio in Liquor Workers Federation, in Havana, June 2, 1959.

67. Interview with José Antonio Hernández, secretary general of Federacion Nacional de Trabajadores de la Industria Metalúrgica y Similares, in Havana, September 13, 1959.

68. Interview with Pedro M. Rodríguez Ponce, secretary general of Sindicato de Empleados Bancarios, Provincia de Matanzas, in Havana, June 6, 1959.

69. Interview with Henry Hammond, U.S. Embassy labor attaché, in Havana, June 2, 1959.

70. Córdova, 1996, op. cit., pages 59–60

71. Interview with Manuel Pérez Llanese, member of Executive of Frente Obrero Revolucionario Democrático Cubano, former leader of Federación Gastronómica, in New York City, October 14, 1960.

72. Interviews with Conrad Bécquer, op. cit., September 14, 1959, and Fabián Pérez, jefe de activistas of Federación Nacional de Trabajadores Bancarios, in Havana, September 14, 1959.

73. "Responde el M–26–7 a Joaquín Ordoqui," *Revolución*, Havana, September 14, 1959.

74. Interview with Gilberto García, op. cit., June 5, 1959.

75. Interview with Antonio Collada, secretario de organización of Federación Nacional de Trabajadores del Ramo de la Construcción, in Havana, September 13, 1959.

76. Interview with Rafael Perdomo y Perdomo, secretary of organization of Federación Nacional de Trabajadores de la Industria Metalúrgica y Similares, in Havana, September 15, 1959.

77. Interview with Fabián Pérez, op. cit., September 14, 1959.

78. Interview with Pedro H. Rodríguez Ponce, op. cit., June 6, 1959.

79. "Declaración de Principios," *Prensa Libre*, Havana, September 11, 1959, page 19.

80. Interview with José María de Aguilera, secretary general of Federación Nacional de Trabajadores Bancarios, in Havana, September 13, 1959.

81. Interview with Fabián Pérez, op. cit., September 14, 1959.

82. Interview with Conrado Bécquer, op. cit., September 14, 1959.

83. Interview with Henry Hammond, op. cit., September 15, 1959.

84. Interview with José María de Aguilera, op. cit., September 13, 1959.

85. Ibid., and interview with Fabián Pérez, op. cit., September 14, 1959.

86. Interview with Rafael Otero, in Havana, January 13, 1959.

87. Interview with Octavio Lloit, op. cit., January 15, 1959.

88. Interview with Conrado Bécquer, op. cit., September 14, 1959.

89. Interview with Luis Viña, op. cit., September 14, 1959.

90. Interview with Reinol González, provisional secretary of international affairs, Confederación de Trabajadores de Cuba, former secretary general of Juventud Obrera Católica, in Havana, January 12, 1959, June 5, 1969.

91. *Boletín Internacional con Noticias de Cuba*, Havana, September 1959, page 6.

92. Interview with Pascasio Lineras, op. cit., January 12, 1959.

93. Interview with José María de Aguilera, op. cit., September 14, 1959.

94. Letter from Robert J. Alexander to Jay Lovestone, September 27, 1959.

95. Córdova, 1996 op. cit., pages 65–66; see also interview with Juan Ramón Alvarez, former official of Sociedad de Dependientes de Restaurantes, in Havana, January 11, 1959.

96. Brown, op. cit., page 73.

97. Córdova, 1996, op. cit., pages 67–68.

98. Ibid., page 69.

99. Ibid., pages 69–70.

100. Quoted in Ibid., page 71.

101. Ibid., pages 71–72.

102. Ibid., page 73.

103. Ibid., pages 73–74, 82.

104. Ibid., pages 75–77.

105. Ibid., pages 77–78.

106. Ibid., pages 83–84.

107. Ibid., page 84; see also *Labor Conditions in Communist Cuba,* 1963, op. cit., page 115.

108. Córdova, 1996, op. cit., page 85.

109. Robert J. Alexander, *Organized Labor in Latin America,* The Free Press of Glencoe, New York, 1965, page 170.

110. Interview with Mario Fontela, former secretary general of Federación de Trabajadores Agrícolas of Cuba, in New York City, October 22, 1960.

111. *Boletín Internacional con Noticias de Cuba,* Havana, September 1959, page 2.

112. Interview with Mario Fontela, op. cit., October 22, 1960.

113. Interview with Eric Garcés, former secretary general of Federación de Músicos de Cuba, in New York City, October 22, 1960.

114. "Sindicato Provincial de Trabajadores de Plantas Eléctricas, Gas, y Agua de La Habana: Comisión Electoral, Resultados," 1959 (mimeographed).

115. Córdova, 1996, op. cit., page 115.

116. Ibid., pages 117–118; see also Serafino Romualdi, "What Castro Has Done To Cuban Labor, Excerpts from Address at the Industrial Research Association, Chicago, Illinois Chapter, February 8, 1962" (mimeographed).

117. Córdova, 1996, op. cit., page 86.

118. Pascasio Lineras, cited in Brown, op. cit., page 34.

119. Córdova, 1996, op. cit., page 87.

120. Ibid., pages 90–91.

121. E. P. Whittemore, "Cuba's Unions Come Full Circle," *New Leader,* New York City, February 5, 1962, page 24.

122. Letter of Robert J. Alexander to Jay Lovestone, January 19, 1959.

123. Córdova, 1996, op. cit., pages 94–97, 125–126.

124. Ibid., page 97.

7

Soviet-Style Labor Movement in Castro's Cuba

After the Castro government's seizure of control of the labor movement from those who had been elected to lead it in 1959, organized labor and its relations with the state—virtually the only employer—underwent a total transformation. This change involved both a reorganization of the structure of the trade union movement and a 180-degree alteration of the role that it had traditionally played.

REORGANIZATION OF THE CTC

The thorough purge of the Confederación de Trabajadores de Cuba and its constituent unions paved the way for a complete reorganization of the CTC, in terms of not only personnel, but structure and basic nature. These changes began when a congress of the Construction Workers Federation decided to put an end to the craft structure that had been characteristic of the unions in that federation. Other changes began to occur in other national affiliates of the CTC.

In March 1961, the Ministry of Labor presented the Executive Committee of the CTC with a proposal for a basic reorganization of the structure of the labor movement. According to the ministry, these changes were accepted "unanimously and enthusiastically" by the CTC Executive. They were issued in the form of a law in August 1961.[1]

This new law altered fundamentally the basic structure of the labor movement. In place of the comparatively loose structure of the CTC as a confederation of rather loosely joined autonomous federations, there was established a highly centralized organization. The federations were replaced by "national industrial unions" (*sindicatos nacionales*), each of which had "sections" instead of "unions." Any existing union organization had to belong to the CTC, making illegal the kind of resistance to top CTC leadership by officials of its affiliates that had sometimes existed in the past. In place of the thirty-four federations, there were established twenty-five national unions (this number was altered several times in subsequent years).

Another important change in the trade union structure, particularly on the local level, was the establishment of workers' militia. Although some steps had been tentatively taken in 1959, in January 1960 the Executive of the CTC ordered the creation of workers' militia in all work centers. By June, the Labor Ministry said that some 70,000 workers in Havana, and about a half million in all of Cuba, had undergone some military training.[2]

The workers' militia had several functions. One of these was obviously paramilitary. The military members were given rudimentary military instruction. The importance of this was demonstrated at the time of the Bay of Pigs invasion in April 1961, when the militia played a crucial role in defeating the invaders.[3]

However, there were also other functions performed by the militia. They became a means of testing the workers' loyalty to the regime—participation in the militia became an important consideration in management's judgment of the performance of workers on the job. Also, as the regime turned in the Marxist-Leninist direction, the militia were more important in helping to indoctrinate the workers in that ideology.

Efrén Córdova noted another function of the militia insofar as local union groups were concerned:

By creating in each workshop a new structure with strong quasi-military bonds, the authority of union leaders began to weaken and was superseded in reality by that of militia chiefs. Questions of trade union discipline were overshadowed by matters relating to the fulfillment of militia duties. Authority no longer accrued to the leader by reason of his position in the union hierarchy, but to militia officers or to those militiamen who were most vocal in their support of the revolution. This meant in practice that local union leaders were relegated to a secondary position and gradually began to lose their hold on the membership.[4]

During this period there were even more critical changes made in the nature as well as the forms of Cuban labor organization. We shall deal with these in subsequent sections of this study.

The process of restructuring the labor movement culminated in the XI Congress of the Confederación de Trabajadores de Cuba, which met November 26–28, 1961. In the process of choosing the 9,650 delegates to that meeting, the trade union democracy that two years earlier had led to spirited contests in virtually all of the country's unions was ended. There were virtually no contested elections this time. In most cases, there was only one list of candidates, which the official organ of the CTC, Vanguardia Obrera, described as evidence of "a demonstration of solidarity." Another periodical noted that in 98 percent of the cases, the workers had voted unanimously for the official list of candidates.[5]

Before the CTC Congress, each of the twenty-five national unions then existing also held a congress. The people attending those meetings and that of the CTC itself included 200 "fraternal" delegates from the Soviet Union, East Germany, Czechoslovakia, and other countries under Communist rule. The mine union's congress bestowed on Nikita Khrushchev the title of "first miner of the world."[6]

The method of electing delegates to at least some of these national unions presaged a change that was soon to become standard throughout the Cuban labor movement. Ursinio Rojas, an oldtime Communist leader of the sugar workers, explained that in his federation's case:

The National Plenary of the FNTA held on December 19 of last year unanimously agreed and all the regional plenaries held in recent days ratified it, that in our Sugar Unions we would have elections with one single Unitary Candidates List that would be discussed previously with the leaders of each Union and the Organizaciones Revolucionarias Integradas in each plantation. This agreement has great importance and reflects how advanced is the revolutionary consciousness among the workers in our sector.[7]

When it came time for the CTC Eleventh Congress to elect new leaders, Lázaro Peña, the veteran Communist who had headed the CTC during the first Batista period, was returned to the post of secretary general. According to E. P. Whittemore, Peña's reassumption of that post amounted to the conversion of his de facto position into a de jure one. Whittemore wrote: "From the time Salvador resigned in March 1960 until the 11th Congress in November the CTC's official spokesman was Jesús Soto, a 'melon' who was one of Salvador's deputies. But in fact Peña ran the Confederation during the eight-month period. And it was Peña who initiated some important changes in Cuban labor both before and during the 11th Congress." Peña was one of the two principal speakers at the Eleventh Congress, although he held no official position in it until his election as secretary general shortly before its conclusion.[8]

Other old-line Communists who were elected to the new thirteen-person Executive Committee included Fausto Calcines, Carlos Fernández R., Ursinio Rojas, and Hector Carbonell. However, there were also listed some of those from the 26th of July Movement who had help purge and completely change the Cuban labor movement—including Jesús Soto, José María de la Aguilera, Rogelio Iglesias, Octavio Lloit, Odón Alvarez de la Campa.

Minister of Labor Martínez Sánchez himself summed up the difference between the Eleventh CTC Congress and the Tenth Congress, in his speech to the former: "Now there are not here traitors and vagabonds who shout 'Veintiseis, Veintiseis,' to oppose the unity of the labor movement, nor are there shouts in the hallways: Melons, Melons! They are not here, but we melons are here and we continue being melons, green on the outside and red on the inside."[9]

RATIONALE OF TRANSFORMATION OF CUBAN ORGANIZED LABOR

The Eleventh Congress of the CTC was a major step in the direction of transformation of Cuban organized labor from a movement that fought for the interests of its members into one adapted to the model that Stalin had established in the Soviet Union a generation before. It was converted into an organization that had the twin functions of disciplining the working class and of carrying out functions formerly thought of as principally the job of management or government, not of trade unions.

The rationalization of this change was that after the revolution Cuba was a workers' state, and that it was the wage workers and peasants who were now in power. Therefore, the effort of individual groups of workers to get higher wages, shorter working hours, and other benefits sabotaged the attempts of the "workers' state" to develop and expand the economy and thus opposed the interests of the working class in general.

Fidel Castro frequently sounded this theme. However, no one did so as explicitly as Minister of Labor Augusto Martínez Sánchez, in his address to the XXVI National Council of the CTC in September 1962: "Today the workers, laborers and peasants, the manual and intellectual workers, are those who are in power, are the owners of the principal means of production and of the natural riches of the country. They are the ones who have in their own hands the destinies of the country."

Martínez Sánchez argued:

The Socialist Revolution has done away definitively with all of the old worm-eaten structure of capitalist exploitation and imperialist domination and on the ruins of a regime of misery, opprobrium, injustice, political manipulation and corruption, is constructing our new society without exploited and exploiters, without the bosses or gentlemen, where he who works and produces is the true and only owner of the country.

The minister continued:

Today, different from what occurred in the past, it is the workers who elaborate, discuss and approve the laws. They are the ones who proposed and suggest measures that should be adopted. They are the ones who discuss, in their assemblies, in the centers of work, the extent and content of these. Never before in the history of our country, have the workers had a participation so active and so direct on all that affects their interests, needs and aspirations.[10]

Some of the North American admirers of the Castro regime have echoed statements such as those of Martínez Sánchez. Thus, Hobart Spalding argued: "Thus by the end of 1961 organized labor had become integrated into the revolutionary process. From that time, workers increasingly made basic decisions affecting their lives, and played a growing role in deciding the future course of Cuba's transition to Socialism."[11]

Efrén Córdova raised doubts about the control of the workers and peasants, or more specifically, organized labor, over the economy, society, and politics of Castro's Cuba:

In pure logic this should signify that trade unionism as the organized movement of the workers and the State as the political expression of its new position of political control should be equalized and their officials be interchangeable. The trade union functionaries should be able to move into and take over functions of government and official and Party functionaries should be transferable to the CTC.

However, Córdova added:

This hypothesis has not been correct. In Cuba the government has been in the hands of professional revolutionaries and politicians of the new kind who have been at Castro's side. It is not common for trade unionists to be called to occupy political-administrative positions, at least not on the highest levels. Some trade unionists have been transferred to responsibilities in the Party, particularly at the local level, but many more have remained for indefinite periods in the CTC. In contrast, those are numerous who have passed from the Party to the highest positions of the CTC, including the secretariat general, given to Miguel Martin in 1966 and to Pedro Ross in 1969 (both militants of Party organizations).

Córdova added, "In 1975 only 6.5 percent of the members of the Central Committee of the PCC were trade union workers."[12] The PCC was Fidel Castro's Communist Party of Cuba, the final form of the single dominant party, first established as the Organizaciones Revolucionarias Integradas, then converted into the Partido Unido de la Revolución Socialista, and finally into the supposedly all-powerful Communist Party of Cuba.

After the formal establishment of the Communist Party of Cuba in 1975, the statutes of the Confederación de Trabajadores de Cuba were altered to provide in their preamble that it and its affiliated unions "openly and conscientiously" accept the direction of the party.[13]

Perhaps nothing illustrates the degree to which the trade unions were made subject to the Party and government, instead of the other way around, as much as the alterations of the secretary generalship of the CTC. In 1961, when the "unity" of the CTC leadership (that is, incorporation of the old-line Communists into its key positions) that Fidel Castro had first openly insisted on during the Tenth Congress was put fully into effect, the Eleventh Congress "unanimously" elected Lázaro Peña, veteran Stalinist, who had been secretary general during the first Batista period, to that position once again. However, at the XII Congress in 1966, at which Castro announced his complete endorsement of "moral" over "material" incentives, which Peña did not support, Peña was removed in favor of Miguel Martín. Two years later, after Castro's "surrender" to the USSR over the Czechoslovakian issue, Martín was "given leave as secretary general of the CTC and was sent to Camaguey with a post of little importance in the provincial branch of the CTC."[14] In 1973, Lázaro Peña was again "unanimously" elected secretary general by the XIII Congress.[15]

This pattern continued in subsequent congresses of the CTC. In July 1978, at the XIV Congress, Roberto Veiga Menéndez, a member of the Central Committee of the Communist Party, who had succeeded to the secretary generalship on the death of Lázaro Peña and was acclaimed by Fidel Castro in his speech closing the session as having done an "extraordinary job," was "unanimously" reelected to the post.[16]

In the Sixteenth Congress in 1989, Pedro Ross Leal became secretary general of the CTC. Efrén Córdova described him as

an "aparatchik" who until then had been a substitute member of the Political Bureau and secretary of the Central Committee of the PCC. Pedro Ross Leal had no trade union experience. Born in the province of Oriente he had long belonged to the Juventud Socialista Popular and participated from the triumph of the revolution in various organizational stages of the PCC. He went to the university, graduating in Political Science. Between 1959 and 1975 he had various management jobs in the agricultural and sugar sectors of the province of Oriente.[17]

As for the right of the workers in Socialist Cuba to participate in decision making either in their place of work or in the economy in general was concerned, there is little indication that such became the case. As early as 1966, in his report to the CTC XII Congress, Secretary General Miguel Martín said: The production assemblies have been transformed into meetings in which the functionaries recite cold statistics without any participation or animated discussion of the workers. The masses are being separated more and more from the solution of problems."

Carmelo Mesa-Lago and Roberto E. Hernández commented, "Martín accepted the opinion that the bureaucrats and the organizations presumed that they had the right to think for the people." They added:

Four years later the situation did not seem to have improved, since the Executive Buro of the CTC criticized "the method which is seen . . . in assemblies, where by agitational harangues there is proclaimed a production goal, instead of a serious analysis with real participation of all workers in the essential details for fulfilling the plan: human resources, disposable raw material, state of the machinery and tools, etc.[18]

In 1969, Maurice Zeitlin, a friendly disposed student of the state of the workers in Castro's Cuba, noted:

At present, despite the apparently ample participation of the workers in discussions and decisions concerning the *implementation* of the objectives of the national economic plan set for their plant, the workers have no role whatever, to my knowledge, in determining the plan itself. They have nothing to say over investment priorities; the decision as to what and how much is to be produced is made by the central planning bodies of the Revolutionary Government, responsible to the Council of Ministers.[19] (Emphasis in the original)

That situation was not to be altered basically in subsequent decades.

In 1973, another North American observer who was friendly disposed toward the Castro regime noted a close association of the union leadership with the management of sugar plantations that he had studied. He said that in most cases, the head of the union was officially the deputy of the plantation manager, and when for some reason or the other the manager had to be away, the union leader took over his position ad interim. However, this observer claimed that this did not involve any conflict of interest on the part of the union official.[20] Perhaps, since both the manager and the union chief had as their goals the achievement of the most possible output at the least possible cost, such was the case.

Writing in the 1990s, Efrén Córdova indicated that the situation with regard to the workers' power to influence policy either on an enterprise or a national level had not been altered:

In principle, the union as representative organ of the dominant class should participate in the elaboration not only of plans but also of the laws. In practice, the unions would be charged in the future with organizing meetings for the *discussion* of the plans for the workers and to *suggest* possible new laws in the accords of their congresses. Later dispositions would slightly broaden their powers with respect to projects of decree-laws and decrees which the Ministry of Labor would submit to the Council of State, since it provided that that ministry would *consult* before with the National Council of the CTC . . . the State would assign the unions more tangible functions with regard to labor security and hygiene; these would not achieve, however, the powers that other socialist countries gave them in connection with labor inspection in general.[21] (Emphasis in the original)

The two basic documents dealing specifically with the workers that were enacted during the period of institutionalization of the Cuban Revolution, the 1976 Constitution and the 1984 Labor Code, raised serious questions about the nature of the state in which the workers were supposedly the ruling class. Efrén Córdova noted that the Constitution

presents three notable characteristics in the case of labor: first, it is more authoritarian and rigid than those of other socialist countries, including the Soviet Union; second it is less generous in conceding rights and benefits than any recent Latin American constitution; and third, it is very backward in terms of social progress compared to the Cuban Constitution of 1940.[22]

In this connection, Córdova noted the vagueness of workers' supposed rights as compared with those of the 1940 Constitution. For instance, that of the 1976 stated that the workers were entitled to annual vacations and weekly periods of rest, in contrast to the 1940 document, which specified a forty-hour workweek and one month's vacation every year. Also the Castro Constitution omitted all mention of a minimum wage.[23]

But the Constitution of 1976, if dealing sparsely with the rights of workers, laid great emphasis on their duties. Córdova noted in this connection that in Article One the document listed three obligations of all workers:

1. the duty to work, a duty which in the letter and spirit of the Constitution weighs on each citizen instead of being stated merely as a social obligation as in other constitutions; 2. the unpaid nature of supposed voluntary labor; and 3. the obligation to carry out entirely the tasks which are associated with each job. . . . Not even the Constitution of the Soviet Union was as explicit in underscoring the importance of those duties.[24]

Córdova also noted that there was no mention in the 1976 Constitution of the freedom of workers to choose their own employment; nor was there any prohibition of forced labor, which is usual in modern constitutions. He also observed that there was a provision to the effect that "none of the rights and freedoms granted in the constitution . . . could be carried out against the existence and objective of the Socialist State or the decision of the Cuban people to construct socialism and communism."[25]

The Labor Code, presumably the basic law governing labor relations, also tended to be vague about the workers' rights, but quite specific about their duties. For instance, one passage provided, "When there happens an interruption of work for causes not imputed to the worker, the worker will be guaranteed a part of his wage, except for cases determined by law," without specifications. Similarly, a provision to the effect that "the transfer of the worker for interruption of the work process, devaluation of his qualifications, restructuring, reorganization, rationalization, partial invalidity, or originating from the disciplinary measure, will be such as is provided in law," without establishing a specific protection for the workers involved.[26]

However, the Labor Code went into great detail about the matter of labor discipline, which was the subject of 65 of the 300 articles in the Code, "which dealt in an explicit way with the duties of the worker, minimum output required, and labor discipline." In addition, other articles dealt with "voluntary" unpaid work. Efrén Córdova noted, "The phrases 'observe labor discipline' and 'strengthening of the discipline of work' appear half a dozen times in Chapter I of the code, containing the basic principles, and then they are repeated frequently throughout the code."[27]

René Dumont, the French Socialist economist who worked more or less closely with Castro and his government in the 1960s, noted as early as 1970 the real nature of the group who ruled Cuba after 1959:

Along with a certain number of positive aspects, the impressive series of economic setbacks, which we have recounted, were not the result of chance. It is necessary to have a better global explanation, related to the nature of power, to the strategy of development and the struggles of vari-

ous social categories, such as those which exist in the interior of the directing group. . . . There under the shadow of Fidel Castro, of the Army
and of the Party, is constituted 'new class,' of privileged directors, a fact
perhaps graver than the series of personal errors of the commander in
chief.

Dumont continued: "What is the ideology of this class? It is
very difficult to say if it has one globally. I think that is very heterogeneous, except for its taste for power and its advantages. It
considers itself a vanguard, but it assigns itself this role, without
being able to justify it, either by its competence, or by a sufficient
conscience."[28] (Emphasis in the original)

This situation as described by René Dumont had not changed
thirty years later.

THE PROCESS OF TRANSFORMATION OF
CUBAN ORGANIZED LABOR

The conversion of Cuban organized labor from the traditional
kind of trade union movement into the Stalin-type appendage of
the government party and of management began right after the
Tenth Congress of the CTC. It started with the process of the unions' "voluntarily" giving up most of the gains that Cuban
organized labor had made for its members during many decades.

One of the first steps taken by the newly purged unions was
to give up any further search for wage increases. This move was
started at a meeting of the Executive Committee of the Sugar
Workers Federation, which agreed to freeze wages at their then
current levels. Subsequently, the same federation agreed to give
up the traditional practice that part of the workers' income was
tied to the price of sugar, so that when the price went up, so did
the return to the workers. In the circumstances of the 1960s and
1970s that meant a very substantial loss of income to the sugar
unionists.[29] The sugar workers also soon gave up their long struggle to prevent bulk loading of sugar instead of loading into ships
in bags.[30]

The example of the sugar workers was quickly followed in
most of the other parts of the labor movement.[31] Also given up
was the right to extra pay for overtime work—to be followed before
long (as we shall see further on) by renunciation of any pay at all
for "voluntary" work outside the normal working hours.

Other long-fought-for rights were also forfeited between the
Tenth and Eleventh Congresses of the CTC. The latter meeting
ratified these "sacrifices." As Efrén Córdova wrote:

The delegates present threw away without much deliberation the right to nine days of sick leave, the Christmas bonus, the maximum work week of 44 hours (substituted by 48 hours). . . . They decided also to renounce the collection of overtime pay needed for the sugar harvest of 1962. And carrying to an extreme their masochistic impulses, they pronounced themselves in favor of revision of all clauses in collective contracts that involved participation in profits or any other type of benefits which were excessive, seemed unaffordable or were not in accord with the march toward socialism. Finally, they authorized the Minister of Labor to purge from the collective agreements any stipulation that could prejudice the development of production, the increase of productivity or the progress of socialism.[32]

This abandonment of the gains the labor movement had made over almost a century was enthusiastically endorsed, and in large degree stimulated, by Fidel Castro, the head of the "workers' and peasants' state." One of his many statements on the subject was made in his speech closing the Eleventh Congress of the CTC. In that discourse, he congratulated the workers on having given up these "mortgages of the past," which he assured his audience were "absurd payments which the revolution cannot give itself the luxury of undertaking." Then he added (as paraphrased by Efrén Córdova):

From now on . . . the workers of Cuba will be able to advance by the paths of socialism, free of complexes and with the assurance that they are developing a wealth and fortifying an economy of which they will be the only proprietors and beneficiaries. They had to follow the example of Russia, he added at the end, since according to information he had, in 20 years the Soviet Union would be producing double that produced by all of the non socialist countries together.[33]

Probably the single most significant right that the workers forfeited after the Tenth CTC Congress was the right to strike. The labor laws passed by the Castro regime took for granted that the workers did not have the right to strike by simply not mentioning the subject. However, Law #924 of January 4, 1961, proclaimed that "all counterrevolutionary activity will be considered cause for separation or dismissal from the job." Listed among such "counterrevolutionary activity" was anything "carried out with the objective of provoking difficulties in the labor centers, [to] paralyze industries and create obstacles to the development of revolutionary measures," a provision clearly indicated that any organized attempts to interfere with production would be considered criminal.[34]

This "voluntary" forfeiting of rights for which the labor movement had fought for so long was not always so voluntary. As late as 1963, the Trotskyist sympathizer with the Castro regime Adolfo Gilly recounted one such case. In September of that year, Lázaro Peña, already CTC secretary general, spoke at a meeting of the heavy construction workers union. The subject of discussion at the meeting was a resolution providing that when a worker's equipment was damaged, the worker involved should be reduced to a lower skill category and so receive the reduced wage appropriate for that category. When the local union leaders hesitated about defending this proposal, Lázaro Peña demanded its passage.

However, Gilly recorded: "The assembly was transformed into a scandal. A worker declared that he would accept that proposition when the leaders abandoned their automobiles and came to work with them. Another recalled his [Peña's] old friendship and collaboration with Batista. Another accused him of seeking privileges. The assembly was suspended in great disorder."

A new assembly "better prepared" by the union leadership met several days later. Gilly noted that fewer workers attended that meeting than the former one. It "approved by a majority this proposition."[35]

These "agreements" underscored the entirely different role of the labor movement took on in the wake of the Tenth CTC Congress and the purge of the labor movement that occurred after that event. Minister of Labor Martínez Sánchez made clear the new kind of labor movement that was being forged in "Socialist" Cuba in his address to the Twenty-sixth National Council meeting of the CTC in September 1962.

In declaring that meeting open, the minister noted, "It is necessary to multiply our efforts on all levels of the trade union movement to fulfill the tasks of production and emulation, the wage scales and labor norms, the new collective contracts, the discussion of the social security project in all centers of work and in the whole country, the issuing of the Labor Book and the other tasks in different labor fronts."[36]

The minister of labor was most explicit in his discussion of the nature of the new type of collective agreements, which, as he said, "acquire a new significance and content."[37] He stressed that any differences between management and labor "do not have an antagonistic character, since both the trade union and the administrations of state organisms have the same interests and pursue the same objectives. For this reason, collective contracts . . . have a content completely opposed to those reached during capitalism."

Minister Martínez Sánchez stressed the importance of the new kind of contract:

The working out of collective contracts is converted into a most important measure directed to guarantee the fulfillment and overfulfillment of the production plans, the increase in the productivity of labor, the improvement of the organization of labor, as well as also raising the responsibility of the state organizations and unions to improvement of the material conditions of life and elevation of the cultural level of all the workers of the enterprises and labor units.[38]

Martín Sánchez then went on to explain what should be included in the new collective agreements. He said, "In the first place, the collective contracts must begin by setting forth the political and economic tasks which our ORI and the Revolutionary Government set before the workers, in each separate branch of our national economy." (The ORI was the first step in formation of what became the Communist Party of Cuba.)

The minister continued:

In the second place, the obligations of the Enterprise and National Union concerning fulfillment and overfulfillment of the state production plan, development of socialist emulation . . . setting forth in this chapter the obligation of the collective in fulfilling the plan of production. . . . These obligations must take concrete form in reducing the cost of production by such and such percent . . . reduce defective production by a determined percent.[39]

At another point in his discussion of the nature of the new kind of collective agreement, Martínez Sánchez said that it must contain "the preparation and elevation of the skills of the workers, discipline in work which consists of informing all the workers about the internal regulations concerning labor, to fight against absenteeism, to observe rigorously the working day established by Law, the protection of work."[40]

After his meeting with the CTC National Council, the minister of labor drew up a model of this new type of collective contract. In a CTC assembly in November 1962 it was accepted.[41]

In his talk before the CTC National Council, the minister made reference to several new laws and regulations concerning the labor movement and the workers in general. In addition to submitting the labor movement to its control de facto, the Castro government passed several important pieces of legislation with this same objective. One of these was the Law of Trade Union Organization, which we have already noted, which decreed the new structure of the trade union movement.

Another fundamental piece of legislation was Resolution No. 5798 of the Ministry of Labor, which dealt extensively with the way the workers were to be organized and treated within each en-

terprise. Minister of Labor Martínez Sánchex explained this in
some detail to the CTC Council. Each economic unit was to prepare a list of personnel, including the total number of those
employed, as well as an analysis of the number in each skill or
occupation. When a post had to be filled, the replacement had to
be from within the enterprise, unless there was no one there
qualified for the job, in which case application for a new worker
had to be made to the Ministry's Employment Directorate.

Decree #5798 also covered working hours, which could not be
altered by any enterprise without permission of the ministry.
Overtime could only be worked if there were no other workers
available to the firm. There was also extensive regulation of paid
vacations.[42]

Special attention was paid in Resolution 5798 to workers' absenteeism. According to Minister Martínez Sánchez:

In cases of arriving late or abandoning work before the time to leave, and
in cases of habitual absentees there is established a gradation of sanc-
tions which go from public censure before the assembly and on the
mural bulletin board of the labor center, to discount from the wage in
proportion to the number of lateness without justification; a transfer or
dismissal from employment could be used for repeaters.

The Minister added:

It is necessary to employ persuasion, convincing, frank and open discussions of the cases of absenteeism before the masses in each work center,
but it is also necessary to adopt concrete measures to prevent the disori-
entation of those who do not respect the new socialist morality, or who
pay no attention to warnings against inappropriate conduct which dam-
ages the Revolution and their own work comrades.[43]

Wages were also dealt with in Resolution #798. It provided
that no changes in wages in an enterprise could be made without
the previous approval of the Ministry of Labor. In the case of a
worker's being promoted to a position with a higher wage than he
or she had been receiving, that worker should receive a wage increase of only 25 percent, and in any case, no additional amount
could be paid the worker that caused his or her wage to exceed
$200 a month. Martínez Sánchez defended this provision, "The
regulation issued tends to resolve, on a provisional basis, a situation created by the conceding of wages which, by their own desire,
the workers agreed to in order to avoid inflation and which is today still in effect."[44]

Subsequent legislation that had a major impact on individual
workers and vastly increased government control over the work

force was the Ley del Expediente Laboral of 1969. This law established the kind of minute control over each worker that Stalin had instituted in the Soviet Union but that the Khrushchev regime had done away with several years before it was introduced in Cuba.

The *expediente* was a species of ledger or workbook, which according to the law itself was "the orderly and chronological accumulation of all the data and antecedents or labor history of the worker." The management of every enterprise was obliged to prepare such a document for every one of its workers, and no enterprise management could employ a worker without presentation of his or her expediente.

The official rationale for such a document was that it would contain all the data necessary for determining the worker's rights under the social security system. However, as Efrén Córdova noted, "In practice the expediente included also references to the attitude of the worker toward the revolution (his participation in voluntary work, his enrollment as a militiaman, his presence at commemorative ceremonies, the reports of the CDR, etc."[45] (The CDRs were the neighborhood committees established to keep close track of the activities of everyone in their jurisdiction.)

STAKHANOVISM AND "SOCIALIST EMULATION"

Among the new tasks assigned to the labor movement by the Castro regime were those of organizing (or participating in the organization of) intense personal competition among the workers (Stakhanovism), which was referred to officially as "Socialist emulation." Workers who spectacularly surpassed their official production quota, or who worked particularly long hours, were given great publicity and praise. Efrén Córdova noted, "The new heroes appeared on television and occupied positions of honor in the presidential tribunal during the grand parades and demonstrations of the regime." He added, "It appears reasonable that the so-called labor exploits were the product of a phenomenon of collective psychosis provoked by the propaganda of the regime and the influence of the charismatic power of Castro."[46]

However, Minister of Labor Martínez Sánchez made clear in a speech to the September 1962 CTC Council meeting that the wider objectives of "Socialist emulation" were to pressure ordinary workers to meet the targets set by the Stakhanovites: "The economic effectiveness of emulation is determined not by the successes achieved by isolated participants, no matter how great they are, but by the increase of the labor productivity of the majority of the workers. The isolated successes and records only indicate how much and how the productivity of labor can be increased." He added, "Socialist emulation is the fundamental form in which is revealed the activity and creative initiative of the workers in their struggle for constant increase in productivity of labor."[47]

The minister also indicated that the organization of the Socialist emulation was one of the fundamental tasks of the labor movement, "because emulation is the objective law of the socialist mode of production and does not mean that it develops spontaneously. The conscious action of the working masses must be directed and organized by the trade union and state organisms."[48]

Socialist emulation became a permanent feature of Cuban labor relations, with the strong support of the Confederación de Trabajadores de Cuba.

WAGE DETERMINATION IN "SOCIALIST" CUBA

Whereas the stimulation of competition among individual workers (which organized labor had traditionally fought) became a major function of the labor movement in Fidel Castro's "socialist" Cuba, the unions were no longer allowed any part in the negotiation of their members' wages, which ceased to be the unions' concern. The fixing of wages became the prerogative of the state, according to a resolution of the Ministry of Labor early in 1960.[49]

As we have noted, existing wage levels were frozen early in 1960. The government thereupon set afoot a process of trying to establish a gradation of wage levels applicable to the whole country. It is clear that, at least in the beginning, the government favored an overall system of piecework wages (which the labor movement had traditionally opposed).

Minister of Labor Martínez Sánchez explained the government's position to the CTC National Council in September 1962. He said that wages should be based on the "norms" set by the government for the particular job at which the worker was employed. As he put it:

This need requires a rigorous control over the expenditure of social labor, which requires, at the same time, the measure of the work done, but to compare it also with what is necessary. The amount of necessary labor can be determined only by establishing the norms of production or of time, which, in turn will determine the remumeration for the work of each worker of the production unit.[50]

Professor Taylor, the "father of Taylorism," could not have stated the situation more clearly.

The Labor Code finally adopted in 1984 stated that wherever possible payment to the worker should be by the piece. The individual worker would be paid in accordance with his or her ability to meet the quota of work established as "normal" by the Ministry of Labor officials charged with that task. If a worker's output fell below that "normal" amount, his or her wage payment was to be reduced by the percentage of shortfall, but if the worker exceeded the expected output target, he or she could receive an additional payment of at most 30 percent of the computed value of the increased output.[51]

The CTC offered no objections to this alteration of the Cuban wage payment system. Quite to the contrary, it endorsed the system. Typical was the following resolution of the Thirteenth Congress of the CTC:

If the worker doesn't fulfill his norm, his salary should be reduced accordingly. . . . If the worker overfulfills his norm his salary should be increased accordingly. . . . For piecework the relationship between wages and finished product is clear and direct. He who makes 15 units is paid for 15 units. He who makes 10 is paid for 10. And he who makes only 8 cannot be paid for more than 8.[52]

The Ministry of Labor first established a course to train experts in determining "norms," and in 1961 some 500 people graduated from this course. However, the ministry was apparently not satisfied with the results of this training course, and in 1962 a number of Soviet "specialists" arrived to train Cuban specialists in labor norms. As Efrén Córdova commented, "It is consequently not strange that the new wage system was not only inspired by socialist principles but was in practice a copy of the Soviet model with adjustments made by the Council of Mutual Aid (COMECON) and the new rigidity which Castro wanted to impose."[53]

As time passed, the establishment of "norms" became increasingly complicated. When they were introduced, there was emphasis on egalitarianism, but difference between the lowest and the highest wage was 1 to 4.5. However, the government found that such a narrow range tended to discourage administrative and technical workers, and in 1970, 1976, 1978, and 1982 there were changes in norms to provide more "appropriate" payment for workers with special skills.

Also, in the beginning the Ministry of Labor people thought that a relatively small number of criteria could be established on a nationwide basis. However, with passage of time, it was decided that different norms should apply to different sectors of the economy, and even to different enterprises within an economic sector. As a consequence, there were by 1989 some 2.5 million different norms applied by different enterprises in the various sectors of the economy.

Norms were set in various different ways. Within an enterprise they were worked out by the management together with the union section leadership. Norms set for a whole industry were established by the appropriate ministry and national industrial union. Norms involving more than one industry were established by the State Committee of Labor and Social Security, "in coordination with the CTC and the appropriate national unions."

The rank and file workers had little to say about the fixing of norms to which they must conform. Efrén Córdova noted:

The official literature emphasized . . . that before implementation the norms must "be analyzed and discussed with the workers." The technicians explained "in detailed fashion" to the workers the procedure used for their elaboration, their basis and how long they would last. All this took place 15 days before the imposition of the norm, which could be reduced in some cases to only three days. The technicians responded in the assemblies to the questions but never or almost never modified their estimates. The workers had no power to approve or reject the norms that in all cases were elaborated from outside.[54]

"Errors" were not infrequently made in the establishment of norms—and therefore of wages. When it was found that many of the workers were able to exceed the output set by the norms, and therefore increase somewhat their wages, the norm setters hastened to raise the norms. In many such cases the workers "responded with indifference or passive resistance. In certain situations the setting of norms could then become involved with labor discipline."[55]

In the government's assumption of control of the whole economy, a special problem was presented by what were called "historic wages." These were cases in which workers and their unions had before the Cuban Revolution or in its first year won wages that were higher than those set by the norms established by the Castro regime. In 1975, it was estimated by the Cuban Communist Party that in 1962, 79.9 percent of the workers in received such wages.

Rather than face potentially serious worker resistance, the Castro government decided that, for the time being, those workers who received the "historic wages" should continue to receive them. However, over the following years, every effort was made to abolish such payments. When a worker retired, his successor got a wage fixed by the official norms, when a worker was transferred from his or her job to one with a wage set by the norms, that worker was paid at the norm rate. By 1972, only 18.9 percent of the workers in agriculture were still receiving "historic wages." In 1977, a decree provided that no more historic wages could be set. As Efrén Córdova commented, "Thus, in a gradual but incessant manner, there were disappearing from the labor scene the last remains of the labor 'ancient regime,' vestiges which represent an embarrassing contrast with the austere wage system of the revolution."[56]

In the period following the economically disastrous 1970 sugar harvest, when the government partially retreated from its previous emphasis on moral incentives, the labor movement was given a role to play in the combination of material incentives, moral incentives, and political reliability that was established to determine how much—in real terms—a worker would receive for his or her labors. Each union was allotted a quantity of certain goods and was left to decide who received these goods, in terms of the workers' needs and their behavior on the job. After extensive discussions of the needs and virtues—or vices—of individual workers, those selected were then given the right to buy the products involved, principally heavier consumer goods, such as radios, televisions, and refrigerators. The prices were often high, but the workers usually bought what was offered to them, since most workers had substantial amounts of cash, since there had been little available to buy except the goods that were rationed, the purchase of which used up only a relatively small amount of their wages.[57]

WORKING HOURS IN "SOCIALIST" CUBA

Hours of work as well as wages went through a drastic transformation in "socialist" Cuba, where presumably the workers ruled. This was reflected in the Constitution of 1976, which proclaimed that the "average" workweek would be forty-four hours—in contrast to the Constitution of 1940, which had established a forty-four-hour workweek as the maximum—and provided that payment for forty-eight hours would continue.

The "normal" limit of 44 hours a week was frequently exceeded. Efrén Córdova noted, "Whether by special laws, by resolutions of the CETSS [State Committee of Labor and Social Security], by dispositions of the trade union leaders or the Party, or by initiative of a group of workers or instigation of the Commander in Chief, the fact is that there is the tendency to establish in whatever way the pernicious practice of extended hours."

There were numerous examples of such increases. A resolution of the CETSS dealing with special workers' groups known as *contingentes* specified a general workday of 12 hours. The CETSS also authorized a ten-hour workday in construction "in cases in which it was requested by chiefs and competent authorities." In the case of the El Patate dam project in 1988, the workers had to labor thirteen hours a day, in accordance with requirements of the party and the CTC. In September of the same year, it was provided that there would be a ten-hour day in a project to rebuild railroad coaches, as well as the requirement that workers give up their Saturday and Sunday rest days.[58]

One way in which the government sought to curb absenteeism was to make the workers of an enterprise collectively responsible for the absence of any of their number. This involved the so-called double shift (*doble turno*), which

signifies that the worker is obliged to double his shift to make up for the unforeseen absence of workers whose job cannot be interrupted. . . . The occurrence of the double shift is determined by the administration in those occupations in which this is agreed to in the collective contract (which is almost always very generous in this respect) and the worker has no other option than to carry out this work. It should be added that cases are becoming increasingly frequent in which double shift is applied in jobs which are not urgent or indispensable and are motivated by the simple desire to accelerate the work or fulfill an agreement.[59]

As Córdova has noted, the provision for a sufficient labor force to cover possible absentees is generally a task of management, "not of the worker who has already carried out his job and completed his shift."[60] However, in Castro's Cuba the device of the double shift was designed, at least in part, to turn workers of an enterprise against those of their number who might be inclined to absent themselves from their jobs.

The 1984 Labor Code provided that workers could be made to work as many as 160 hours a year beyond the normal workday, compared to 120 hours in the USSR. However, the State Committee of Labor and Social Security was authorized to increase this number of overtime hours.[61]

There were other ways in which under the new system the workers lost much of their leisure time. One was compulsory attendance at after-hours "ideological meetings." According to one early study of this subject: "Another indirect method of extending the length of the work day is to be found in the periodic ideological sessions which are held at the place of employment. These sessions, which average one or two hours each, several times per week, are attended by workers on a 'voluntary' basis but in reality utilize the concept of the 'captive audience.' "[62]

The labor movement, which traditionally had sought to limit the working day, offered no opposition to the extension of the work period after the 1960–1961 transformation of the CTC and its subordinate organizations. On the contrary, the CTC boasted about this change. For instance, the CTC periodical *Trabajadores* of June 5, 1989, praised a mechanic in the Empresa Nacional de Envases Industriales y Comerciales who sometimes worked for thirty hours straight without interruption. The same periodical on May 1, 1989 pointed with pride to a construction worker who had worked fifteen to sixteen hours a day and as a result was given a seat on the principal platform of the May Day demonstration.[63]

One procedure for increasing the workweek was the particular province of the Confederación de Trabajadores de Cuba. This was the so-called Domingo Rojo (Red Sunday), that is, the organization of union members to give up Sunday as a day of rest. Efrén Córdova noted: "It falls generally to the CTC to bring about the necessary mobilization for work carried out on Red Sunday. The central trade union group indicates the objects of that work, and fixes the number of workers who will be necessary in each case. Sometimes it indicates with the greatest magnanimity that the work will extend for only eight hours."[64]

GRIEVANCE PROCEDURE IN "SOCIALIST" CUBA

Historically, trade unions in Cuba and elsewhere had two basic tasks. One was to negotiate collective contracts with the employers, the other to bring about the establishment of a grievance procedure whereby the collective agreements could be enforced as they applied to individual workers. In this second case, there were—as in the negotiations of collective contracts—profound changes after the Tenth CTC Congress and the subsequent purge of the leadership of the labor movement.

Between 1961 and 1964, the government established Grievance Commissions. However, from early on, there was unhappiness with the functioning of these bodies. As a result, in April 1962, the government enacted the Law of Labor Justice. According to Minister of Labor Martínez Sánchez:

This law enlarges the jurisdiction of the Comisiones de Relaciones, which were dealing with and resolving labor matters, declaring them organs capable with and resolving everything concerned with Social Security, maternity, help in cases of injury, old age and death, indemnization for common and work accidents and common and professional diseases, as soon as the new Law of Security is enacted.[65]

However, government leaders continued to be unhappy with the performance of the Grievance Commissions, particularly because of their frequent siding with the workers in the cases that they handled. Thus, Fidel Castro himself claimed, "Many members of the Comisiones de Reclamaciones seem to encourage absenteeism and vagrancy." "Che" Guevara, then minister of industry, also claimed, "The Comisiones de Reclamaciones are a nuisance which create contradiction," and added that these bodies "could carry out a very useful task if they would change their attitude. The fundamental thing is to produce." Carmelo Mesa-Lago and Roberto E. Hernández commented, with regard to these complaints, "Thus, some Comisiones de Reclamaciones, in spite of their little power, attempted to support the workers against the administration of state Enterprises."

As a result of the unhappiness of top government leaders a new Law of Labor Justice was enacted in 1964. Martínez Sánchez noted, "The new law will strengthen discipline in work and will increase production and productivity." He added that the new law would be applied against

that type of worker who is still present in the labor centers, undisciplined workers, and against them there must be disciplinary measures. We still encounter shirkers, and against them there must be disciplinary measures. We still encounter workers who have not made the leap in revolutionary development, and have a certain predisposition to discuss and protest any measure of the Administration.

The new law dealt with a variety of violations of labor discipline: "lateness, absence, disobedience, negligence, offence to supervisors in word and deed, damage to equipment, fraud and robbery." It provided a variety of punishments for such offenses, including loss of honors given for meritorious service, banning from holding certain jobs, fines of up to 25 percent of a worker's wage for a maximum of four months, transfer to another labor center, and suspension from work for as much as a month, loss of vacation rights, and finally, dismissal from the job.[66]

The new law established Consejos de Trabajo (Labor Councils) in every enterprise, consisting of five members elected by the workers. In order to qualify for membership on such a council, a worker needed "to have a socialist attitude toward work, be disciplined and not to have any absences." There were also established Councils of Regional Appeal, consisting of three people named by the Ministry of Labor, an administrator of a state enterprise, and a representative of the union. Finally, there was a National Review Commission made up of two from the ministry, two from the administration of state enterprises, and one from the CTC. In the last instance, the Ministry of Labor was given power to decide cases without right of appeal and to change the personnel of the various grievance bodies.[67]

Mesa-Lago and Hernández commented with regard to this law:

In view of the requirements to be a member of the Consejos de Trabajo, the composition of the Regional Appeal Councils (in which the representatives of the Ministry of Labor and of the administration of enterprises are the majority), and the ample powers given by the law to the Ministry of Labor to resolve conflicts directly and on appeal, it is obvious that the control of the Government in matters of discipline and labor conflicts is enormous.[68]

UNPAID WORK

One of the most important innovations introduced into the labor movement by the Castro regime was the organization by the government—and the trade unions—of unpaid work on a massive scale. It began soon after the CTC Tenth Congress and the subsequent purge of the Confederación de Trabajadores de Cuba and its constituent organizations.

There were certainly both ideological and economic reasons for the Cuban government to encourage, organize, and virtually compel the use of unpaid labor. The ideological motives for such a development were perhaps most clearly stated by "Che" Guevara: "Voluntary work should be looked at for its economic importance or for its present value to the state. Ultimately, voluntary work is the element that most actively develops the workers' conscience, preparing the road to a new society."[69]

Economic factors were also a reason for the Castro government's, with the acquiescence of the new labor leadership, pushing for workers to labor without payment—what was officially called "voluntary labor." For one thing, the revolution had caused important changes in the labor market. Large numbers of agricultural workers moved to the cities, particularly Havana and Santiago, where they found employment in the rapidly expanding government, as well as in industries and other enterprises taken over by the regime. Pledged to eliminate unemployment, the government could not deny these people employment, even when there was little for them to do.

At the same time, those remaining in agriculture, particularly in the sugar industry, as a result of the limitation of their income that began early in 1960, had little incentive to work hard, leading important figures in the government to accuse them of working only three or four hours a day, instead of the eight that had been the normal workday.

Finally, the increasing shortage of consumer goods from 1960 on, due in part at least to growing difficulties with the United States, from which Cuba had traditionally received many such products, and leading in 1961 to the imposition of rationing, meant that increased wage payments could only lead to serious inflation. One answer to this situation was for workers to work without pay.

Efrén Córdova conceded that "in the period of transformation, the majority of those who responded to the campaign for voluntary labor did so spontaneously." However, he added that "many were obliged to participate in it through social pressure or were compelled by the propaganda of the heads of government."[70]

However, by 1961 the recruiting of "volunteer" workers to labor without pay was more organized, and the CTC established machinery to prod its members to continue to work with no pay. It first set up a Department of Voluntary Labor, with branches in the various provinces, and then installed a secretary of voluntary labor as a member of its Executive Bureau.[71] Carmelo Mesa-Lago noted in 1969, "Since 1962 voluntary workers have been recruited because of pressure from trade unions and managers of state enterprises, and have been organized in battalions and brigades under Communist party guidance."[72]

Mesa-Lago analyzed the types of "voluntary" labor in Socialist Cuba:

Five types of unpaid labor may be distinguished in Cuba: (1) work performed by employed workers outside of regular working time, (2) work done by unemployed women, (3) work performed by students as a method of socialist education, (4) work accomplished by politico-administrative prisoners as a means of "social rehabilitation," and (5) work included as part of the compulsory military service.[73]

By 1963 the government enacted "Reglamentos para la Organización de la Emulación Socialista," specifying official regulations concerning voluntary labor. Mesa-Lago commented:

The state has regulated the performance of unpaid labor by introducing several measures: criticism among voluntary workers, annual contracts binding the workers to achieve a determined number of unpaid hours of labor, management and trade union checks on the amount and quality of the labor done, weekly reports by the battalions on their own performance and that of others, inspection teams to keep discipline and discover flaws, and penalties for disciplinary violations of the state regulations.

Students in all levels of the educational system were recruited to do unpaid work, some of it during the schoolday, but also in the hours after classes had finished, and particularly during weekends and their summer vacations. Several hundred thousand students were mobilized for this type of "voluntary" labor.[74]

An important role in mobilizing children and teenagers for "voluntary" labor was played by the Union of Pioneers (UPC), composed of children ranging in ages from six to twelve, and the Communist Youth, both dependencies of the Communist Party. They organized "columns and detachments in the textile industry, in construction, in the maritime industry, in the exploitation of nickle and in other sectors."

These various groups were formed into Ejercito Juvenil Trabajo (EJT, Youth Labor Army) in 1973, which also included some military conscripts, and it was "called upon from time to time to work in the most arduous jobs of construction and agriculture. . . . The EJT also applied the principles of socialist emulation."[75]

Two kinds of people who were involved in "voluntary" labor whose participation was clearly not voluntary were political prisoners and army conscripts. The first of these categories included both citizens who were guilty of "subversive" activities and those administrative personnel who had "erred" grievously in the performance of their duties. In both cases, the people were interned in work camps, where they labored at whatever their prison guards specified.

In 1963, for the first time in Cuban history, military conscription was established by the Castro government. There were clearly at least two motivations for this move. One was the Castro regime's continuing fear of a U.S. invasion attempt; the other was the desire of the government to mobilize those young people who were neither employed in a regular job nor going to school.[76]

However, the tendency toward militarization of work went considerably beyond the use of people formally drafted into the armed forces. Maurice Zeitlin noted in 1969, "There are signs that 'labor brigades' organized along military lines, as well as the actual utilization of 'conscript labor' are already quite important in agricultural work, especially in sugar-cane harvesting."[77] Such semimilitarization of workers was to become a permanent part of the Cuban scene.

Certainly the high point of mobilizing people for unpaid work was the 1970 sugar harvest. In the attempt to reach the goal of

10 million tons of sugar in that harvest, people were "volunteered" from virtually all the rest of the economy to harvest sugar. One former official of the Castro government described to me an example of how the "volunteers" were recruited for that and previous harvests. The Cuban representative at the International Sugar Conference, he was on a visit home to report on his work in the midst of the annual harvest drive. He had occasion to get a haircut, and while he was there, a "recruiter" for the local Committee for the Defense of the Revolution entered the barbershop. After determining who the people there were, he indicated who among them was going to "volunteer" for cutting cane.[78]

In Castro's speech at the July 26, 1970, annual commemoration of his and his followers attempt to seize the Moncada barracks in 1953, he reported on the 10-million-ton drive, and particularly on its impact on the rest of the economy. He noted that the campaign had seriously damaged virtually every other sector, and recited the decline in output, the failure to meet the year's production goals, for almost all other parts of the economy. In explaining each such case, Fidel Castro said that it was due to the diversion of workers and of transport facilities for the sugar harvest.[79]

The massive efforts to recruit "voluntary" labor that characterized the 1970 sugar harvest were never repeated. However, the recruiting and organizing of people for unpaid labor continued to be a major policy of the Castro regime. As late as 1994, *Trabajadores*, the official newspaper of the CTC, noted with regard to the province of Las Tunas, that "Julian López, member of the Central Committee and first secretary of the Party in the province, recognized the work of the Tunas voluntary cane cutters who fulfilled by 120 percent the plan for cutting cane in the harvest."[80]

CTC CONGRESSES AND THE NEW ROLE OF CUBAN ORGANIZED LABOR

Once it had been thoroughly purged in 1960, the Confederación de Trabajadores de Cuba offered no resistance to the transformation of organized labor from a movement defending the rights of the workers into one whose principal jobs were enforcing labor discipline and doing everything possible to stimulate production and productivity of workers. Quite to the contrary, it conformed in every way to the new orientation. Nowhere was this clearer than in the successive congresses of the CTC.

The Twelfth Congress, in August 1966, saw the implementation of a new method of choosing delegates to the highest body of the confederation. Preliminary elections were held in the 10,962 sections of the national unions affiliated with the CTC, and these sessions produced 45,508 possible delegates.

Then, within each workplace there was formed a committee consisting of representatives of the Communist Party, the Communist Youth, the union, and the administration of the enterprise. That body "proceeded to purge the initial list of those not considered reliable or lacking in merit to be named as delegates." The names of those who passed this preliminary screening were then given to a "higher body," which once again studied the merits and demerits of those people under consideration.

Efrén Córdova noted, "The criteria used by these commissions were principally membership in the party, being a militiaman, accumulated hours of voluntary labor, diplomas, awards and recognition obtained on the job, attendance of courses of ideological training, and naturally, the labor book of those concerned to note labor discipline and index of productivity."[81]

The Twelfth Congress paid unusual attention to "international" questions, such as support of guerrilla activities in various Latin American countries, racial discrimination in the United States, and condemnation of the Vietnam War. Insofar as domestic matters were concerned, the resolutions of the meeting dealt with reform of the CTC statutes, with stronger support for agriculture, "and strengthening labor discipline."

Córdova noted that all of the resolutions adopted by the Twelfth Congress had been prepared beforehand by the Organizing Committee of the Congress, and no delegate was moved to propose any additional ones: "Nor did anyone ask for explanations when the posts of recording secretary, and legal matters, accident prevention and social security secretaries were eliminated. Nor were there any requests for information about any unclear point in the report on activities or about the impact of some resolution which might affect the members in a direct way."[82]

By the late 1960s, the virtually complete failure of the organized labor movement to fight for the rights and interests of the workers was quite clear. This was commented on both by friendly foreign observers and some government leaders.

Maurice Zeitlin noted in 1969:

As to the trade unions . . . from what I could observe, and from the vague and infrequent references to them by the workers I interviewed, they seem to have "withered away." The workers do not have an *independent organization* which takes the initiative in the plant, industry, or country as a whole, to assure, let alone demand, improved working conditions or higher wages; no organization exists, as an autonomous force, to protect and advance the immediate interests of the workers, as they see them, independent of the prevailing line of the Communist Party, or policies of the Revolutionary Government. The distinction in practice between the role played by the Ministry of Labor and that of the CTC-R, the Workers Federation—if clear in the formal sense—is not clear to ordinary workers. Nor, indeed, does this distinction seem clear to some of the government officials and national leaders I spoke with.[83]

One of the party and government leaders who made the same kind of observation was Carlos Rafael Rodríguez, a onetime minister in the cabinet of Fulgencio Batista and in 1969 a top figure in Castro's Communist Party. He told Zeitlin that "the unions are transmission belts of the Party directives to the workers but have insufficiently represented the workers to the Party or the Revolutionary Government. They cannot merely be instruments of the Party without losing their purpose."[84]

However, it is clear that these "failures" of the labor movement were in fact encouraged by the Castro regime. This was made clear by Raúl Castro in 1972:

Under capitalism the trade unions are the instruments that organize and lead the working masses in the struggle for their just demands. . . . However, when the working class is in power the role of the trade union is changed. . . . There are no antagonisms between the working class and the revolutionary power. . . . One of the principal functions of the trade unions under socialism is to serve as a vehicle for the orientation, directives and goals which the revolutionary power must convey to the working masses. The trade unions are the most powerful link between the party and the working classes. That is one of their principal mission. . . . Moreover, the work of the trade unions helps and supports that of the administration. . . . The principal tasks are the productivity and work discipline; more efficient utilization of the work day, norming and organization; quality, conservation and most efficient and rational use of both material and human resources.[85]

The Thirteenth Congress of the CTC, which met in November 1973, seven years after the previous one, reflected Fidel Castro's retreat from total endorsement of "moral" incentives. It passed a resolution that cited Karl Marx's *Critique of the Gotha Program* to the effect that payment to everyone should be "according to his capacity, to each according to his work." It then praised the abolition of payment to workers when they had to work overtime, arguing that the need to be paid to work overtime in order to reach the pre-established production goals was a "vice."

This Congress also demanded the end of payment of historic wages. It likewise urged abolition of special retirement rights for workers who had outstanding production records.

A special resolution was passed by the Thirteenth Congress dealing with workers' participation in state and administrative planning of enterprises. It said that "production and service assemblies" should be held in each enterprise at least once a month, with an agenda prepared by the enterprise administration and the local union section, and that the fundamental purpose of such a meeting should be "the fulfillment or overfulfillment of the production plan."[86]

One supposed purpose of this congress was to give more life and a greater role to the labor movement. In the discussions preceding the congress, it had been described as too dominated by the party and government.[87]

However, the resolution of the Thirteenth Congress dealing with the relationship of the unions with the party and the government did not seem likely to achieve the end in view. Although it proclaimed that the union movement was "autonomous," it added, "They recognize openly and conscientiously the direction of the Party as a vanguard group and the maximum organization of the working class; they make it their own to follow the policy and slogans of the party."[88]

The votes in favor of all of the subjects discussed at the Thirteenth Congress were little short of unanimous. According to the official account of the meeting, they varied from 99.1 percent to 99.4 percent.[89]

The Fourteenth Congress of the CTC met in the last days of December 1978. As had become traditional, there were congresses of the national unions just prior to the CTC meeting. In them, thirteen different "theses" had been adopted by overwhelming votes. For example, one dealing with "the economic activity of the Unions" passed with 1,842,808 votes in favor, 968 against, and 1,512 abstentions.[90]

Some twenty-nine different resolutions were passed by this CTC Congress. Efrén Córdova commented extensively with regard to these. He noted that there was "no novelty" in resolutions dealing with unpaid labor, socialist emulation, and collective contracts.

Córdova then observed, "In reaffirming in effect the role of voluntary labor it gave it a breadth that would cover all economic activities as well as the carrying out of works of a social character, the ideological tasks, the work done in saluting the historic anniversaries and the Red Sundays, the establishment of which was attributed to the National Committee of the CTC."

Córdova continued:

The resolution on socialist emulation not only summed up the objectives, principles and kinds of emulation, but sought to give impulse vigorously to the "conscientious, enthusiastic and permanent struggle of all the workers and work collectives to fulfill and overfulfill the agreements reached." If the resolution on collective agreements ratified the abandonment of the term formerly used ("collective pledges") its objective continued being that of giving priority to the fulfillment of the plan of production and service, determination of the organization and normalizing of work, including punctual attendance at work, the improvement of the quality of the products and control of socialist emulation as well as the organization and control of voluntary labor and the enforcement of the internal rules of order.[91]

Between the Fourteenth Congress in 1978 and the Fifteenth Congress in February 1984, the leadership of the CTC did work with outstanding production records. These increases amounted to some 670 million pesos a year, according to Fidel Castro's report to the Second Congress of the Communist Party late in 1980. He said that this had been possible because of notable increases in the late 1970s in labor productivity. But these were also years of substantial increases in Soviet aid to Cuba and rising sugar prices.[92]

Perhaps this temporary change in attitudes of both union leaders and enterprise managers accounted for a change at the country's largest textile plant, Textilera Ariguanabo, in the small town of Bauta in the province of Havana. In September 1987 a six-hour shift was introduced for the production workers in the plant, but with wages still being paid for eight hours. As a North American who studied labor relations in that plant noted, this change made work there very attractive, drawing in many new workers, so that the work force could be carefully selected. Wages paid there were relatively high. Nonproduction workers still stayed on the job for eight hours. She also reported that the change in working time was made on the orders of national planners, because of marked labor turnover in the plant and the fact that studies had shown that productivity of the workers fell markedly in the last two hours of work, and accidents on the job notably increased.

This observer reported that work norms were generally met in the plant. She also commented that the workers worked for the material benefits, and some received almost double the standard wage through extra compensation for surpassing their work quota.[93]

There would seem to have been little discussion of the relative improvement of the workers' lot in the Fifteenth Congress. However, there were the usual new resolutions urging the need to overfulfill production plans, particularly in the sugar industry.[94]

The "liberalization" of wages and working conditions did not last long. It gave way to "a new policy of austerity which was conceived of as part of the campaign for rectification of errors. The fact that there existed in enterprises an excessive number of workers with consequent repercussions on the wage bill brought the government not only to reduce the workforce but also to moderate the increase in wages."[95]

Official figures indicated that the average wage of Cuban workers in 1988 was "twenty-six pesos less than that received by an industrial worker at the beginning of 1959 and much below that earned by an office worker. As for the minimum wage, it was only eleven pesos higher than that established by Batista in 1958 when the peso was equivalent to the dollar."[96]

A document of the Central Committee of the Communist Party giving instructions to government institutions "reiterated . . . the policies initiated in 1987 to avoid the presentation of new cases of workers who received wages above the one provided in the labor rules or that there be wage increases without corresponding rise in material production of services."[97]

The Sixteenth Congress of the CTC took place in January 1990, a few months after the fall of the Berlin Wall, and the beginning of the disintegration of the Communist bloc of Eastern Europe. Insofar as Cuba was concerned, the period before the Sixteenth Congress had been marked by the "rectification of errors" stage of the revolution, during which Fidel Castro had totally reversed the modest relaxation of the Cuban regime's policies— allowing peasant markets and modest proliferation of control over self-employed artisans, and modest wage increases—that he had allowed in the late 1970s and the beginning of the 1980s.[98]

Events in Eastern Europe produced few echoes in the CTC Congress. However, the "rectification" campaign of Castro did. The major "thesis" document submitted to and adopted by the meeting was entitled "The Unions in the Process of Rectification." It and other resolutions of the Congress restated old themes. Efrén Córdova commented, "The majority of those resolutions repeated the same things dealt with in previous congresses: the promotion of volunteer labor, socialist emulation, strengthening of labor discipline, the increase of productivity, the fulfillment or overfulfillment of production plans, use of the working day, and elimination of waste of material, human and financial resources."[99]

This last congress of the CTC before the disappearance of the Soviet Union and the resulting tremendous economic crisis for Cuba was reported by Radio Rebelde as demanding of the workers "an insistence on full dedication and consecration to work."

Radio Rebelde reported (as paraphrased by Efrén Córdova) that the CTC congress had called for

greater vigilance of the union in controlling arrivals and exists from the workplace, a stricter application of disciplinary regulations and a decrease in the incomes arising from prizes and awards. The process of rectification of errors involved . . . greater need for the workers to adopt attitudes in accord with the revolution if they expected to get work in an enterprise, retain their jobs, be promoted to better paying posts, be selected for training courses or avoid being transferred to less desirable jobs. It was a program of great austerity, in which priority was given to moral rather than monetary payment, and also of great severity in working conditions.[100]

Efrén Córdova summed up the differences between all of the CTC Congresses after the Tenth and what he called "real trade union congresses." He noted, "The latter mixed eulogies and criticisms, formulated protests and approbation, praise and accusations and all of this was carried out in a vibrant atmosphere of those who were concerned with improving labor conditions." Córdova posed the question, "Of what importance is it that 500,000 workers had passed sixth or ninth grade if then they were incapable of making the slightest contribution to the discussion of questions which were vital for them and their families?"[101]

Of course, the CTC and its subordinate groups were the only legal labor movement in Castro Cuba. This status was enshrined in both the Constitution of 1976 and the subsequent Labor Code. To attempt to challenge this monopoly position was a criminal offense. Córdova noted:

In April 1983 the Supreme Popular Tribunal condemned to 30 years in prison the workers Ezequiel Díaz, Angel Martínez, Carlos García, José L. Díaz and Benito García Olivera for violating article 53 of the Constitution. Before, they had been condemned to death. The crime? To attempt the creation of an independent trade union federation. Even the defending lawyers were condemned to long prison terms. In 1989 another worker, Isidoro Padron, was shot for the same crime of wanting to found an independent union.[102]

A GLIMPSE AT A LOCAL UNION SECTION

A North American scholar, Gail Lindberg, who had studied at considerable length labor relations in the Textilera Ariguanabo outside Havana, sketched the way in which the local union there was organized, and what it did, in 1987–1988, when she studied it. She noted that there were 5,641 unionized workers in the plant. They were divided into six sections, corresponding to the six departments of the plant.

The union in this textile plant did not have dues checkoff. The treasurers of the various sections collected dues when the workers received their pay, which was in cash. Professor Lindberg noted that she had been told that only fourteen people in the plant did not pay dues, because of religious scruples. She said that these workers were regarded as "strange people" by their fellows.

There were 467 union officials in the plant. Sixty-nine of these were section leaders, thirteen for each section. There were also several intermediate levels of officials. At the top of the local was a thirteen-member bureau, of which three were full-time union leaders; the others worked for the union after hours. Some 58 percent of all of the leaders were men, 42 percent women, 39 percent under thirty years of age.

Professor Lindberg was also interested in the racial and political composition of the union leadership. She found that 80 percent were white, 12 percent black, and the rest mestizo. She could not get information on the racial composition of the workers as a whole. She discovered that 20 percent of the leaders were Communist Party members. Most were from the town of Bauta, where the factory was located.

A system of indirect election was used to choose the top officials of the union, a process that occurred every two and a half years. The procedure started with assemblies of the members of each of the six sections, which had to have an attendance rate of at least 70 percent. There, nominations were made from the floor, and there had to be at least two candidates for each post. There was then a secret ballot. Above this level, the process became "more intricate." Membership in the higher levels of the union in the plant was determined by "selected members" of those elected on the section level. Those serving at this intermediate level chose the thirteen-member bureau of the plant union.

The three full-time union officials in the factory were the secretary general, secretary of organization, and secretary of socialist emulation. While serving in their union jobs, they received the same wages they had received before assuming these positions. Professor Lindberg concluded that it was these three who really ran the union. She added that the socialist emulation secretary had the "most difficult" job in the union leadership. At the time she observed the situation, he had been able to induce only 2,000 of the 5,641 workers to give voluntary labor.

The union leadership had several tasks, aside from trying to boost production and productivity. For one, they decided which workers would get housing that the plant had at its disposal, making the decision on the basis of both the worker's need and his or her work history. The union officials also were supposed to protect the health and safety of the workers, a job that Professor Lindberg concluded they did not do adequately. For example, they refused to recognize the existence of "black lung disease," which arises from waste in the air of a textile plant, although it was apparently clear that this malady did exist on a considerable scale.

Professor Lindberg had not been able to find out how "security" was organized in the plant. However, she did know that several of her acquaintances had received training in the field in East Germany.[103]

Efrén Córdova noted the major role played by the party unit in any workplace. He said that it had "a primordial presence in the labor center: its base organizations are made up of the nuclei which exist in each factory or workshop. The officials of the nucleus watch over the fulfillment of the objectives of the Party, stimulate the competitiveness of its militants and examine the conduct of those who work in the center."[104]

PASSIVE RESISTANCE?

One cannot help but raise the question of how it was possible that a labor movement with such militant traditions as that of Cuba could be so completely transformed into one so utterly subordinated to the ruling party and the government as occurred in the Castro regime. One has to ask also whether or not, in spite of the obvious subordination of the leadership of the Cuban labor movement, there was not in fact some kind of resistance—even passive resistance—by the rank and file of the unionized workers to this transformation.

In discussing these questions, at least three points are very clear. On the one hand, there has undoubtedly been throughout the existence of the Castro government a core of unconditional supporters of Fidel Castro and the regime that he headed. Whether aroused by the personal charisma of the dictator, which certainly existed and was long enduring; by his appeals to patriotism and the constantly repeated warning of dangers (from inside as well as outside Cuba) to national sovereignty; or by honest Marxist-Leninist convictions, this core of true believers gave enthusiastic support to all calls for sacrifice and subordination of the individual workers' own well-being to the supposed well-being of the working class in general, and the nation as a whole.

A second clearly important factor was that the Castro regime quickly developed a very efficient machinery of repression. In the earlier years, any union official, or even any ordinary worker, had clearly before him or her the example of what had happened to those trade unionists who had tried to defy the will of El Maximo Lider at the Tenth CTC Congress and in the succeeding purge of the labor movement. Dismissal from union posts and their basic jobs, imprisonment, exile, and even execution had been the fate of those who had sought in any degree to resist the transformation of the labor movement.

It was soon true that

In each work center of any importance there was present in some form the State Security. Sometimes it was visible and known presence; in others its agents worked in a secret and hidden form. In addition to the agents who worked in the General Directorate or Counterintelligence of the Ministry of Interior were the informants or *sources* whose information was channeled through the Guide of the Informer and was subsequently processed in the computers of the State Security. The Guide of the Informer had fifty-five points, of which no less than fifteen referred to labor problems, including one concerning participation in voluntary labor.[105]

Furthermore, early in the regime were established the famous Committees for the Defense of the Revolution (CDRs), which were organized in every neighborhood and had the primary job of spying on everyone in their jurisdiction, reporting to the police and other authorities the slightest sign of unhappiness with the regime, and preventing discontent from taking organizational form. Maurice Zeitlin described them as having the function of "being fully informed about the actions of their neighbors."[106] He cited an article in *Cuba Socialista* that described the CDRs as a "system of collective revolutionary vigilance, in which everyone knows who everyone is, what each person who lives in the block does, what relations he had with the tyranny, to what he is dedicated, whom he meets and what activities he follows."[107]

There were also other "security" forces that had equally extensive control over the workers in their places of employment. The "workbooks" that all workers had to have, listing in detail what the regime regarded as the pluses and minuses of their behavior, would serve to make the great majority of workers very cautious about doing anything that might be interpreted an opposition to the regime—or even unhappiness with the management of the enterprise in which they were employed.

A third factor was that with the passage of time, a new generation grew up that had no memory of or experience with the militant labor movement which had existed before 1960 and may well have come to regard the transformed movement as the "normal" one. The importance of this insofar as the leadership of the CTC was concerned was underscored when the Fourteenth Congress of the CTC in December 1978 created a massive turnover in the confederation's leadership. As Efrén Córdova noted:

Perhaps having achieved the Castroite ideal of that new organization which had as its principal function the unrestricted support of the regime, there were left out many of the old unionists who had figured as leaders in previous congresses. With the exception of Agapito Figueroa, Ursinio Rojas and some others of less significance, none of the leaders who had been elected in the XI, XII and XIII congresses appeared now in the National Council or in National Committee of the CTC. . . . Instead it was preferred to fill those posts with new people formed in the 20 years of revolution, people who combined the spirit of heroes of labor with the capacity to assimilate the Marxist ideology and to show unbreakable loyalty to the Commander in Chief.[108]

During the two years that followed the Tenth Congress there was certainly overt opposition by some unionists to the transformation that was taking place in their movement. We have noted the resistance in the Electrical Workers Federation and some other groups to the labor purge after the Tenth Congress. But, when open protest became virtually impossible, a fair number of workers resorted to sabotage. Such incidents were particularly noticeable and frequent in the last months of 1960 and the beginning of 1961. Employees of radio and television station CMQ set fire to some of the equipment there, and there were spectacular fires in leading Havana stores. Telephone workers also engaged in sabotaging the functioning of the phone system. These and other activities were coordinated by several underground labor groups, most notably the Movimiento Revolucionario 20 de Noviembre, founded by David Salvador, among others, and the Movimiento de Recuperación Revolucionaria.[109]

Virtually all such underground activity became impossible after the so-called Bay of Pigs invasion, organized by the CIA in April 1961, when the Castro regime rounded up virtually everyone about whose adherence to the regime there was the least possible doubt. A number of the participants in this invasion were people with "Batistiano" reputations, which greatly reduced the support of workers and others for any opposition to the Castro regime.

In subsequent decades, workers' objections to the regime's supermobilization of labor—and the union movement's participation in it—mainly took the form of passive resistance.

Although this was seldom admitted in meetings such as union congresses, there is some reason to believe that transformation of the labor movement after the Tenth Congress was not as totally accepted or endorsed with as wild enthusiasm as was claimed at those congresses, or by both labor movement officials and political leaders, such as the Castro brothers and successive ministers of labor.

The constant emphasis in successive labor congresses on the evils of "absenteeism" and "tardiness" would seem to indicate that many workers were not accepting the tight discipline to which the CTC and its affiliates were committed. As one early study of labor conditions in Castro Cuba said, "Absences and lack of punctuality in work had never been a really serious problem while the private enterprise system existed in Cuba."[110] Also, the endorsement of coercive measures to make the workers meet the work quotas assigned to them would also seem to be evidence that, unable really to influence the setting of these quotas, large numbers of workers were showing their unhappiness with then by failing to meet them voluntarily.

Occasionally, leading government officials recognized publicly the existence of such passive resistance by the workers. The Kingston, Jamaica newspaper *The Sunday Gleaner* reported in August 1970:

In a recent three-hour television address in Havana, Capt. Jorge Risquet, the Minister of Labor, attributed the country's mounting economic problems principally to widespread passive resistance by the workers. . . . Captain Risquet acknowledged that there was no rapport between Cuban workers and their superiors—the state administrators and Communist party and labour union officials.[111]

Maurice Zeitlin also quoted Risquet as saying about the same time that "a vanguard with Communist consciousness at work has been developing, but at the same time there is still a rear guard whose conduct reflects the ideology of the capitalist past . . . there has also been an accentuation and spread of absenteeism, negligence, and inadequate use of the workday."[112]

Perhaps the old joke that circulated in the final phases of the Soviet Union became applicable to Castro's Cuba: the workers explain that "we pretend to work and they pretend to pay us."

LABOR LEADERS IN EXILE

Those Cuban leaders who were forced into exile established several organizations, based in the United States, but with members or branches in some Latin American countries as well. At least until the massive roundup of opponents or possible opponents of the regime at the time of the Bay of Pigs invasion in April 1961, they were also able to maintain at least some contact with underground labor elements within Cuba.

There were sharp divisions among the exiled trade unionists. One group, led by Eusebio Mujal, consisted of leaders who had supported him down to the victory of the revolution. That group, the so-called Authentic CTC (CTC Auténtica), reportedly consisted of fifty-six former union leaders, including people who had been officers of twenty-four national union federations.[113] As late as 1962, Mujal was reported to have made a four-day surreptitious trip to Cuba.[114]

Another group formed in exile consisted of people who had continued to hold union offices for longer or shorter periods during the second Batista regime but had been opposed to Mujal and those people associated with him. These formed the Consejo Obrero Revolucionario Independiente de los Trabajadores Cubanos en el Exilio (Independent Revolutionary Labor Council of Cuban Workers in Exile), the Executive Committee of which consisted Marco Antonio Hirigoyen of the Havana transport workers, Antonio Collada of the construction workers, Angel Cofiño of the electrical workers, and Vicente Rubiera of the telephone workers.[115]

The principal organization established by the exiled 26th of July labor leaders and others who had opposed the Mujal regime in the CTC was the Frente Obrero Revolucionario Democrático Cubano (FORDC). Its objective, according to one of its founders, was "to bring together all workers' groups of a democratic type . . . working against the Castro dictatorship."[116]

Established in October 1960, the FORDC included José Antonio Hernández of the metal workers, Manolo Fernández (the first major union leader to be purged, in December 1959), Eric Garcés, the 1959 head of the Musicians Federation; Luis Moreno, elected head of the Tobacco Workers Federation in 1959; Mario Massi, former secretary general of the Chemical Workers Federation; and Mario Fontela, founder and elected first secretary general of the Federation of Agricultural Workers in 1959, all of whom were from the 26th of July Movement. Others included the Auténticos Pascasio Lineras of the Textile Workers Federation, and Antonio Collada, who had been elected secretary of organization of the Construction Workers Federation in 1959, and César Lancis, former head of the Medical Travelers Union. Finally, there were such anti-Mujal pre-1959 union leaders as Rogelio Roig of the Autobuses Modernos bus drivers union; Marco Hirigoyen, onetime secretary general of the Transport Workers Federation; and Angel Cofiño of the Electrical Workers Federation.[117]

The document recording the formation of the FORDC contained a list of demands for which it was working. Some were frankly political, such as the full reestablishment of the democratic Constitution of 1940. Others were labor and trade union in nature, such as the ending of the wage cuts instituted by the regime, reestablishment of collective bargaining, and the right of workers to negotiate for wage increases and other benefits.

The FORDC proclaimed that it was not "either with the ignominious past or the present terror." It was opposed to the people who had exploited the labor movement during the Batista regime and against those who were "renouncing all economic and social demands at the present time on behalf of a hypothetical happiness in the future."[118] The FORDC completely rejected the urgings of Serafino Romualdi that it join forces with the CTC Auténtica headed by Eusebio Mujal.[119]

The FORDC had a number of activities. For several years it published a monthly periodical, in which it recounted the sad events that were affecting the labor movement and the Cuban workers in general and urged support from trade union movements in other countries. It particularly sought to persuade Latin American port and maritime workers to boycott Cuba; several of its members dealt on the spot with unions in Colombia, Venezuela, and Mexico. The FORDC was endorsed by the Confederation of Workers of Venezuela at the CTV's Fourth Congress in December 1961.[120]

In the early years, members of the FORDC were able to get into Cuba on occasion, to work with the underground opposition there. Thus, Rogelio Roig spent six months there in late 1961 and early 1962.[121] Some of the FORDC members were arrested during these excursions into Cuba, including Luis Moreno; Enrique Oviedo, former executive member of the Chemical Workers Federation; and Eric Garcés.[122]

CONCLUSION

Cuban organized labor under the Castro regime presents the only case in the Western Hemisphere of the conversion of a previously militant labor movement into one patterned after the model originally established by Joseph Stalin in the Soviet Union in the late 1920s and early 1930s. This was certainly not what most of the new leaders who seized control of the labor movement after January 1, 1959, had planned or desired.

During most of 1959 the new union leaders—the great majority of whom were in Fidel Castro's own 26th of July Movement—sought to revive the militancy of the Confederación de Trabajadores de Cuba and its affiliates. They engaged in vigorous collective bargaining and aspired to make organized labor more independent of the government than it had been since the establishment of the CTC in the late 1930s.

The great majority of the 26th of July Movement labor lead-ers—as well as the relatively small number from the Auténtico Party and the Directorio Revolucionario—were strongly opposed to working with the Communists of the Partido Socialista Popular to convert Cuban organized labor into a Soviet-style trade union movement. That they had the overwhelming support of the rank and file was amply demonstrated by the local union elections, the federation congresses held in the first half of 1959, and the elec-tions for delegates to the Tenth Congress of the CTC.

However, beginning in November 1960, Fidel Castro and those who remained associated with him seized control of the Cuban labor movement and turned it in an entirely different direction from the one the workers had voted for in the first months of the revolution. They did this partly by appeals to the charisma of Fidel and by references to threats to the security of the revolution and of Cuba itself. But for the most part, they did so by the sug-gestions and actual exercise, of force. The government carried out a ruthless purge of the elected trade union leadership, substitut-ing for it a new group composed of Fidel loyalists, opportunists, and orthodox Communists—capping this process with the choice in 1961 of Lázaro Peña, the Communist who had headed the CTC during the first Batista regime, as secretary general of the confed-eration.

Thereafter, the labor movement was supine. It was converted into an instrument of the Castro government, and on a local basis an instrument of the managers of the government enterprises that had become universal in the economy. The trade unions were converted from organizations dedicated to serving the interests and reflecting the ideas of their worker members into organiza-tions designed to enforce discipline in the workplace, and to do everything possible to increase production and productivity. In-stead of opposing, it supported vast wage reductions, much longer working hours, and work without pay for its worker members.

All of this was done in the name of a supposed workers' and peasants' state. However, the workers had little or no say in de-termining the regime or their own working and living conditions. In fact, in Cuba as elsewhere in the Communist-controlled re-gimes, the real rulers of the "workers' state" were the "new class" of professional revolutionaries and politico-bureaucrats who con-trolled the politics, economy, and all other aspects of the country. In the last instance, indeed the control was in the hands of the chief representative of that class, Fidel Castro.

NOTES

1. Efrén Cordova, *Clase Trabajadora y Movimiento Sindical en Cuba, Volumen II (1959–1996)*, Ediciones Universal, Miami, 1996, page 145.

2. Efrén Córdova, *Castro and the Cuban Labor Movement: Statecraft and Society in a Revolutionary Period (1959–1961)*, University Press of America, Lanham, MD, 1987, page 199.

3. Jorge G. Castañeda, *Compañero: The Life and Death of Ché Guevara*, Alfred A. Knopf, New York, 1997, page 200.

4. Córdova, 1987, op. cit., page 203.

5. Córdova, 1996, op. cit., pages 127–128.

6. Ibid., page 128.

7. *Combate*, Havana, September 29, 1961.

8. E. P. Whittemore, "Cuba's Unions Come Full Circle," *New Leader*, New York, February 5, 1962, page 25.

9. Córdova, 1996, op. cit., pages 128–129.

10. Augusto R. Martínez Sánchez, *La Política Laboral de Revolución Socialista, XXVI Consejo de la CTC-R*, Editorial CTC, La Habana, 1962, pages 6–7.

11. Hobart Spalding, *Organized Labor in Latin America*, New York University Press, New York, 1977, page 242.

12. Córdova, 1996, op. cit., page 141.

13. Ibid., page 249.

14. Carmelo Mesa-Lago and Roberto E. Hernández, *La Organización del Trabajo y el Sistema Salarial en Cuba*, reprinted from *Revista de Política Social*, Julio–Septiembre 1972, page 8.

15. Córdova, 1996, op. cit., page 224.

16. Ibid., page 295.

17. Ibid., page 381.

18. Mesa-Lago and Hernández, 1972, op. cit., page 43.

19. Maurice Zeitlin, *Revolutionary Politics and the Cuban Working Class*, Harper Torchbooks, New York, 1970, page xl.

20. Interview with John Dumoulin, U.S. anthropologist, in New Brunswick, NJ, October 8, 1973.

21. Córdova, 1996, op. cit., page 147.

22. Efrén Córdova, *El Trabajador Cubano en el Estado de Obreros y Campesinos*, Ediciones Universal, Miami, 1990, page 34.

23. Ibid., page 35.

24. Ibid., page 37.

25. Ibid., pages 36–37.

26. Ibid., pages 48–50.

27. Ibid., pages 49–50.

28. René Dumont, *Cuba est-il socialiste?*, Editions du Seuil, Paris, 1970, page 221.

29. Córdova, *Clase Trabajadora y Movimiento Sindical en Cuba, Volumen II*, 1996, op. cit., page 171.

30. *Labor Conditions in Communist Cuba*, Cuban Economic Research Program, University of Miami, 1963, page 27.

31. Córdova, 1996, op. cit., page 171.

32. Ibid., page 143; see also Serafino Romualdi, "What Castro Has Done to Cuban Labor, Excerpts from Address at the Industrial Relations Research Association, Chicago, Illinois Chapter, February 8, 1962" (mimeographed).

33. Córdova, 1990, op. cit., page 27.

34. *La Situación Laboral en al Cuba Castrista*, Publicaciones ORIT-CIOSL, Mexico, n.d. (circa 1962), page 8.

35. Quoted in Oscar Tiseyra, *Cuba Marxista: Vista por un Católica*, Jorge Alvarez Editor, Buenos Aires, 1964, pages 107–108.

36. Martínez Sánchez, op. cit., page 8.

37. Ibid., page 27.

38. Ibid., pages 27–28.

39. Ibid., page 28.

40. Ibid., page 29.

41. Mesa-Lago and Hernández, op. cit., page 17.

42. Martínez Sánchez, op. cit., pages 9–10.

43. Ibid., page 11.

44. Ibid., page 12.

45. Córdova, 1996, op. cit, pages 158–159.

46. Ibid., pages 196–197.

47. Martínez Sánchez, op. cit., page 38.

48. Ibid., page 39.

49. Córdova, 1990, op. cit., page 157.

50. Martínez Sánchez, op. cit., page 33.

51. Córdova, 1990, op. cit., pages 30, 170–171.

52. Cited in Trotskyist periodical *Class Struggle*, New York City, December 1973.

53. Córdova, 1996, op. cit., page 166.

54. Ibid., pages 200–201.

55. Ibid., pages 201–202.

56 . Ibid., pages 169–170.

57. Interview with Lourdes Casals, Cuban-American professor at Rutgers University, in New Brunswick, NJ, October 15, 1974.

58. Córdova, 1990, op. cit., pages 111–112.

59. Ibid., page 117.

60. Ibid., pages 117–118

61. Ibid., page 119.

62. *Labor Conditions in Communist Cuba*, op. cit., page 39.

63. Córdova, 1990, op. cit., pages 122–123.

64. Ibid., page 131.

65. Martínez Sánchez, op. cit., page 13.

66. Mesa-Lago and Hernández, op. cit., page 19.

67. Ibid., page 20.

68. Ibid., page 21.

69. Carmelo Mesa-Lago, "Economic Significance of Unpaid Labor in Socialist Cuba," *Industrial and Labor Relations Review*, Cornell University, Ithaca, NY, April 1969, page 344.

70. Córdova, 1996, op. cit., page 190.

71. Ibid., page 192.

72. Mesa-Lago, op. cit., page 342.

73. Ibid., page 340

74. Ibid., page 342.

75. Córdova, 1990, op. cit., pages 139–140.

76. Mesa-Lago, 1969, op. cit, page 343.

77. Zeitlin, op. cit., pages xxxvii.

78. Interview with Miguel Tarrab, former Cuban representative on International Sugar Council, in Lubbock, Texas, March 6, 1969.

79. *Granma Revista Semanal*, Havana, August 2, 1970.

80. *Trabajadores*, newspaper of Confederación de Trabajadores de Cuba, Havana, June 20, 1994, page 4.

81. Córdova, 1996, op. cit., page 211.

82. Ibid., pages 217–218.

83. Zeitlin, op. cit., pages xxv-xxvi.

84. Ibid., page xxx.

85. Carmelo Mesa-Lago, *Cuba in the 1970's: Pragmatism and Institutionalization*, University of New Mexico Press, Albuquerque, 1974, page 80.

86. Córdova, 1996, op. cit., pages 226–227.

87. Interview with Lourdes Casals, op. cit., October 15, 1974.

88. Córdova, 1996, op. cit., pages 226–228.

89. Ibid., page 239.

90. Ibid., page 292,

91. Ibid., page 297.

92. Ibid., pages 343–345.

93. Interview with Gail Lindberg, member of faculty of Empire State College, speaking to Columbia University Latin American Seminar, New York City, December 6, 1990.

94. Córdova, 1996, op. cit., page 350.

95. Córdova, 1990, op. cit., pages 158–159.

96. Ibid., page 15.

97. Ibid., page 165–166

98. Ibid., pages 55–57.

99. Córdova, 1996, op. cit., page 379.

100. Ibid., page 381.

101. Ibid., page 351.

102. Córdova, 1990, op. cit., page 197.

103. Interview with Gail Lindberg, op. cit., December 6, 1990.

104. Córdova, 1990, op. cit., page 77.

105. Ibid., page 77.

106. Zeitlin, op. cit., page xlvi.

107. Ibid., page 16.

108. Córdova, 1996, op. cit., pages 295–296.

109. Ibid., page 119.

110. *Labor Conditions in Communist Cuba*, op. cit., page 44.

111. *The Sunday Gleaner*, Kingston, Jamaica, August 16, 1970.

112. Zeitlin, op. cit., page xxxu.

113. "Labor Exiles Lead Cuban Fight on Castro," *AFL-CIO News*, Washington, DC, November 2, 1960.

114. Interview with Serafino Romualdi, Latin American representative of American Federation of Labor-Congress of Industrial Organizations, in New York City, October 8, 1962.

115. C.O.R.I., Consejo Obrero Revolucionario Independiente de los Trabajadores Cubanos en el Exilio, Open Letter to "Los trabajadores que sufren en la Cuba rebelde, Los Trabajadores Cubanos en el destierro, Los Trabajadores Libres del Mundo," Miami, May 1, 1967.

116. Interview with Manuel Traiano, official of Frente Obrero Democrático Revolucionario Cubano, in New York City, October 22, 1960.

117. Interview with Marco Hirigoyen, former secretary general of Transport of Workers Federation of Cuba, in New Brunswick, NJ, May 25, 1962.

118. *Frente Obrero Revolucionario Democrático Cubano FORDC*, newsletter of FORDC, October 1960.

119. Interview with Pascasio Lineras, secretary of propaganda, Sindicato Textil Ariguanabo, subsequently textile workers' leader of Organización Auténtica, and member of Executive of Frente Obrero Revolucionario Democrático Cubano, in New York City, October 14, 1960.

120. *Cuban Labor*, organ of Frente Obrero Revolucionario Democrático Cubano, New York, May 1, 1965, July 1965.

121. Interview with Rogelio Roig, member of Executive of Frente Obrero Revolucionario Democrático Cubano, in New Brunswick, NJ, May 8, 1962

122. Interview with Marco Hirigoyen, op. cit., May 25, 1962.

Bibliography

BOOKS AND PAMPHLETS

Robert J. Alexander. *International Trotskyism 1929–1985: A Documented Analysis of the Movement*, Duke University Press, Durham, NC, 1991.

Robert J. Alexander. *Organized Labor in Latin America*, The Free Press of Glencoe, New York, 1965.

Robert J. Alexander. *Presidents of Central America, Mexico, Cuba and Hispaniola, Conversations and Correspondence*, Praeger, Westport, CT, 1995.

Juan Arévalo. *Nuestras Actividades Sindicales en Relación con el General Machado y Su Gobierno*, Ediciones de Acción Socialista, Havana, 1947.

Juan Arévalo. *Problemas de la Unidad Obrera en America*, Havana, 1946.

Carleton Beals. *The Crime of Cuba*, J. P. Lippincott Co., Philadelphia, 1934.

Jorge G. Castañeda. *Compañero: The Life and Death of Ché Guevara*, Alfred A. Knopf, New York, 1997.

Confederación de Trabajadores de Cuba: *Respuesta a la Asociación de Industriales*, Havana, April 1951.

Contrato Colectivo de Trabajo Concertado Entre la Federación Sindical de Trabajadores Telefónicos de Cuba y la Cuban Telephone Company, Havana, May 27, 1950.

Efrén Córdova. *Castro and the Cuban Labor Movement: Statecraft and Society in a Revolutionary Period (1959–1961)*, University Press of America, Lanham, MD, 1987.

Efrén Córdova. *Clase Trabajadora y Movimiento Sindical en Cuba, Volumen I (1819–1959)*, Ediciones Universal, Miami, 1995.

Efrén Córdova. *Clase Trabajadora y Movimiento Sindical en Cuban Volumen II (1959–1996)*, Ediciones Universal, Miami, 1996.

Efrén Córdova. *El Trabajadore Cubano en el Estado de Obreros y Campesinos*, Ediciones Universal, Miami, 1990.

Carlos del Toro. *El Movimiento Obrero Cubano en 1914*, Instituto del Libro, La Habana, 1969.

René Dumont. *Cuba est-il socialiste?* Editions du Seuil, Paris, 1970.

El Movimiento Obrero Cubano Documentos y Articulos, Tomo II, 1925–1935, Instituto de Historia del Movimiento Comunista y de la Revolución Socialista de Cuba, Adjunto al Comité Central del Partido Comunista de Cuba, Editorial de Ciencias Sociales, La Habana, 1977.

El Movimiento Revolucionario Latino Americano, Report of the First Conference of Latin American Communist Parties, Buenos Aires, 1929.

Federación Sindical de Trabajadores Telefónicos. *Cooperativa de Trabajadores Telefónicos de Cuba: Reglamento 1951*, Havana, 1951

Foreign Labor Information. Labor in Cuba, United States Department of Labor, Bureau of Labor Statistics, Washington, DC, May 1957.

Jorge García Montes and Antonio Alonso Avila. *Historia del Partido Comunista de Cuba*, Ediciones Universal, Miami, 1970.

Historia del Movimiento Obrero Cubano 1865–1958, Tomo I, 1865–1935, Instituto de Historia del Movimiento Comunista y de la Revolución Socialista de Cuba anexo al Comité Central del Partido Comunista de Cuba, Editoria Política, La Habana, 1985.

Historia del Movimiento Obrero Cubano 1865–1958, Tomo II, 1935–1958, Instituto de Historia del Movimiento Comunista y de la Revolución Socialista de Cuba anexo al Comité Central del Partido Comunista de Cuba, Editoria Política, La Habana, 1985.

Phillip J. Jaffe. *The Rise and Fall of American Communism*, Gergen Press, New York, 1975.

Labor Conditions in Communist Cuba, Cuban Economic Research Project, University of Miami, 1963.

La Situación Laboral en la Cuba Castrista, Publicaciones Especiales ORIT-CIOSL, Mexico, n.d., (circa 1962).

MACLAS Latin American Essays, Middle Atlantic Council of Latin American Studies, Volume VI, 1993.

Augusto Martínez Sánchez. *La Politica Laboral en la Revolución Socialista, XXVI*, Consejo de la CTC-R, Editorial CTC, La Habana, 1962.

Memoria de los Trabajos Presentados al Congreso Nacional Obrero, Imprenta y Papeleria La Universal, La Habana, 1915.

Carmelo Mesa-Lago. *Cuba in the 1970s: Pragmatism and Institutionalization*, University of New Mexico Press, Albuquerque, 1974.

Carmelo Mesa-Lago and Robert E. Hernández. "La Organización del Trabajo y el Sistema salarial en Cuba," reprinted from *Revista de Politica Social*, Julio-Septiembre, 1972.

Eusebio Mujal. *Contesta a la C.G.T. de la Argentina*, Editorial CTC, Havana, n.d., (circa 1951).

Moises Poblete Troncoso. *El Movimiento Obrero Latinoamericano*, Fondo de Cultura Económica, Mexico, D.F., 1946.

Mario Riera Hernández. *Historial Obrero Cubano 1574–1965*, Rema Press, Miami, 1965.

Serafino Romualdi. *Presidents and Peons: Recollections of a Labor Ambassador in Latin America*, Funk and Wagnalls, New York, 1967.

Hobart Spalding. *Organized Labor in Latin America*, New York University Press, New York, 1977.

Evelio Telleria. *Los Congresos Obreros en Cuba*, Editorial de Ciencias Sociales, La Habana, 1984.

Oscar Tiseyra. *Cuba Marxista: Vista por un Católico*, Jorge Alvarez Editor, Buenos Aires, 1964.

Maurice Zeitlin. *Revolutionary Politics and the Cuban Working Class*, Harper Torchbooks, New York, 1970.

NEWSPAPERS AND PERIODICALS

Acción Socialista, magazine of Juan Arévalo, Havana.

The ACES Bulletin (Association for Comparative Economic Studies).

AFL-CIO News, newspaper of American Federation of Labor-Congress of Industrial Organizations, Washington, DC.

Boletín Internacional con Noticias de Cuba, Havana.

Class Struggle, Trotskyist newspaper, New York City.

Combate, daily newspaper, Havana.

CTC, magazine of Confederación de Trabajadores de Cuba, Havana.

Cuban Labor, periodical of Frente Obrero Revolucionario Democrático Cubano, New York City.

Current History, monthly periodical, Philadelphia.

El Mundo, daily newspaper, Havana.

Frente Obrero Revolucionario Democrático Cubano FORDC, newsletter of FORDC.

Granma Revista Semanal, weekly edition of official newspaper of Communist Party of Cuba, Havana.

Industrial and Labor Relations Review, Cornell University, Ithaca, NY.

International Press Correspondence, periodical of Communist International.

Mundo Obrero, Communist labor periodical, Havana.

New Leader, newspaper of Social Democratic Federation, New York City.

New York Times, daily newspaper.

Prensa Libre, daily newspaper, Havana.

Revolución, newspaper of 26 de Julio, Havana.

The Sunday Gleaner, newspaper, Kingston, Jamaica.

Superación, labor newspaper, Havana.

Trabajadores, newspaper of Confederación de Trabajadores de Cuba, Havana.

INTERVIEWS

José María de Aguilera, secretary general, Federación de Trabajadores Bancarios, in Havana, September 13, 1959, and September 14, 1959.

Humberto Aguirre, responsable of 26 de Julio in Delagacion #2 of Hermandad Ferroviaria, in Havana, January 11, 1959.

José Miguel Juan Aizpurua, responsable of 26 de Julio in Hermandad Ferroviaria on Ferrocarriles Occidentales, in Havana, January 11, 1959.

Juan Ramón Alvarez, former official of Sociedad de Dependientes de Restaurantes, in Havana, January 11, 1959.

Juan Arévalo, reformist union leader and sometime Socialist, in Havana, August 8, 1947.

Jesús Artigas, secretary general of Federación Nacional de Trabajadores de la Medicina, subsequently Treasurer of Confederación de Trabajadores de Cuba, in Havana, August 4, 1947.

Alberto Bago Elias, treasurer of Confederación de Trabajadores de Cuba of Cofiño, in Havana, August 4, 1947, March 17, 1952.

Modesto Barbeito, secretario sindical of Asociación Libertaria de Cuba, subsequently official of Federación de Trabajadores de Plantas Eléctricas, in Havana, August 6, 1947, July 15, 1952, January 13, 1959.

Leandro Barrera, secretario agrario of Federación Nacional de Trabajadores Azucareros, in Havana, June 2, 1959.

Armando Baudet, building manager of Federación de Trabajadores Azucareros, in Havana, June 18, 1954.

Antonio B. Bayer, secretario de propaganda of Acción Revolucionaria Guiteras, in Havana, August 8, 1947.

Conrado Bécquer, secretary general, Federación Nacional de Trabajadores Azucareros, in Havana, September 14, 1959.

Juan Beguer, secretary general of Caja de Retiro de Trabajadores Gastronómicos, in Havana, July 16, 1952.

Fidel Benitez, secretary general of Textile Workers Union of Mariano, in Havana, January 14, 1959.

Orlando Blanco, secretary of organization of Sindicato de Trabajadores de Plantas Eléctricas de la Habana, in Havana, May 30, 1959.

Earl Browder, former secretary general of Communist Party of the United States, in Yonkers, NY, March 23, 1953.

Manuel Carvallo, secretary general of Federación Minera, in Havana, June 1, 1959.

Lourdes Casals, Cuban-American professor at Rutgers University, in New Brunswick, NJ, October 15, 1974.

Reinaldo Cassin González, treasurer of Colegio Nacional de Pedagogos, in Havana, June 5, 1959.

Jesús Coca Mutis, secretary general, Federación de los Trabajadores de Comercio, member of Executive Committee of Confederación de Trabajadores de Cuba of Cofiño, in Havana, August 3, 1947.

Angel Cofiño, secretary general of Confederación de Trabajadores de Cuba; secretary general of Federación de Trabajadores de Plantas Eléctricas, in Havana, August 12, 1947.

Antonio Collada, secretary of organization of Federación Nacional de Trabajadores del Ramo de la Construcción, in Havana, September 13, 1959.

Vicente Collado, coordinador de Secciones Sindicales of Federación de Trabajadores de Plantas Eléctricas, in Havana, September 14, 1959.

Sr. Cornejo, member of Comisión Obrera Nacional of Auténtico Party, a leader of Sindicato Omnibuses Aliados, in Havana, June 5, 1959.

John Correll, U.S. Embassy labor attaché, in Havana, January 12, 1959.

Pedro Domenech, secretary general of Cinematográficas Federation, in Havana, March 17, 1952.

John Dumoulin, U.S. anthropologist, in New Brunswick, NJ. October 8, 1973.

José Enseñat Polit, secretary general of Sindicato de Marineros, Fogoneros y Similares, and secretario de relaciones of Federación Obrero Marítima Nacional in Havana, August 8, 1947.

María Luisa Fernández, leader of 26 de Julio in Sindicato Metalúrgico Continental Can, in Havana, January 11, 1959.

Carlos Fernández R., subdelegate before Official and Employers Organizations of Confederación de Trabajadores de Cuba headed by Lázaro Peña, member of Communist Party, in Havana, August 11, 1947.

Roberto Ferrer Guzman, Responsable of 26 de Julio in Federación de La Habana, in Havana, January 11, 1959.

Mario Fontela, former secretary general, Federación de Trabajadores Agrícolas de Cuba, in New York City, October 22, 1960.

Eric Garcés, former secretary general, Federación de Musicos de Cuba, in New York City, October 22, 1960.

Antonio Gil Brito, secretary general of Federación Obrera Marítima Nacional, in Havana, September 14, 1959.

Gilberto García, secretary general of Juventud Obrera Católica, in Havana, September 14, 1959.

Robert Gladnick, head of International Ladies Garment Workers Union in Puerto Rico, in Santurce, P.R., June 25, 1959.

Gilberto Goliat, member of Executive Committee of Confederación de Trabajadores de Cuba (Cofiño faction), subsequently secretary general of Federación Obrera Marítima, in Havana, August 10, 1947, March 18, 1952.

Javier González, leader of Sección Obrera of 26 de Julio in Liquor Federation, in Havana, June 2, 1959.

Reinol González, acting secretary of International Affairs, Confederación de Trabajadores de Cuba, former secretary general, Juventud Obrera Católica, secretary general, Union de Trabajadores Cristianos, in Havana, June 12, 1959.

Alfredo González Freitas, secretary general of Federación Nacional de Vendedores y Similares, secretary of correspondence, Confederación de Trabajadores de Cuba of Angel Cofiño, in Havana, August 8, 1947.

Gerardo González López, member of Executive of Federación de Obreros del Ramo de la Construcción, in Havana, June 1, 1959.

Ignacio González Tellechea, leader of Maritime Workers Federation of Cuba, in New York City, December 10, 1955.

Humberto Grillo, responsable of 26 de Julio in Federación Ganadera, in Havana, January 11, 1959.

Henry Hammond, U.S. Embassy labor attaché, in Havana, June 2, 1959.

José Antonio Hernández, secretary general, Federación Nacional de Trabajadores de la Industria Metalúrgica y Similares, in Havana, September 11, 1959, September 13, 1959.

Marco Hirigoyen, secretary general, Federación del Transporte, member of Buro of Confederación de Trabajadores de Cuba, in Havana, March 15, 1952, in New Brunswick, NJ, May 25, 1962.

Roberto Hoyos, organization secretary of Federación de Petroleo y Minas, in Havana, March 17, 1952.

César Lancis, former secretary general of Federación de Viajantes, secretary general of Comisión Obrera Nacional of Auténtico Party, in Havana, June 5, 1959.

Pascasio Lineras, secretary of propaganda, Sindicato Textil Ariguanabo, subsequently textile workers' leader of Organización Auténtica, and member of Executive of Frente Obrero Revolucionario Democrático Cubano, in Havana, August 4, 1947, January 12, 1959, in New York City, October 14, 1960.

Gail Lindberg, member of faculty of Empire State College, speaking to Columbia University Latin America Seminar, New York City, December 6, 1990.

Irving Lippe, labor attaché of U.S. Embassy, in Havana, March 17, 1952.

Octavio Lloit, director of propaganda, Confederación de Trabajadores de Cuba, in Havana, January 15, 1959.

Neill Macaulay, history professor at University of Florida, former lieutenant in Rebel Army of Fidel Castro, in Rio de Janeiro, Brazil, August 27, 1965.

José Mandado, president of Sociedad de Dependientes de Hoteles, Restaurantes y Fondas, in Havana, September 6, 1949.

José Luís Martínez, secretary general, Federación Nacional de Trabajadores de la Industria Azucarera, in Havana, March 17, 1952.

José Martínez, secretary general, Federación de Trabajadores de Calzado, in Havana, June 2, 1949.

Pedro Martínez, head of labor affairs for Directorio Revolucionario, in Havana, January 13, 1959.

Adalberto Martínez Cobiello, member of Executive of Sindicato Cinemategráfico de La Habana, member of Comisión Obrera Nacional of Auténtico Party, in Havana, June 5, 1959.

Martín Martínez Ezcurra, secretary of culture, Federación Nacional de Trabajadores Telefónicos, in Havana, March 20, 1952.

Luis Alberto Monge, Costa Rican labor leader, former secretary general of Organización Regional Interamericana de Trabajadores, in Havana, January 12, 1959.

Luis Moreno, provisional secretary general and subsequently secretary general, Federación Tabacalera, in Havana, January 14, 1959.

Castro Moscú, secretary of interior of Federación de Trabajadores Gastronómicos, in Havana, March 16, 1952.

Eusebio Mujal, secretary general, Confederación de Trabajadores de Cuba, in Havana, September 4, 1949, September 10, 1949.

Guido Muñoz Ponce de Leon, Directorio Revolucionario leader in Electrical Workers Federation, in Havana, January 13, 1959.

Raúl Muñoz Robledo, secretary of organization of Sindicato Bancario de La Habana, in Havana, June 6, 1959.

Rafael Otero, former leader of Hermandad Ferroviaria, ORIT representative on east coast of South America, in Havana, January 13, 1959.

Rafael Perdomo y Perdomo, secretary of organization, Federación Nacional de Trabajadores de la Industria Metalúrgica y Similares, in Havana, September 15, 1959.

Fabián Pérez, jefe de activistas of Federación Nacional de Trabajadores Bancarios, in Havana, September 14, 1959.

Carlos Pérez Bega, responsable general of Sindicato de Trabajadores de Laboratorios, Droguerias y Farmacias, in Havana, June 1, 1959.

José Pérez González, member of Buro de Dirección of Confederación de Trabajadores de Cuba, labor leader of Partido Acción Unitaria, in Havana, July 25, 1953.

Manuel Pérez Llanese, member of Executive of Frente Obrero Revolucionario Democrático Cubano, former leader of Federación Gastronómica, in New York City, October 14, 1960.

Marifeli Pérez Stable, associate professor of sociology, SUNY Old Westbury, speaking to Columbia University Latin American Seminar, New York City, February 7, 1991.

José Plana, member of Provisional Executive of Confederación de Trabajadores de Cuba, member of Executive, Union de Trabajadores Cristianos, in Havana, June 5, 1959.

Herbert Samuel Powell, member of Executive of Federación Nacional de Trabajadores de la Industria Azucarera, in Havana, March 17, 1952.

Alfredo Rancano, responsable of 26 de Julio in Federación Gastronomica, in Havana, January 12, 1959.

Rodolfo Riesgo, editor of Juventud Obrera Católica publications, in Havana, January 12, 1959.

Pedro M. Rodríguez Ponce, secretary general, Sindicato de Empleados Bancarios, Provincia de Matanzas, in Havana, June 6, 1959.

Rogelio Roig, member of Executive of Frente Obrero Revolucionario Democrático Cubano, in New Brunswick, NJ, May 8, 1962.

Serafino Romualdi, Latin American representative of American Federation of Labor, assistant secretary of organización Interamericana de Trabajadores, in New York City, October 8, 1962.

Emilio Rubido, secretario de propaganda, Sindicato de Licoreros y Refresqueros de La Habana, member of Comisión Obrera Nacional of Auténtico Party, in Havana, June 5, 1959.

Vicente Rubiera, secretary general, Federación de Trabajadores Telefónicos, in Havana, August 4, 1947, March 20, 1952.

Isidoro Salas Alvarez, member of Buro Nacional Azucarero of Federación Nacional de Trabajadores Azucareros, in Havana, January 15, 1959.

David Salvador, delegate of 26 de Julio in charge of Confederación de Trabajadores de Cuba, in Havana, January 10, 1959, January 11, 1959, June 10, 1959.

Calixto Sánchez, head of Federación Aerea Nacional, in Havana, July 15, 1952.

Luis B. Serrano Tamayo, secretary general, Federación Nacional de Trabajadores Tabacoleros, in Havana, March 19, 1952.

Emilio Surí Castillo, secretario de asistencia Social, Federación Nacional de Trabajadores Azucareros, secretary general, Comisión Obrero Nacional of Partido Auténtico, subsequently, secretary general of Federación Nacional de Trabajadores Azucareros, in Havana, August 4, 1947.

Miguel Tarrab, former Cuban representative in International Sugar Council, in Lubbock, Texas, March 6, 1969.

Manuel Triano, official of Frente Obrero Revolucionario Democrático Cubano, in New York City, October 22, 1960.

Antonio Torres, member of Provisional Executive of Confederación de Trabajadores de Cuba, in Havana, January 11, 1959.

Simeon Torres, secretary general, Federación de Obreros del Ramo de la Alimentación, in Havana, June 1, 1959.

Sra. de Valdivia, wife of Raúl Valdivia, ex-President of Sugar Workers Federation, in Havana, January 13, 1959.

José Vega, secretary of propaganda of Federación Nacional de Trabajadores Azcareros, in Havana, June 2, 1959.

Esteban Ventosa, member of Provisional Committee of Federación de Trabajadores de la Industria Azucarera, in Havana, January 16, 1959.

Luis Viña, secretario de actas, Federación Obrera Marítima Nacional, in Havana, June 1, 1959.

Fausto A. Waterman, a leader of Comisión Obrera Nacional of Partido Auténtico, subsequently secretary of youth and sports affairs of Confederación de Trabajadores de Cuba, in Havana, August 9, 1947.

MISCELLANEOUS

Robert J. Alexander. "Notes of Meeting of Comisión Obrera Nacional of Partido Auténtico, Havana, June 5, 1959" (typewritten).

"Al Pueblo de Cuba en General, y a los Trabajadores en Particular: Unidad Obrera," signed by Vicente Rubiera Feito, Angel Cofiño García and Eusebio Mujal Barniol, undated but 1949 (throwaway).

Robert Kenneth Brown. "The Impact of Revolutionary Politics on the Autonomy of Organized Labor in Cuba, 1959–1960," University of Colorado Master's Thesis, 1965.

Barry Carr. "Sugar and Soviets: The Mobilization of Sugar Workers in Cuba—1933," paper prepared for the Tenth Latin American Labor History Conference, Duke University, April 23–24, 1993.

"Confederación de Trabajadores de Cuba 1 de Mayo de 1951" (throwaway).

Confederación de Trabajadores de Cuba. "Acta de la Reunion del XVIII Consejo Nacional de Trabajadores de Cuba, Celebrado en el Segundo Piso del Palacio de los Trabajadores, Site en San Carlos y Penalver en la Ciudad de la Habana el Dia 25 November de 1950" (mimeographed).

C.O.R.I. Consejo Obrero Revolucionario Independiente de los Trabajadores Cubanos en el Exilio, Open Letter to "Los trabajadores que sufren en la Cuba Rebelde, los Trabajadores Cubanos en el destierro, Los Trabajadores Libres del Mundo," Miami, May 1, 1957.

"Hacia el Triunfo de las Demandas Azucareras" (mimeographed).

La Habana, Comisión Electoral, Resultados," 1959 (mimeographed).

Letter of Robert J. Alexander to Jay Lovestone, January 19, 1959.

Letter of Robert J. Alexander to Jay Lovestone, September 27, 1959.

Letter to "Estimado Compañero" signed by Angel Cofiño García and Vicente Rubiera F. for Comité Obrero Nacional Independiente, and

Helio Nardo and Modesto Barbeito for Asociación Libertaria de Cuba, March 25, 1949 (mimeographed).

Letter to José Pardo Llada from H. Samuel Powell, March 5, 1952 (mimeographed).

Serafino Romualdi. "What Castro Has Done to Cuban Labor," Excerpts From Address at the Industrial Research Association, Chicago, Illinois Chapter, February 8, 1962 (mimeographed).

"Sindicato de Trabajadores de Camiones de Carga por Carretera y Sus Anexos: Lider Nacional," Havana, January 1952 (throwaway).

Index

meets with Fidel Castro and
David Salvador to choose new
CTC Executive, 201; praises
Law of Labor Justice as
strengthening labor
discipline, 236; praises "new
kind" of collective contract
stressing fulfillment of
production norms, 226, 227;
refuses to recognize new
Federación de Trabajadores
Agrícolas, 203; speaks to
opening session of CTC Tenth
Congress, 199
Martínez Villena, Rubén, 42, 43,
49
Marx, Karl, 242
Matos, Huber, 161, 172, 173
McDonald, David, 196
McKinley, William, 2
Mella, Julio Antonio, 37, 38
Mendieta, Carlos, 107, 115
Menocal, President. See García
Menocal, Mario
Mesa-Lago, Carmelo, 221, 237,
238, 239
Mestre, Guillermo, 144
Metal Workers Federation, 191
Miners Federation, 185
Ministry of Communications, 63
Ministry of Industries, 174
Ministry of Labor, 78, 112, 114,
121, 127, 184, 198, 215,
231, 236
Miolán, Angel, 138
Monge, Luis Alberto, 148
Moreno, Luis, 252, 253
Movimiento de Recuperación
Revolucionaria, 250
Movimiento de Resistencia
Cívica, 151, 158
Movimiento Revolucionario 20
de Noviembre, 250
M26J. See 26th of July
Movement
Mujal, Eusebio:
active in Second Congress of
CTC, 99; announces
dissolution of CON, 143;
attacked by Marcos

Hirigoyen, 140; attacks
Argentine CGT, 123; attends
founding congress of CTAL,
81; becomes Batista ally, 6;
becomes head of CON, 98;
becomes secretary general of
CTC, 116, 119; close
relationship of, with
Auténtico governments, 142;
comments on new leadership
of CTC on unification of CTC
and CGT, 122; cooperation of
Jesús Soto with, 205; critical
of Auténtico and Ortodoxo
parties, 124; deal with
Batista embarrassing to him,
137; elected to Executive
Committee of ORIT, 123;
founded CON with Sandalio
Junco, 142; has contact with
Batista's new minister of
labor, 136, 137; has group of
unquestioning supporters in
CTC, 142; heads CTC
Auténtica in exile, 252;
imposes close control of
Ninth CTC Congress, 146,
147; insists on Raúl Valdivia
taking post in Batista
cabinet, 144; leader of
Auténtico labor faction, 61;
named secretary of
organization of CIT, 122;
opponents of Mujal play
major role in anti-Batista
underground, 169; principal
lieutenant of Sandalio Junco,
61; promises Serafino
Romualdi to take CTC out of
CTAL, 122; protests of, get
elections in Autobuses
Modernos after March 10
coup, 140; relations of, with
Batista discussed at ORIT
Bogotá Congress, 195;
removes Cofiño from
leadership of Electrical
Workers Federation, 153;
receives subsidies from
Auténtico government, 142;

About the Author

ROBERT J. ALEXANDER is a Professor Emeritus of Economics, Rutgers University. One of the country's most respected scholars of Latin American politics and economic affairs, Professor Alexander is the author or editor of 40 earlier books.